ART IN ITS TIME

Art writing normally contrasts art with "everyday life." This book explores art as integral to the everyday life of modern society, providing materials to represent class and class conflict, to explore sex and sexuality, and to think about modern industry and economic relationships. Art, as we know it, is not common to all forms of society but is peculiar to our own; what art *is* changes with people's conceptions of the tasks of art, conceptions that are themselves a part of social history. The history of society does not shape art from the outside, but includes the attempts of artists to find new ways of making art and thinking about it.

The essays in *Art in Its Time* offer a critical examination of the central categories of art theory and history. They propose a mode of understanding grounded in concrete case studies of ideas and objects, exploring such topics as the gender content of eighteenth-century theories of the sublime and beautiful, the role of photography in the production of aesthetic "aura," the limits of political art, and the paradox by which art, pursued for its own sake with no thought of commercial gain, can produce the highest-priced of all objects.

Employing an unusually wide range of historical sources and theoretical perspectives to understand the place of art in capitalist society, *Art in Its Time* shows a way out of many of the cul-de-sacs of recent art history and theory.

Paul Mattick is Professor of Philosophy at Adelphi University. He is the author of *Social Knowledge* and editor of *Eighteenth-Century Aesthetics and the Reconstruction of Art*. He is also editor of the *International Journal of Political Economy* and has written criticism for *Arts*, *Art in America*, and *Artforum*, among other publications.

ART IN ITS TIME

Theories and practices of
modern aesthetics

Paul Mattick

Routledge
Taylor & Francis Group

LONDON AND NEW YORK

First published 2003
by Routledge
11 New Fetter Lane, London EC4P 4EE

Simultaneously published in the USA and Canada
by Routledge
29 West 35th Street, New York, NY 10001

Routledge is an imprint of the Taylor & Francis Group

Typeset in Baskerville by
The Running Head Limited, Cambridge
Printed and bound in Great Britain by
MPG Books Ltd, Bodmin

British Library Cataloguing in Publication Data
A catalogue record for this book is available from the British Library

Library of Congress Cataloging in Publication Data
Mattick, Paul, 1944–
Art in its time: theories and practices of modern aesthetics/Paul Mattick
p. cm.
Includes bibliographical references and index.
1. Art and society. 2. Aesthetics, Modern. I. Title: Art in its time. II. Title.
N72.S6 M36 2003
700'.1'03—dc21

01–415–23920–6 (hbk)
01–415–23921–4 (pbk)

For Ilse Mattick
with love and admiration
and for three friends who should be remembered
Serge Bricianer
Louis Evrard
Gherasim Luca

CONTENTS

ILLUSTRATIONS

PREFACE

In writing this book I have depended greatly on the work of many people, inadequately represented in my footnotes, with whom I have discussed over the years the issues treated here. I thank in particular Jeffrey Barnouw, Annie Becq, Timothy J. Clark, Susan Denker, Judith Goldstein, Valerie Jaudon, Richard Kalina, Sylvia Plimack Mangold, Sally Markowitz, Joseph Masheck, Maureen Ryan, Richard Shiff, and Barry Schwabsky. Two art historians have been of special importance: Meyer Schapiro gave me, along with an example combining immense learning with a flexible and sensitive language for the description of works of art, the single most important piece of advice I received when I began my study of art: to draw everything I wanted to look at seriously. And Alan Wallach, who first gave me the idea that I could try to understand my reaction to a picture, in terms both of its physical form and of my historical relation to it, was for years a companion in my attempts to understand a domain of experience in which he is also deeply involved.

I have been privileged to encounter art not only as a set of finished objects but as process; I owe much to the artists who have discussed their work and ideas about art, history, and society with me. In particular, Rochelle Feinstein first led me into the world of contemporary art, and I am honored to acknowledge the pleasure and stimulation of years of friendship with the late Sidney Tillim, whose brilliance as an artist combined depth and subtlety of thinking with formal inventiveness steeped in history and so critically alive to the present moment. Long ago, Frans Brüggen helped me see and hear the relation of art, as a mode of action, to the social worlds in which it is produced and consumed.

Katy Siegel read the entire manuscript, offering criticisms and suggestions both material and formal that considerably improved the book. She has also considerably improved my life as a whole.

I acknowledge two sources of funds that made it possible for me to take time off from teaching for research and writing: the J. Paul Getty Trust and the Dedalus Foundation. Regina Di Pietro helped with production of the manuscript. Muna Khogali was an encouraging and otherwise exemplary editor. Claire L'Enfant is at the source of this project.

Finally, I am grateful to schools and editors who invited me to prepare earlier versions of the essays collected here. Chapter 2 was originally given as a lecture to the Department of Art, College of William and Mary. Chapter 3 appeared in Paul Mattick (ed.), *Eighteenth-Century Aesthetics and the Reconstruction of Art* (Cambridge: Cambridge University Press, 1993). Portions of Chapter 4 formed an essay included in Peggy Brand and Carolyn Korsmeyer (eds), *Feminism and Tradition in Aesthetics* (University Park: Pennsylvania State University Press, 1995). A German version of Chapter 5, "Kunst im Zeitalter der Rationalisierung," was included in Brigitte Aulenbacher and Tilla Siegel (eds), *Diese Welt wird völlig anders sein. Denkmuster der Rationalisierung* (Pfaffenweiler: Centaurus, 1995). An early version of Chapter 6 appeared in the September 1990 issue of *Arts* magazine, now sadly no more. Chapter 7 came into existence as a talk commissioned by Grantmakers in the Arts for their 1993 annual conference; an edited version appeared in Andrew Patner (ed.), *Alternative Futures: Challenging Designs for Arts Philanthropy* (Washington: Grantmakers in the Arts, 1994). An ancestor of Chapter 8, "Aesthetics and anti-aesthetics in the visual arts," was included in the *Journal of Aesthetics and Art Criticism* 51:2 (1993). Chapter 9 appeared in *Critical Inquiry* 24 (1998). Chapter 10 was first given as a lecture in the Fordham University Fine Arts Lecture Series, 1998, and Chapter 11 began as a paper read at the 1999 annual meeting of the American Society for Aesthetics.

1

INTRODUCTION

The ten chapters that follow this introduction were first written, over about as many years, as lectures and essays for a variety of audiences and occasions. Assembled to form a book they present at once the problem of disjointedness and a tendency to repetition. I have left the latter alone, for the most part, in the hope of diminishing the effect of the former. Reading them through to revise them for the present publication, I was pleased to discover to what extent they are bound together by the recurrence of a small number of artists and writers on art: Eugène Delacroix, Marcel Duchamp, Piet Mondrian, Barnett Newman, Pablo Picasso, Jackson Pollock, Joshua Reynolds, and Andy Warhol; along with Charles Baudelaire, Walter Benjamin, Pierre Bourdieu, Clement Greenberg, Immanuel Kant, Karl Marx, Jean-Jacques Rousseau, and Friedrich Schiller, among others. The fabric created by the warp and woof of the works of these figures displays, if not an overall design, a coherent set of basic themes: the eighteenth-century origin of the modern practice of art; the nature of modernity as a period of social history and the place of art in it; the salience of gender categories in the theory as well as the practice of art; the conceptual opposition of art and commerce; the dynamic character of the social category of art, changing theoretically and practically along with the society in which it has its life.

By emphasizing the intimate relation between art and other historically specific features of modern society, I am violating a fundamental aspect of the idea of art, the contrast with what art writers generally call "everyday" or "ordinary" life (a common variant is exhibited in the title of Arthur Danto's first book-length contribution to aesthetics, *The Transfiguration of the Commonplace*[1]). While its underlying conception is seldom made explicit, it is clear that the contrast is meant to signify a radical separation of art from the social (and individual) circumstances in which it is produced and enjoyed, which then can only appear as its historical "context."[2]

---

1 Cambridge: Harvard University Press, 1990.
2 See P. Mattick, "Context," in Robert S. Nelson and Richard Shiff (eds), *Critical Terms for Art History* (Chicago: University of Chicago Press, 1996).

Art, in the first place, is supposed to transcend its historical moment: the category unites products from all epochs and areas, a unity represented physically by museum collections and intellectually by art history as a study of products from every human society. The museum physically separates art from the hustle and bustle of modern life, creating an apparently independent universe in which—in the words with which Gurnemanz in *Parsifal* describes the ritual of the Grail that Wagner no doubt identified with the mystic power of art—time has become space. Similarly, art history presents an autonomous narrative structured by such categories as tradition, influence, style, medium, and technique, a domain of relations between artworks.

In the second place, art represents a mode of value—aesthetic value—independent of practical interest. From the eighteenth century, when Kant characterized the aesthetic attitude to an object (in contrast with the moral or instrumental point of view) as marked by disinterest in its existence, to the twentieth, when the US Supreme Court defined "obscenity" in terms of the absence of artistic value, art's significance has been distinguished from other modes of social importance.

With no apparent use-value, the work of art seems to acquire its exchange-value simply by the expression in money of the art-lover's desire. The miracle is that these objects can achieve prices higher than those of any other human products. This well-known paradox suggests a problem with the distinction of the aesthetic realm from that of the everyday. And a moment's thought suggests that art as actual thing exists nowhere but within the "everyday life" from which its cultural construction separates it. The artist must pay rent on the studio, buy paint, seek dealers and buyers; his or her product, if it succeeds in entering the stream of art, will find a place in a home, a museum, a reproduction in a book or postcard. The work of art, to have a chance of entering that stream, must show its kinship to other things called art and so to the social world in which artists and art have their places.

That moment's thought, however, has not as a rule disrupted the flow of aesthetics, art theory, and criticism from the eighteenth century until quite recently. This fact itself is evidently a key to the nature of art, and must be central to an engagement with the literature of art that wishes to provide a path to understanding this social reality constituted, like others in most societies, by activities both represented and misrepresented by the concepts and theories evolved to describe them. To put the same point in other words, these essays are meant as elements of a critical analysis of the ideology of art.

To call a discourse ideological is to read it differently than did its originators: in particular, to identify at its basis a set of assumptions not explicitly recognized by them. While the inhabitants of a mode of social life typically experience their cultural conventions as not only normal but natural, an outsider may seek to understand those conventions as the product of particular historical circumstances. This might be described as the anthropological point of view; to understand one's own culture with some independence from its ideology, as I am attempting to do in this book, one must view it from something like an outsider's perspective. Comparing it to other cultures is helpful; a variant required in any case is to view it historically, in the double sense of having not only an origin but also an imaginable endpoint in a future fundamental social transformation.[3]

Characteristic of modern ideology is the idea that culture has a history of its own, with a logic of thoughts operating independently of the other factors acting on the thinkers of those thoughts. It may even seem—as it did to the thinkers of the Enlightenment, to Hegel, and still to many contemporary thinkers—that social history as a whole is regulated by the progress of thought. This appearance acquires strength, as Marx and Engels pointed out in their influential treatment of ideology, from the existence of professional thinkers within the social division of labor.[4] As the activity in which a particular group of people specialize, consciousness ceases to look like the necessary aspect of all social activity it is and appears as an autonomous domain, with its own history.

Only in relatively modern times has the set of practices grouped since the eighteenth century as the fine arts become an important element of ideology in this sense, demanding to be considered historically autonomous, part of the domain of "mind" alongside law, morality, religion, and philosophy, as opposed to that of productive labor or quotidian life generally. This peculiarity of the modern idea of art cannot be explained within the terms set by that idea. Art developed along with the commercialized mode of production that became capitalism, and it is only by understanding art as an aspect of this mode of production that the supposed antagonism between them (central to aesthetics)— and so the idea of art's autonomy—can be understood.

How difficult it can be to attain the outsider's anthropological perspective can be gauged by considering Terry Eagleton's popular (at least among academics) effort to confront aesthetic theory as ideology, a book that itself employs the vocabulary of that ideology in speaking, for example, of the "debasement" of art as a branch of commodity production.[5] Eagleton's argument is that aesthetics, the intellectual product of a social system that both places its highest value on human subjectivity and requires the subject's submission to class oppression, at once expresses basic ideological themes of modern society and provides a powerful challenge to those themes. In its freedom from social and economic utility—threatened by commodification—art provides "a utopian glimpse of an alternative to this sorry condition,"[6] in principle shareable by everyone. Such an argument, despite its author's wishes, restates fundamental elements of the

---

3 For a detailed exploration of this issue, see P. Mattick, *Social Knowledge* (London: Hutchinson, 1986).

4 K. Marx and F. Engels, *The German Ideology*, in *Collected Works*, vol. 5 (London: Lawrence and Wishart, 1976), pp. 36, 45.

5 Terry Eagleton, *The Ideology of the Aesthetic* (London: Verso, 1990), p. 2.

6 Ibid., p. 65.

aesthetic ideology against which it is directed; in particular, the idea of a polarity between creative freedom and the compulsions of the market.

Renaissance artists laid the groundwork for the modern ideology of art when they struggled for social status by insisting that they practiced not a craft but a liberal art, the object-making hand merely fulfilling the dictates of the imaginative mind. The nineteenth-century modernization of art that replaced working to the order of religious, state, and private patrons with producing on speculation for the market redefined it as the expression of individual genius. In fact, artworks are produced by independent entrepreneurs (or, latterly, professionals, employed by nonprofit cultural or educational institutions) rather than by wageworkers. Art can therefore incarnate free individuality, validating the social dominance of those who collect and enjoy it, and signifying a cultural end to which the making of money becomes only a means. The freedom of the artist, including his or her freedom to starve, provides a model for that of the ruling elite (who have the education and leisure necessary for the appreciation of art) purchased by the unfreedom of the many. It is precisely its distance from market considerations, its "non-economic" character, that gives art its social meaning—and its market value.

Aesthetics, along with the artistic ideologies at work in critical and pedagogical theory and in the history and psychology of art, consists of theoretical constructions open like other discursive products to critical analysis. But if, in accordance with such analysis, art is seen to derive its meaning not from some autonomous realm of spiritual significance but from the social world in which it exists, art objects themselves must be able to embody ideology. It is not in principle difficult, though it may take ingenious and scholarly work, to identify ideological elements in the aspects of artworks that have or can be given linguistic representation, such as Zola's biologism or the vision of a fruitful natural order crowned by aristocratic ownership presented by some English landscape painting around 1800. But since the nineteenth century the question of artistic meaning has increasingly been addressed in terms of a contrast between the "content"—stateable in words—of artworks and their nondiscursive "form." Especially after the development of abstract art, the purely aesthetic element in art has been identified with those attributes—color, line, and handling, in the case of painting, for instance—peculiar to particular artistic media. Can ideology be interpretively identified in artistic form?

This question provides a meeting point for two important problems: the relation between experience and what is said about it in words; and the means and nature of the production of meaning in non-discursive modes of signification, such as gesture, sound, and imagery. The first of these arises as soon as ideology is understood as a systematic rendering of social practices—such as behavior at home, school, and work, voting or not voting, reading newspapers, watching television—that people ordinarily engage in without thinking too much about what they are doing. What is decisive in social life, as Raymond Williams says, "is not only the conscious system of ideas and beliefs, but the whole lived social process as practically organized by specific and dominant meanings and values."[7] Williams wrote of "structures of feeling," meaning "not feeling against thought, but thought as felt and feeling as thought: practical consciousness of a present kind."[8] This may be compared to Pierre Bourdieu's concept of "habitus," dispositional schemata of action and perception, learned in the family and reshaped as individuals move through social institutions like school and workplace. Habitus includes, for instance, the unconscious details of carriage, tone of voice, vocabulary, and differentiated response—reactions of enjoyment, displeasure, or indifference—to objects and activities, that allow people to sort each other out by social class. It involves for some a sense of being at home with works of art, and a felt assumption of a high place for art in the scale of social values. We can think of ideology as a systematizing (and simplifying, since abstracting) presentation of such structures of feeling and action as natural forms of experience. Thus the doctrine of "aesthetic experience" defines art, a cultural practice, as the natural producer of a particular psychological response (if only on the part of certain, properly sensitive individuals).

But why should language be seen as the only medium for such systematization? Even within the linguistic domain, the plot summary of a novel leaves out much that readers might look for in the work, and that a writer might have labored to put into it; no description of a painting is a substitute for the visual experience of the picture itself; and the question of the "meaning" of music antedated the development of abstract composition, in eighteenth-century debates about the relation between music and text in opera. Yet it is hard to see how a piano sonata or an abstract painting can be understood as exhibiting features of an ideology. Can the meanings inherent in such works, or identifiable in the formal aspects of narrative or descriptive art, be capable of ideology, presenting people's experience of their social existence in ways that occlude the historical specificity of that experience?

Theodor Adorno argued that it was the very irreducibility of an artwork to its description—a version of Kant's idea of the autonomy of art, its independence as a mode of meaning and value from other modes of experience—that constituted its social significance. Music, the most abstract art, provided the clearest case. Adorno saw the music of Viennese classicism as ideological by virtue of its submission to formal laws of composition, by which "it closes itself off against the manifest portrayal of society in which it has its enclaves," hiding class conflict with harmonically structured wholeness.[9] He believed that the new music of the second Viennese school, in contrast, was "no longer an ideology," because in its hermeticism and refusal to please an audience it "surrendered the deception

---

7   R. Williams, *Marxism and Literature* (Oxford: Oxford University Press, 1977), p. 109.
8   Ibid., p. 132.
9   T. W. Adorno, *Philosophy of Modern Music*, tr. Anne G. Mitchell and Wesley V. Blomster (New York: Continuum, 1973), p. 129.

of harmony" and made the alienation of the oppressive class system in which music has its being audible in the rigors of serial technique.[10]

Despite the brilliance of Adorno's writing the relation he discovers between Arnold Schoenberg's liberation of dissonance and the avowal of social disharmony is only a suggestive analogy. Elsewhere he compares serial composition to bureaucratic rationalization and the relation between theme and variation in sonata form to the dialectic of individual and society. Such analogies or allegorical readings can be stimulating and even revealing, but they can also be arbitrary or mechanical. At best they point to further, deeper questions about the origin of the seeming similarity between such disparate orders of social reality as economic organization and compositional technique.

The relation between the two tends to be mediated in cultural theory by some conception of "world view" or "class outlook."[11] Such conceptions demand further exploration of the relation between artistic activity and the social groups to whose outlook it supposedly gives formal definition. One path art historians have taken into this territory is the study of patronage, ranging from examination of the constraints set on earlier artistic activity by the religious or courtly commissioners of work to more recent examples such as the effect on Abstract Expressionist painting of its utilization by the American ruling class as a propaganda weapon in the Cold War. Serge Guilbaut, for instance, concluded with regard to the latter case that American "[a]vant-garde art succeeded because the work and the ideology that supported it, articulated in the painters' writings as well as conveyed in images, coincided fairly closely with the ideology that came to dominate American political life after the 1948 presidential elections."[12] (I consider a related argument of T. J. Clark's, formulated partly in response to Guilbaut's, in Chapter 10.) Whether such claims are true or not must in the end be decided by the plausibility of interpretations of the actual images; study of the uses made of art provide only a temporary escape from the question of how form in art can constitute ideology.

This can only be because—to repeat—art does not exist in a world of its own, sealed off from the conceptualizing performed in language. In Meyer Schapiro's words, "there is no 'pure art,' unconditioned by experience; all fantasy and formal construction, even the random scribbling of the hand, are shaped by experience and by nonaesthetic concerns."[13] The mute experience of an art object is no different from any other lived event. Just as all language is an

---

10 Ibid., p. 131.

11 On the difficulty of such explanations, see Meyer Schapiro, "Philosophy and worldview in painting," in *Worldview in Painting—Art and Society. Selected Papers* (New York: Braziller, 1999), pp. 11–71.

12 S. Guilbaut, *How New York Stole the Idea of Modern Art: Abstract Expressionism, Freedom, and the Cold War*, tr. Arthur Goldhammer (Chicago: University of Chicago Press, 1990), p. 3.

13 M. Schapiro, "Nature of Abstract Art," in *Modern Art: 19th and 20th Centuries* (New York: Braziller, 1978), p. 196.

articulation of nonverbal as well as verbal practices, so nondiscursive form—visual, aural, and other—shares its world of meaning with that constructed in speech. Not only can a mode of depiction or mark-making be, for instance, described as literally "free," meaning ungoverned by convention or a definite idea of an image's final configuration. Images and sounds can also metaphorically exemplify (to use Nelson Goodman's terminology[14]) the same descriptions as other things (giving us gloomy colors, happy tunes, or mechanical shapes), in this way establishing links to them.

Schapiro gives an example, drawn from the appeal of machinery to modernist painters after the First World War:

> The older categories of art were translated into the language of modern technology; the essential was identified with the efficient, the unit with the standardized element, texture with new materials, representation with photography, drawing with the ruled or mechanically traced line, color with the flat coat of paint, and design with the model or the instructing plan. The painters thus tied their useless archaic activity to the most advanced and imposing forms of modern production; and precisely because technology was conceived abstractly as an independent force with its own inner conditions, and the designing engineer as the real maker of the modern world, the step from their earlier Expressionist, Cubist, or Suprematist abstraction to the more technological style was not a great one.[15]

Ideology can be identified in such artistic work in the location of "modernity" in engineering (and indeed in what might be analyzed as ideological forms in the presentation of machine-made things), ignoring the historical specificity of the ways in which the mechanization of production was being accomplished. The advance of capitalist production—including, in the USSR, its state-directed analogue—was equated visually with the progress of universal norms of rationality and efficiency (a matter discussed in some detail in Chapter 5).

We can say, then, that ideology can be identified in artistic form where the latter can be conceptually linked, by maker or receiver, to other areas of social practice. Ideological content, in form and subject-matter alike, is for this reason not univocal, as Schapiro pointed out in a discussion of Diego Rivera's Mexican murals: "in so far as the revolutionary work of art projects slogans, phrases, and their counterpart images, in so far as it forms a spectacle rather than determines an action, its effect in stirring the imagination may be manipulated in contrary ways".[16] It is open, that is, to contrary interpretations. As an artifact, thrown by

14 See N. Goodman, *Languages of Art* (Indianapolis: Hackett, 1976), Part II.
15 M. Schapiro, "Nature," p. 210.
16 M. Schapiro, "The patrons of revolutionary art," *Marxist Quarterly* 1:3 (1937), p. 465.

its maker into the public realm, a revolutionary poster can be recycled as a testimony to a collector's liberal sympathies with the downtrodden, or to the autonomy of artistic form. Ideology is a matter of the uses to which a work of art is open.

The essays presented here are concerned with the use of both art and theories about it for the elaboration of social meanings. Chapter 4, for instance, investigates how eighteenth-century writers both employed gender categories for the interpretation of artworks and established those categories by reference to aesthetic concepts, while artists united aesthetic doctrine and sexual ideology in the formal construction of their works. Chapter 6 considers the efforts made by a number of artists in the 1920s to redefine art itself in terms of the rationality identified as the spirit of modern industrial society, efforts involving conscious attempts to create formal embodiments of a social ideology. My discussions of artworks in such cases are not meant to illustrate theoretical positions but to demonstrate the interaction of verbal and visual ideology.

These essays are intended as contributions neither to aesthetics nor to the history of art, but to what I think of as "historical criticism" or "critical history," taking the categories of artistic creation and aesthetic theorizing for its analytical object. They aim not to provide a synoptic view, but to study a few cases of theory and practice that seem to me to clarify the functioning of "art" as a category of modern life. I start with the eighteenth century, because it seems to me that this is when the conception of art first acquired something like its modern form. But my main interest is in the art of the century just ended. It was the century in which the idea of the "modern," the name industrial capitalism claimed for itself, became a central preoccupation of artistic production and thought, and so in which the relation of art to the rest of social life has come most sharply in view. Recognizing that art is not historically autonomous but an element of the complex social totality in which we live makes it not less but more interesting, emotionally engaging, and—at its best—exalting. While the twentieth century is now over, the problems its artists posed remain for anyone who tries to understand the workings of the modern world.

2

SOME MASKS OF MODERNISM

The days when one could sit down with an easy mind to write an account of something called "modernism" are over. One might have thought that the opposite would be the case since it has become common, over the past 25 years or so, for writers on culture to insist that this term labels a phenomenon of the past. At least in the restricted field of art history, the closure of "modernism," thus detached from the original reference to the chronological present, might have been expected to have given the concept definability as a stylistic term. But it has not. Earlier definitional orthodoxies, such as that embodied in Alfred Barr's famous diagram of the history of abstract art, or Clement Greenberg's various formulations, no longer have their former power. The complexity, incompleteness, and hesitation that mark a notable recent attempt at a con-ceptualization, T. J. Clark's *Farewell to an Idea*,[1] suggest that the purported end of modernism has if anything made the task more difficult.

If we agree, in the search for a plausible minimum definition, to apply the label "modernist" to art which orients itself self-consciously to the social-historical reality called "modernity," the source of the problem is clear: there is agreement neither on the limits or the content of the historical period referenced nor on what to take as the "orientation" of artistic practice to the wider field of social experience. As Raymond Williams put it,

> Although modernism can be clearly identified as a distinctive move-ment, in its deliberate distance from and challenge to more traditional forms of art and thought, it is also strongly characterized by its internal diversity of methods and emphases: a restless and often directly com-petitive sequence of innovations, always more immediately recognized by what they are breaking from than by what, in any simple way, they are breaking towards.[2]

1 T. J. Clark, *Farewell to an Idea: Episodes from a History of Modernism* (New Haven: Yale University Press, 1999).
2 Raymond Williams, *The Politics of Modernism* (London: Verso, 1989), p. 43.

We might as well admit, therefore, that an account of modernism should range over a field of artistic practices, seeking not to define an entity but to make explicit both the relationships holding elements of that field together as a classification we have become accustomed to making, and the gaps between them that show the historical falsifications inherent in this intellectual custom.

Modernity

"Modern" is itself a modern word, developed originally to express the sense that the "rebirth" of western European culture after what then became the "Dark Ages" was not just a revival of ancient virtues but the creation of something new, with a character all its own.[3] The term *modernus* had come into existence in Medieval Latin, as an antonym to *antiquus*, and these terms were used already in the twelfth century for the two sides of a controversy between the adherents of antique poetry and the practitioners of a new poetics. But essential to the idea of this contrast as it developed after the Renaissance was the conception of history as a progress through a sequence of distinct stages. In this conception the present day is not just a period of time, but a period of history, characterized by features differentiating it from other eras, such as Antiquity or the Middle Ages. Thus we have a series of contrasts with earlier periods, expressed in such images as Enlightenment's overcoming of the darkness of the feudal age, or in the mythology of the "organic," "traditional" community of the preindustrial past so basic to early sociology. Set against such contrast categories, modern politics, learning, science, art are conceived of as more than contemporaries; they are aspects of a unity: modernity.

Something fundamental in this conception was correct: the appearance of "modernity" as cultural category was a response to the development of a new commercial and then industrial mode of social life. It is not an accident, and is more than symbolically appropriate, that Descartes's *Discourse on Method*—the initiating document of modern philosophy, written in French not Latin and beginning with the rejection of classical and scholastic tradition—was written amidst the commercial bustle of seventeenth-century Amsterdam. As is indicated by the use, during the last half-century, of the locution "modern society" as a euphemism for capitalism, and of "modernization" for the destruction of non-capitalist social formations and the expansion of the market together with the institution of wage labor, "modernity" can be taken as a name of the social order which, originating in the late medieval period, by the eighteenth century was already becoming the determining presence in Europe and North America, and which today, in various forms, covers the globe. The advent of this social order impressed itself on the consciousness of people with the speed and violence with

---

3 For the history of "modern" and "modernity," see Chapter 1 of Matei Calinescu's excellent *Five Faces of Modernity* (Durham: Duke University Press, 1987).

which it displaced existing patterns of social activity, above all with the experiences of the agricultural and industrial revolutions and the political upheaval which began as the French Revolution but soon affected all Europe. In the course of the nineteenth century the pace of change accelerated; the fifty years before the First World War both saw the fastest rates of economic growth in history and the invention of the technology which was to dominate most of the twentieth century in both industry and private consumption. It saw also the spread of this system across the globe until by 1900 Britain, Germany, and France not only had extensive empires, along with other European nations and the US, but together controlled 60 percent of the world market for manufactured goods.

With the growth of this system, and the rise to social power of the industrialists, merchants, and financiers whose way of life was bound up with its dominance, "modern" became a term of praise as well as a description. While in seventeenth-century English, for example, "modern" had negative connotations, by the later 1700s it was increasingly used as a term of approbation, signaling a positive interest in novelty, in change, as basic to and emblematic of the new society and the values of its rulers.

Art

The difficulty of locating a beginning for modernism as a mode of artistic practice can be connected to the fact that "art" itself, as a social institution and category of thought, only came into existence with modern society. Art is thus a product of or, better, an aspect of modernity. Meyer Schapiro has discovered roots of the modern sense of the arts in the "conscious taste" of eleventh- and twelfth-century spectators "for the beauty of workmanship, materials, and artistic devices, apart from the religious meanings," to be found in the products of what was then called "art" (i.e. products of skill). But here already it is linked with "urban development" and "the social relationships arising from the new strength of the merchants and artisans as a class" which mark this period as an early step toward the development of capitalist society.[4] Further development came with the appreciation of well-made objects and, above all, in the new

---

4 Meyer Schapiro, "On the aesthetic attitude in Romanesque art," in *Romanesque Art*, Selected Papers, vol. 1 (New York: Braziller, 1977), p. 2. Schapiro's description of the attitude to art and artists that we share with the late Medieval world summarizes the "secular cult of art": "rapture, discrimination, collection; the adoration of the masterpiece and recognition of the great artist personality; the habitual judgement of works without reference to meanings or to use; the acceptance of the beautiful as a field with special laws, values, and even morality" (p. 23). For an enlightening study of the Renaissance transformation of this outlook into that of modern aesthetics, see David Summers, *The Judgment of Sense* (Cambridge: Cambridge University Press, 1987). Larry Shiner's excellent *The Invention of Art: A Cultural History* (Chicago: University of Chicago Press, 2001) was published too late for me to consult; it is not only the first but will probably long be the best introduction to the history of the modern conception of art.

status claimed for painting and sculpture in the Italy of the Renaissance and then in northern Europe. By the eighteenth century, painting, music, dance, and architecture were established alongside poetry as essential graces of the life of the nobility and church hierarchy. But it is really only after the mid-1700s that the category of "art"—specifically, "fine art"—stabilized as a name for objects and performances valued primarily not for their contribution to the grandeur or dignity of a person, regime, environment, or ceremony but in themselves (and what this can mean is the chief problem in understanding art as a social institution). They were detached from their original contexts, collected, exhibited in museums (or performed in concert halls), and acquired a genealogy as members of a genus of object. Once this has happened, people begin to make objects for such collections—art objects.

It is not hard to read "art" as a carrier of aristocratic values, taken up by the bourgeoisie along with land-ownership and good manners. The art object is the non-practical, non-mass produced thing, the product of free, creative genius rather than mechanical following of instructions. (This is still visible in Clement Greenberg's identification of what he called "modernism" with "quality," contrasted with "kitsch," commercial, vulgar things.) It is made for its own sake, not for money. But in the process by which paintings, sculpture, and music pass from the older ruling classes to the new their character is transformed. Art is henceforth not only supposed to decorate and glorify the lives of the great; it becomes *culture*, the product of labor, both the expression of individual talent and the incarnation of the glories of the past—the labor of mankind on the path of self-development.

Eighteenth-century versions of art history tell a story of peak and decline, with classical Greece being one high point, equaled only by the High Renaissance. Art is exemplified by the Antique, whose products represent a timeless ("classic") standard of value against which the present is to be judged. The embodiment of social virtue and rationality, not only independent of but older than the Christianity of the immediate feudal past, the Antique figures as the non-historical, nature within the domain of culture. Modernity, in contrast, is seen as marked by the increase of social and individual fragmentation, implying the definitive loss of the (imaginary) unified social world of the ancients, due to the division of labor and the market system.

By the early nineteenth century, art has begun to be seen as an ideal sphere in which the reintegration of the individual personality and of the social totality, unachieved in concrete reality, can be attained. Art is gradually redefined also as the search for beauty in individual experience. And experience is of necessity present-day experience. Thus art becomes oriented to modernity; it becomes not just an art of its time but an art of *this* time; it ends by becoming "modernist."

Art as such, not just the "classic" art of the past, is now to be the embodiment of the Antique, of the eternal, of higher values than the mercantile ones of vulgar life. Thus it works by finding otherwise secret correspondences between the elements of fragmented experience, and by discovering classical beauty amidst the chaotic movement of the modern city. In "looking for that quality which you must allow me to call 'modernity'"—writes Baudelaire in his essay on Constantin Guys—the painter of modern life "makes it his business to extract from fashion whatever element it may contain of poetry within history, to distill the eternal from the transitory." For, Baudelaire explains, "by 'modernity' I mean the ephemeral, the fugitive, the contingent, the half of art whose other half is the eternal and the immutable."[5] Modern art seeks the eternal, that which art is supposed to embody, in the ever-changing new that characterizes modern society.

We may compare this appreciation of modernity with that of a contemporary of Baudelaire's:

> Constant revolutionizing of production, uninterrupted disturbance of all social relations, everlasting uncertainty and agitation distinguish the bourgeois epoch from all earlier ones. All fixed, fast-frozen relationships, with their train of venerable ideas and opinions, are swept away, all new-formed ones become obsolete before they can ossify. All that is solid melts into air, all that is holy is profaned and men at last are forced to face with sober senses the real conditions of their lives and their relations with their fellow men.[6]

These often-repeated words from the *Communist Manifesto* tell only half the story toward which Baudelaire was feeling his way. Continuation of this social system, as of any, means stability of patterns of social relationships as a basis for continuing change. Later on, in *Capital*, Marx argued that the "constant revolutionizing of production" activated at once the reproduction of the social system and the generation of its eventual overthrow. Whatever its eventual fate, its continual reproduction gives society the appearance of nature, outside history. Means of production seem always to have been "capital"; the crucifix, removed from a church and taken to the museum for aesthetic contemplation, seems always to have been "art."

An example

An example will clarify the import of these generalizations. Given the extent of the domain to which "modernism" can plausibly be applied, the choice of an illustrative object is almost arbitrary. Risking cliché, I choose a painting whose special place in the history of modernism is indisputable: Picasso's *Demoiselles d'Avignon* (Figure 2.1), now in the Museum of Modern Art, New York. Although it was painted in 1907 and has become a cultural icon, it can give a sensation of newness

---

5 Charles Baudelaire, "The painter of modern life" [1863], in *The Painter of Modern Life and Other Essays*, tr. Jonathan Mayne (London: Phaidon, 1964), pp. 11–13.

6 Karl Marx, *The Communist Manifesto* [1848], (New York: W. W. Norton, 1988), p. 58.

even today. This seems due in part to the bright, fresh color, and to the overall intensity produced by the presence of that color throughout the painting. It is due too to the presence of a quickly brushed on, sketchy line in various places (such as the leg and foot of the leftmost figure and the side of the rightmost). And it is due, I suspect, to the range of differences across the picture—differences in style of representation, in the application of paint, from thin to thick, in the use of paint to create flat surfaces or modeled ones. This produces a suggestion of change, of rethinking and reworking, in principle continuable indefinitely (the picture has often been described as unfinished, though there is no evidence that Picasso thought of it as such).

Finally, still today, it has a shocking quality, due above all to the distortion of

Figure 2.1 Pablo Picasso, *Demoiselles d'Avignon*, June–July 1907, © 2003 The Estate of Pablo Picasso; ARS (Artists Rights Society), New York and DACS (Design and Artists Copyright Society), London. Courtesy of The Museum of Modern Art/Licensed by SCALA/Art Resource, NY.

the faces of the figures on the right. (This quality is all the more powerful because of the large size of the painting, 8 feet by 7 feet 8 inches.) All of these features can be taken as tokens of "modernity": newness, freshness, shock. If the picture looks this way to us today, imagine how it must have appeared when it was first seen. It was certainly Picasso's intention to do something new with this painting. It marks a break (despite elements of continuity) with his own immediately preceding manner of painting, as well as with that even of other avant-garde artists. Its size makes a claim to importance. In the event, it made a strong impression on its earliest viewers—a negative one: collector Leo Stein called it "a horrible mess," and among Picasso's fellow artists, Henri Matisse intensely disliked it, André Derain made fun of it, and Georges Braque, soon to become his close artistic collaborator, reacted violently against it.[7]

The painting represents a curtained room with five women in it; one, at the left, holds a curtain open, allowing us in, while at the right another looks out at us. In front of her a squatting woman with her back to us turns her head to face us. In front, at the center of the picture, is a table with fruit and a Spanish drinking vessel, a *porrón*. Picasso's circle seems to have referred to the picture as "The Philosophical Brothel" or "The Avignon Girls," using *filles* to indicate their profession. The subject was intentionally obscured when it was first publicly exhibited, in 1914, by substituting "*demoiselles*." Now that the picture has entered into art history, it is obvious to the educated viewer that the women are prostitutes. Women at the service of men, they are related to earlier female groups who play important roles in the history of French painting, like the inhabitants of the harem represented in Jean-Auguste-Dominique Ingres's *Turkish Bath* (1862, Musée du Louvre) and Eugène Delacroix's image of Algerian women in their apartment (1834, Musée du Louvre). Enclosed in luxurious interiors, these women are separated from the (male) worlds of action and of mundane affairs; they are presented to us for the pleasure of looking just as they themselves are represented as living works of art. They are emblems at once of beauty and of sexual submission; the meaning of that submission is softened by the exotic locale, which both adds to their allure as mysterious creatures and sidesteps the question of their contemporary European equivalents.

In comparing these pictures to Picasso's I am reminded of another passage from the *Communist Manifesto*, where Marx treats nakedness not as an element of melting beauty but as a metaphor for the revelation of a hitherto hidden, harsh truth: "The bourgeoisie has stripped of its halo every occupation hitherto honored and looked up to with reverent awe . . . In place of exploitation veiled by religious and political illusions, it has put open, shameless, direct, naked exploitation."[8] Again, Marx would come to see the falsifying simplification of this view; in

7 See Hélène Seckel, "Anthology of early commentary on *Les Demoiselles d'Avignon*," in W. Rubin, H. Seckel, and J. Cousins (eds), *Les Demoiselles d'Avignon* (Studies in Modern Art 3) (New York: Museum of Modern Art, 1994), pp. 211–56.

8 Marx, *The Communist Manifesto*, p. 58.

addition to born-again religion and fresh political illusions, capitalism covered its shame above all with economic categories, hiding exploitation behind "free" market transactions and "optimizing" price formation. Nonetheless, modeling the opposition between commerce and art, prostitution has appeared steadily since the start of the nineteenth century as love's opposite. Though attempts have been made to resolve this antithesis ideologically by such disparate though related myths as those of the golden-hearted whore and the murderous client, prostitution remained—and remains—a thorn in the tender bourgeois conscience demanding constant artistic transfiguration.

In the "modern" art of the nineteenth century the commercial character of the enjoyment of beauty became a central subject for representation, in the form of paintings, lithographs, and photographs of prostitutes and their close cousins actresses, dancers, poor working girls. "In that vast picture-gallery which is life in London or Paris," wrote Baudelaire in the essay already cited, "we shall meet with all the various types of fallen womanhood . . . at all levels." In that living picture gallery as in art, "in truth, they exist very much more for the pleasure of the observer than for their own."[9] The whore is a nearly perfect symbol for capitalist culture, representing the domination of the most basic human relationships by monetary exchange, with the casting of human activity as a commodity to be bought and sold. (I say "nearly perfect" only, because even here we are within a Romantic convention; corresponding to the presence of prostitution throughout the arts of the late nineteenth and early twentieth centuries is the near absence of paid labor in any other form.) The prostitute can stand also for art itself, if we wish—just as beauty in the abstract can be seen as incarnated in the female—the thing of beauty for sale to the aesthetic consumer.

Manet's *Olympia* of 1863 (Musée d'Orsay) had presented an image of a prostitute that shocked its first viewers. This painting had disturbed both by the way it is painted—its violation of conventions of the nude—and by the frankness with which Olympia directs her gaze at the painting's viewer. Hers is the face of an individual aware of her position in relation to her customers; the image, like the woman, disdained sentimental veils. Picasso's strategy is a radically different one: of the five figures we see, none has an individual face.

The tendency toward generalization through simplification that we see here was a common feature of the advanced art of the period between 1900 and the First World War. André Derain's *Bathers* (Museum of Modern Art) is a good example (Figure 2.2). Painted in the same year as the *Demoiselles*, it shares important features with the latter besides the masklike faces: the subject-matter of the female nude, the lack of interaction between the figures, suggesting a sense of their isolation as individuals, the integration of the figures into their environments. On the other hand, Derain, despite his use of outline and strong colors, remains attached to the classical tradition of figure painting; his picture still evokes the physical

9 Baudelaire, "Painter," pp. 37, 35.

Figure 2.2 André Derain, *Bathers*, 1907, © 2003 ARS, New York, ADAGP, Paris, and DACS, London. Courtesy of The Museum of Modern Art/Licensed by SCALA/Art Resource, NY.

beauty of female bodies in a landscape. Derain's nudes are simply there for us to look at, while Picasso's confront us like Olympia. Derain presents us with nature; Picasso with the city, and a commercial establishment: with modernity. At the same time, in contrast to Manet's paintings and pictures like the monotypes of prostitutes Degas made in the late 1870s, we are not here shown signs of historical specificity. Picasso's women do not wear modern clothing or appear in a recognizable architectural setting. "Modernity" in this work means not some present moment, but a category of experience. Correspondingly, it is not a figure in it but the *painting* that is modern.

The effect of modernity is made all the more striking by its visible contrast with classical tradition. It includes two basic themes of European painting, both symbolizing the presence of nature within a context of culture: the female nude and the still life. The two women in the center have stylized faces, like two versions of the same face. This face, though apparently based in part on archaic Iberian sculpture, might be called a cartoon version of the face of classical beauty; it goes with these women's bodies, which, descended from Greek statues of Venus, are variations on the languid bodies of the odalisque (the one on the left is even, as Leo Steinberg has pointed out, in a reclining position, though she has been tipped upright for us).[10] They bear the drapery of the antique nude;

10   Leo Steinberg, "The philosophical brothel," *October* 44 (Spring 1988), p. 27 ff.

where genitals are exposed neoclassical convention is upheld: no pubic hair. But their visages are parodies of antiquity, exaggerating the stereotypical character of the classical ideal; the classicizing gesture is countered by the distortion of form in body and face. They are, after all, not goddesses, but whores.

And the whore, beauty for sale, is, according to Baudelaire, "a perfect image of the savagery that lurks in the heart of civilization."[11] In the *Demoiselles* the savagery is spelled out not just in the masks of the figures at right and left but in the violence with which the bodies, and their environment, are cut up into sharp-edged pieces and then reassembled. That is, savagery is not just the subject but is also the method of the painting; it is not something we contemplate but something we are confronted with. Unlike Derain's women, Picasso's are not figures seen against a ground. Instead the area around them, taking form as curtain folds, forms together with them a fabric that both conveys a sense of three-dimensionality and thrusts it forward. Note, for example, the way the area to the left of the squatting woman comes forward like a folded solid, as does the gray shape in the center of the cut-out space within her right arm. At the same time the table, with its aggressive prow echoing the pointed melon and the *porrón*, pushes up into as well as against the image. Not only is the women's sexuality directed at us, we are drawn into their space.

This pictorial destabilization of the relation of the spectator to the image can be taken as another token of the modernity of the experience of looking at it. It calls a convention into question: that the picture represents a view of a reality passively awaiting a viewer, a reality (whether that of classical mythology or Bible story, or of physical nature) fixed and eternal. On the one hand it makes it clear that what we are looking at is a painting, not a window on reality. On the other, it suggests a reality that is uncertain, within which one cannot be sure what is what and where one is in relation to it.

This effect is implicit in a Romantic picture like Delacroix's *Death of Sardanapalus* (1821–8, Musée du Louvre; see Figure 4.2), in which the perspectival inconsistency of the pictured space allows it to present an image which can be thought of as both the picture we are looking at and the vision of the royal aesthete for whose benefit the display and destruction of feminine beauty is arranged. Perspectival paradox operates to analogous effect in Édouard Manet's *Bar at the Folies-Bergères* (1881–2, Courtauld Institute; Figure 2.3). This picture can be seen as an exploration of varieties of looking: the mirror behind the bar shows the spectators of the evening's entertainment, one with binoculars, as well as a customer looking at the barmaid, who in turn looks out at him and us. And we look at all of it, front and back, thanks to the mirror in a painting that is here clearly shown not to be the mirror of reality earlier writers on art compared it to. These various lookers have different social positions: the spectators in the distance are being entertained; the barmaid is working behind the bar, to serve the

---

11 Baudelaire, "Painter," p. 36.

Figure 2.3 Édouard Manet, *Bar at the Folies-Bergères* (© Courtauld Institute Gallery, Somerset House, London)

customer and to be looked at by him, and by us. And what is our relation to him? The picture's famous violation of perspective allows for no resolution of this problem. His relation to her, as customer, is part of what the picture presents to us, but it is a relation into which the picture draws us.

Picasso's early sketches for the *Demoiselles d'Avignon* included two men along with the women: a sailor sat at the table, while a student entered the room from the left and the women turned to look at him.[12] In the picture's final form, the women look out at the spectator. The student's position in the sketches is now occupied by a masked, hieratic female figure, seemingly about to pull a curtain closed upon the room; the sailor has vanished, though his table remains, still bearing the sign of masculine sexuality in the *porrón* and the rather phallic still life. The sailor can be taken as an embodiment of physicality, specifically of male sexuality, the student as representing the powers of the mind. (The student is identified by a book he holds; in other early studies he also carries a skull, an attribute that relates this image to other pictures in which a medical man identifies a woman as an embodiment at once of sexual pleasure and of death, combined particularly, since the

12 For an exhaustive study of the sketched and painted prehistory of the *Demoiselles*, see *Les Demoiselles d'Avignon*, vol. 1 (Paris: Musée Picasso, 1988).

19

seventeenth century, in the form of syphilis.[13]) Absent from the picture these two figures are fused into one—and this person is not hard to identify: it is Picasso himself, a compound of fleshly feeling and controlling intelligence, recognizing the power of female sexuality while also mastering it, forcing it to submit to his art.

But if Picasso, having dropped his symbolic disguises, is now the person to whom the Avignon *filles* direct their attention, the spectator's position in relation to his picture is determined by this fact. The place of the story told in the original sketch, of men in a brothel, is now taken by the fact of our looking at the painting, and in this event we are forced to confront the fact that we are looking through Picasso's eyes. We are offered a view of reality only as it has been shaped by Picasso's hand, to express his sense and thoughts of it. The language it is painted in was in 1907 not a conventional or traditional one, not one viewers shared, even other artists. Today, when that language is familiar to the amateur of modern art, it still signals its original historical moment and so its inventor's solitude and his freedom. It is a picture of women, but we must see it as "a Picasso."

Though the two men are no longer in the picture, two kinds of women make themselves seen (or perhaps three). Besides the antique beauties of the center are the masked figures to the left and right. They lack the round breasts and sexy gestures of their companions. And above all those at the right wear masks made to frighten, not please. They do not display themselves, but look out inscrutably or hostilely, while their companion to the left, looking at them, stands like a guardian of the scene.

While the faces of the central figures reflect Picasso's interest in early Iberian sculpture at the time he was working on the *Demoiselles*, the masks have more distant origins. It seems that Picasso had finished a version of the painting when he visited the ethnographic museum of the Trocadéro; he later spoke of the objects he saw there as not

> just like any other pieces of sculpture . . . They were magic things . . . *intercesseurs*, mediators . . . against everything . . . They were weapons. To help people avoid coming under the influence of spirits again, to help them become independent. They're tools. If we give spirits a form, we become independent . . . I understood why I was a painter.[14]

No doubt there is an important personal aspect to the spirits Picasso wished to master: his work records a lifetime of struggle with and against women. But this

---

13 See the discussion in William Rubin, "Picasso," in W. Rubin (ed.), *"Primitivism" in 20th Century Art: Affinity of the Tribal and Modern*, vol. 1 (New York: Museum of Modern Art, 1984), p. 254.

14 From a conversation of 1937, reported in André Malraux, *Picasso's Mask* (New York: Holt, Rinehart, and Winston, 1976), pp. 11–13, cited in Rubin, Seckel, and Cousins, *Les Demoiselles d'Avignon*, p. 219.

private struggle has a public dimension. Throughout the modern period in the West woman has represented both nature tamed into beauty and nature that threatens disorder and the destruction of civilization; both maternal love and nurturance and structures of social convention threatening to overwhelm and swallow up the individual (typified as male). To approach closer to the subject of the *Demoiselles*, the prostitute is both lover and destroyer, a provider of pleasure and the carrier of venereal disease. Her love is a commodity bought and sold: let the buyer beware. There are deep and complex terrors here indeed to attempt to control by means of form.

But why should forms from a distant culture have this power for Picasso? Nothing is more modern than the presence of these foreign objects in Picasso's picture, which is of a piece with Picasso's own presence in Paris, the metropolis to which he was pulled from economically underdeveloped Spain. Just as the continent was knit together by the dominance of a few economic centers, Europeans were brought into serious contact with the rest of the world by the growth of trade. By the seventeenth century this had become large-scale colonization. In the middle of the nineteenth century the Musée naval was established at the Louvre to display objects collected by French companies operating under the protection of the navy; in 1878 the ethnographic museum which Picasso was to visit in 1907 was founded to display the variety of objects stemming from cultures around the world of the sort once called "primitive" and today more politely described as "tribal." In the same year such things were put on show at the Universal Exposition in Paris. Since contemporary "tribal" cultures were imagined to represent the way of life of prehistoric man, such displays were meant to illustrate the progress of mankind from savagery to modern civilization. By the same token they illustrated the power of capitalism, its ability to assimilate all the world's products (and peoples).

This meant the detachment of such objects from their original contexts, and their assembly in the distinctively modern environment of the exposition and the museum. They were not at first seen as art, but as tools and ritual objects. Indeed, it was the attention they earned, around 1900, from artists that transformed them into art. Western artists, in other parts of Europe as well as in France, saw these objects as the direct expression of their makers' subjectivity, relatively independent as they are of external appearances. They were "primitive" not just in the sense of being crudely made—though this perceived aspect was valued in opposition to conventional refinement—but also in the sense of being original, the earliest and therefore basic form of art.

The interest in "primitive" art reflected the modern separation of artists from the customers for their handiwork. Unlike Medieval or Renaissance image-makers, modern artists did not produce works to order, in a visual language shared by artist and patron. Painting, separated from such earlier functions as decoration and glorification of the upper classes, appeared an autonomous realm of value—"aesthetic value"—so that not function but the formal properties of artworks came to be definitive of art itself. And so, while "primitive"

21

objects acquired the status of art because of their formal properties—their properties as "autonomous" artworks—their having this status helped to endow the subject-matter of modern art, consciously concerned with those formal properties, with an ahistorical, timeless character.

Just as Antiquity was seen in the late eighteenth century as a golden age before the fall into modernity, the "primitive" was seen by the modern artist as outside history, culture in the domain of nature. Eighteenth-century prints portrayed Pacific natives and Native Americans as classical Greeks;[15] Picasso's painting, in contrast, portrays modern women as wearing what look like African masks for faces. The economic forces of modern society which tore these masks (along with natural riches and, earlier, human beings themselves) from Africa and the Pacific and made them resources for Western artistic production are hidden here, precisely because of Picasso's success in using these forms to represent his, modern, experience of woman, society, and art in a guise apparently timeless because supposedly primeval.

The "primitive" here represents not (like the Antique) an ideal to which society aspires, but an inner essence lurking beneath the veneer of culture. It is both threatening, spelling chaos and destruction, and liberatory, implying freedom from convention—a freedom best exercised by the artist who like Picasso replaces convention in giving form to these spirits. Primitivism thus expresses a sense of the instability of modern society, and at the same time represents this experience as eternal, rooted in the nature of things; just as the modern prostitute is seen in an image like this one as an incarnation of the essential force of female sexuality. In the same way, the artist claims to find in his personal resources the elements of a universal language of form, independent of social-cultural determination.

History

We can no longer see such works other than through the lens formed by the history that separates us from them. When William Rubin thoughtlessly writes of Picasso's painting that "the center, left- and right-hand demoiselles communicate progressively darkening *insights* [my emphasis] into the nature of femininity" he is speaking with the voice of an age gone by.[16] The views not only of women but of the nature of art implicit in this picture are simply no longer acceptable as they might have been, at least in certain avant-garde circles, in 1907 or 1913 or even 1940. It is hard today to imagine that art is a universal language or think of

---

15 See, for example, the illustration in Rubin, *"Primitivism,"* p. 6.

16 Rubin, "Picasso," p. 252. That he actually means it is shown by a later passage in which he speaks of Picasso's "deep-seated fear and loathing of the female body," matched with "craving for and ecstatic idealization of it," as "inherently banal material" that is yet "so amplified by the spirit of genius that it emerges as a new insight—all the more universal for being so commonplace" (pp. 251–4).

the artist as a kind of natural force or believe in "modernism" as a single line of aesthetic development peculiarly expressive of the nature of the modern world.

To say all this, however, is not to say that we are in a "post-modern" age. The society we live in is essentially the same as the one Picasso inhabited in 1907, even if critics, artists, and professional intellectuals—along with many others— have lost a sense of historical purpose and direction. Now that capitalism has unfolded its nature on a global scale, bringing—as Marx predicted long ago— human disasters along with the human powers it has unleashed, the limits of conscious human control over the imperatives of the accumulation of capital have become apparent. (Thus the architects' and planners' dream of the all-new city was powerless in the face of the imperatives of real estate and business investment, which controlled the actual forms of urban development.) But if the belief in progress that once powered the responses to capitalist development that went by the name of modernism has faded, the process of capital accumulation continues. It is hard today not to agree with Walter Benjamin's wartime vision of history as a "catastrophe which keeps piling wreckage upon wreckage" at our feet; it is still, as he said, a storm which "irresistibly propels" us "into the future to which" our backs are turned.[17]

---

17 Walter Benjamin, "Theses on the philosophy of history" [1940], in *Illuminations: Essays and Reflections*, tr. Harry Zohn (New York: Schocken, 1969), pp. 251–8.

3

ART AND MONEY

The set of social practices we call "art" is a phenomenon of the society that gave itself the name "modern." Appreciation of products of the arts in the premodern sense of the term (as craft) is seemingly to be found in earlier European, and many other, cultures, and the beginnings of something like the modern conception were already visible in the theory and practice of the cinquecento *arti del disegno*. However, as art historian P. O. Kristeller emphasized in a classic essay, "the system of the five major arts, which underlies all modern aesthetics and is so familiar to us all, is of comparatively recent origin and did not assume definitive shape before the eighteenth century."[1] One may say even that the conception of art which contemporary use of the word takes for granted was not fully evolved before the later nineteenth century, and perhaps not until the "formalism" of the twentieth, with its transcendent aesthetic centered on the autonomously meaningful object. Nonetheless, the eighteenth-century birth of aesthetics as a discipline concerned with the theory of art and nature as objects of appreciation may be taken as marking the crystallization of a field of activities, concepts, and institutions that has since played a leading role in social life.

Given that modern society has been based like none other in history on commerce, it is a striking paradox that, in discussion of the arts from the eighteenth century to the present, "commercial" has been a synonym for "low." In the same way, "mass" has been a derogatory term for culture in a globally integrated social order founded on mass production and consumption. Even a Marxist critic like Clement Greenberg in 1939, who described the artistic avantgarde as attached to the capitalist ruling class "by an umbilical cord of gold," at the same time characterized the mass-cultural counterpart to that avant-garde as the commercialism to which he gave the German name of kitsch.[2] The ideological importance of this conception of art can be seen in the almost reflex

---

1 P. O. Kristeller, "The Modern System of the Arts," in his *Renaissance Thought II* (New York: Harper Torchbooks, 1965), p. 165.
2 Clement Greenberg, "Avant-garde and kitsch," in his *Art and Culture* (Boston: Beacon Press, 1961), p. 8.

action taken to turn aside any threat to it, as when aesthetician Arthur Danto takes Andy Warhol's *Brillo Boxes* to exemplify the very distinction between art and mundane commercial products questioned by such work. As Pierre Bourdieu has observed, "Art cannot reveal the truth about art without snatching it away again by turning the revelation into an artistic event."[3] This is, of course, an effect of "art" only as that is the historically situated social practice we know. This chapter is an attempt to trace the appearance of the ideological opposition of art and commerce as it emerges in the art writing that both reflected and helped structure the development and institutionalization of that practice in the later eighteenth century.

Progress and decline

Despite its distinctive modernity, central to the construction of art we are discussing here was the reference made in texts and images to an imagined Antiquity. There was first of all the idea that modern art represented a revival of the achievements of the Greeks and Romans, after the destruction of culture during the Dark Ages. The initiating work of art history, Vasari's *Lives of the Painters* of 1550, describes "the attainment of perfection in the arts" in the early classical period, followed in the later Roman Empire by "their ruin" and then, at the hands of Cimabue, Giotto, and their successors, "their restoration or, to put it better still, their rebirth." Thus "the beginning of the good modern style" in sculpture was based on Ghiberti's imitation of "the works of the ancient Romans, which he studies very carefully (as must anyone who wants to do good work)."[4] Two centuries later, in a work that fixed the centrality of Hellenic art for German culture, Winckelmann made the imitation of the Greeks the foundation of his discussion of the tasks of modern art, declaring that "the only way for us to become great or, if this be possible, inimitable, is to imitate the ancients."[5]

By this dialectic of "ancient" and "modern" a present-day institution was projected into the past and so given classic status. The works of the past, despite being to a great extent unknown, also functioned as standards of value against which the achievement of the moderns could be measured. According to Vincenzo Galilei, writing in 1581, the sixteenth-century revival of the art of music was unable to achieve the level of excellence reached by the ancient

---

3 Pierre Bourdieu, "The production of belief: contribution to an economy of symbolic goods," in *The Field of Cultural Production* (New York: Columbia University Press, 1993) p. 80. See also, in the same volume, "The historical genesis of a pure aesthetic," pp. 241–6.

4 Giorgio Vasari, *Lives of the Artists*, tr. George Bull (Harmondsworth: Penguin, 1965), vol. 1, p. 32, p. 112; for a stimulating discussion of the circumstance that "an essential element of modernity, as the Italians conceived it, lay in the worship of antiquity," see Francis Haskell and Nicholas Penny, *Taste and the Antique* (New Haven: Yale University Press, 1982) (quotation from p. 1).

5 J. J. Winckelmann, *Reflections on the Imitation of Greek Works in Painting and Sculpture* (1755), tr. E. Heyer and R. C. Norton (La Salle: Open Court, 1987), p. 5.

Greeks.[6] Nineteen years later, however, Ottavio Rinuccini stated that the conventional opinion of the inferiority of modern to ancient music "was wholly driven from my mind" by Peri's setting of *Dafne*.[7] Vasari claimed that the modern revival of the visual arts went beyond imitation, emphasizing "the excellence that has made modern art even more glorious than that of the ancient world."[8]

Pessimism was to surface, however, in the Quarrel of the Ancients and Moderns carried on by writers in a number of European countries from the later seventeenth into the start of the eighteenth century, who debated whether the progress evidently made by the sciences beyond the learning of the ancients could also be claimed for the arts. (Notable here, in the very terminology used, is the explicit idea of modernity as an epoch defined by contrast to antiquity.) But a darker vision was already implicit in the metaphor of rebirth still operative today in the concept of the Renaissance, for life implies eventual death. It is important to understand, wrote Vasari, that

> from the smallest beginnings art attained the greatest heights, only to decline from its noble position to the most degraded status. Seeing this, artists can also realize the nature of the arts we have been discussing: these, like the other arts and like human beings themselves, are born, grow up, become old, and die.[9]

According to Hume, it is a fundamental maxim of cultural progress that "when the arts and sciences come to perfection in any state, from that moment they naturally, or rather necessarily decline, and seldom or never revive in that nation, where they formerly flourished."[10] And Winckelmann described his monumental *History of Ancient Art* as "intended to show the origin, progress, change, downfall of art" as it developed ineluctably through the stages of "the necessary," "beauty," and "the superfluous." Once perfection has been reached, he explained, further advance being impossible, art "must go backwards, because in it, as in all the operations of nature, we cannot think of any stationary point."[11] In Denis

6　See the translation of selections from the *Dialogo della musica antica e della moderna* in Oliver Strunk (ed.), *Source Readings in Music History* (New York: Norton, 1950), pp. 302 ff.

7　Dedication of *Euridice* (1600), in Strunk, *Music History*, p. 368.

8　Vasari, *Lives of the Artists*, p. 249; see also p. 160, for Brunelleschi's advance over ancient architecture. Such sentiments had been previously expressed in Alberti's *Della pittura* of 1435; see the translation by John R. Spencer, *On Painting* (New Haven: Yale University Press, 1966), pp. 31–40, 58.

9　Vasari, *Lives of the Artists*, p. 46.

10　David Hume, "Of the rise and progress of the arts and sciences" (1742), in *Essays Moral, Political, and Literary*, ed. E. F. Miller (Indianapolis: Liberty Classics, 1987), p. 135.

11　Johann J. Winckelmann, *History of Ancient Art* (1764), tr. G. H. Lodge (New York: Ungar, 1968), vol. 1, pp. 3, 29; vol. 2, p. 143. For a discussion of Winckelmann's use of the cycle of progress and decay as the framework of his history, see Alex Potts, "Winckelmann's Construction of History," *Art History* 5:4 (1982), pp. 371–407.

Diderot's version of this scheme, "In all times and everywhere the bad gives rise to the good, the good inspires the better, the better produces the excellent, and the excellent is followed by the bizarre" and the "mannered."[12]

Vasari saw the plastic arts reaching a climax in his own time, in the work of Michelangelo. But by the last third of the seventeenth century, Francis Haskell reminds us, "the feeling developed that the age of very great painters was over—painters whose reputations would, like those of Raphael, Titian and Correggio, the Carracci, Poussin and Rubens, continue to grow and to solidify into eternity."[13] In the eighteenth century it was commonly accepted that there had been but four great periods in the history of the arts: ancient Athens, Rome under Augustus, the Italian Renaissance (associated particularly with the reigns of Julius II and Leo X), and the age of Louis XIV. As that century approached its close, Sir Joshua Reynolds declared in his lectures to the Royal Academy not only that the work of the ancients is the foundation of all later painting and sculpture, but "that the Art has been in a gradual state of decline, from the Age of Michael Angelo to the present, must be acknowledged."[14]

Such ideas did not conflict as strongly with the general progressivism of the eighteenth century as may be imagined. Scholars have long recognized that the Enlightenment, for all the faith in the present and future signaled by its names in various languages, was deeply marked by "historical pessimism."[15] The vision of progress leading to decline had an important source in classical images of

12 Denis Diderot, *Salon de 1767*, in *Oeuvres complètes*, ed. H. Dieckmann, J. Proust, and J. Varloot (henceforth DPV) (Paris: Hermann, 1975–), vol. 16, p. 213; see also the essay *De la manière*, in ibid., pp. 521–30. Diderot's remarks are directed specifically against the rococo style of the period of the Régence, in response to which he is arguing for the return to the *grand goût* embodied in the Antique. The striking similarity, to Diderot's critique, of Clement Greenberg's diagnosis of the cultural decline of capitalism is a remarkable testimony to the stability of the practice of art as a feature of "modern" society: Greenberg evokes an "Alexandrianism" in which the "same themes are mechanically varied in a hundred different works, and yet nothing new is produced." In his scheme, of course, the role of the *grand goût* is played by "avant-garde culture" ("Avant-garde and kitsch," p. 4).

13 Francis Haskell, *Rediscoveries in Art: Some Aspects of Taste, Fashion and Collecting in England and France* (London: Phaidon, 1976), p. 22.

14 J. Reynolds, *Discourses on Art*, ed. R. R. Wark (New Haven: Yale University Press, 1975), p. 280. This sense of "the discrepancy between a remote, ideal era and the true facts of the present," as Robert Rosenblum has observed, is given pictorial form in Reynolds's parody of the *School of Athens* (National Gallery of Ireland, Dublin); see Rosenblum, "Reynolds in an international milieu," in N. Penny (ed.), *Reynolds* (London: Weidenfeld and Nicolson, 1986), p. 44. A similar thought is provoked by the same artist's *Mrs. Siddons as the Tragic Muse* (Huntington Art Gallery, San Marino), which recycles none other than Michelangelo's Sistine image of Isaiah to portray a leading stage actress of the time.

15 See Henry Vyverberg, *Historical Pessimism in the French Enlightenment* (Cambridge: Harvard University Press, 1958).

human history (and indeed of that of the cosmos itself) as cyclical.[16] With the advance of the eighteenth century, however, the idea of degeneracy comes to be associated with specific aspects of modernization intrinsic to the rise of a market economy, commonly associated at the time with the concept of "luxury."

The critique of luxury, as symptomatic of the worship of money for its own sake rather than as an instrument of social well-being, was itself a well-worn classical theme (as Voltaire observed, "luxury has been railed at for two thousand years in verse and in prose" although "it has always been loved").[17] Aristotle's contrast of *oikonomia*, the proper ordering of the household, with *chrematismos*, concern with the making of money, was still present within the conceptual structure, as well as the name, of the "political economy" of the eighteenth century. Similarly, Horace's complaint that "when once this corroding lust for profit has infected our minds, can we hope for poems to be written that are worth . . . storing away in cases of polished cypress?" provided a theme for that period's writers on art.[18] It was expressed in various forms, as a function of differing historical contexts as well as of the particular interests of different writers, who drew the line between the commerce needed to provide a social basis for the arts and the excessive love of luxury that corrupts, in different ways; its presence, despite the fundamental differences that distinguish eighteenth-century discourses of art from more recent ones, is a sign of the continuity of those discourses.

16 To mention the sources most important for modern European thinkers: Plato expounds a doctrine of cyclical creation and destruction of the world in the *Statesman*, among other places; Aristotle states as a commonplace in the *Metaphysics* (1074b.II) that the arts and sciences have many times been lost and regained (see also *Politics*, 1264a.I, and *De caelo*, 270b.19). Polybius's account of history as a cycle of kinds of government was revived in Italy by Villani, Guicciardini, and Machiavelli (the last an important source for later versions of the idea; for a discussion in reference to the eighteenth century, see J. G. A. Pocock, *The Machiavellian Moment* (Princeton: Princeton University Press, 1975).

17 Voltaire, *Philosophical Dictionary*, tr. Peter Gay (New York: Basic Books, 1962), p. 367.

18 Horace, *On the Art of Poetry*, in *Classical Literary Criticism*, tr. T. S. Dorsch (Harmondsworth: Penguin, 1965), p. 90. In the words of another Latin text central to the education of an eighteenth-century person of letters, Longinus's *On the Sublime*, "the love of money, that insatiable craving from which we all now suffer, and the love of pleasure make us their slaves . . . the love of money being a disease that makes us petty-minded" (*Classical Literary Criticism*, p. 157). On classical expressions of the conflict of art and money, see Gregory Nagy, "The 'professional muse' and models of prestige in Ancient Greece," *Cultural Critique* 12 (1989): pp. 131–43; and Leonard Woodbury, "Pindar and the mercenary muse: *Isthmian* 2.1–13," *Transactions of the American Philological Association*, 99 (1968), pp. 521–42. For the distinction between money-making and the ends properly aimed at by the exercise of crafts, see Plato, *Republic*, 345c ff.; and Aristotle, *Politics*, I.9. On the contrast between *oikonomia* and "economy," in the modern sense, see the discussion in Keith Tribe, *Land, Labour and Economic Discourse* (London: Routledge and Kegan Paul, 1978), Chapter 5.

Luxury and corruption

On the one hand, some argued, the opulence of modern society, when compared to the medieval past or to the "rude" or "barbarous" condition of the native cultures of the New World, could be traced to the development of commerce, which stimulated the diversification and improvement of production. Thus it is originally through foreign trade, according to Hume, that

> men become acquainted with the *pleasures* of luxury, and the *profits* of commerce; and their *delicacy* and *industry* being once awakened, carry them on to improvements in every branch of domestic as well as foreign trade . . . [P]resenting the gayer and more opulent part of the nation with objects of luxury which they never before dreamed of, raises in them a desire of a more splendid way of life than what their ancestors enjoyed . . . Imitation soon diffuses all those arts, while domestic manufacturers emulate the foreign in their improvements, and work up every home commodity to the utmost perfection of which it is susceptible.[19]

Growing wealth leads to a growing taste for luxuries, and with them the arts; in Montesquieu's words, "Wealth is the result of commerce, luxury the consequence of wealth, and the perfection of the arts that of luxury."[20]

Montesquieu admits, however, that "commerce corrupts pure morals."[21] This corruption is above all visible in the decline of patriotism, the readiness to defend one's native land; while commerce makes men more industrious, it also renders them less courageous. This is due not only to the "softening" effect of devotion to pleasure but also specifically to the fostering of self-centeredness in a market society. "The system of commerce often comes down to this principle: each should work for himself, as I work for myself; I demand nothing from you without offering you its value; so should you do."[22] Under such conditions the sentiment of "generosity" withers as each thinks only of himself. Even Hume, apostle of what historian J. G. A. Pocock has called "commercial humanism," distinguishes "innocent" from "vicious" luxury, which appears when gratification "engrosses

---

19 "Of Commerce" (1752), in *Essays*, p. 264.

20 "L'effet du commerce sont les richesses, la suite des richesses le luxe, celle du luxe la perfection des arts" (*L'Esprit des loix*, revised edition, XXI.6, in *Oeuvres* (Amsterdam and Leipzig: Arkstée et Merkus, 1764), vol. 2, pp. 291–2).

21 Ibid., p. 257 (*Esprit*, XX.1): "Le commerce corrompt les moeurs pures; c'étoit le sujet des plaintes de Platon." A footnote offers as example the Gauls, said by Caesar to have declined to military inferiority due to the commerce of Marseilles.

22 "Le système du Commerce se réduit souvent à ce principe: que chacun travaille pour soi, comme je travaille pour moi; je ne vous demande rien qu'en vous en offrant la valeur; faîtes-en autant" (ibid., p. 257 n).

all a man's expense, and leaves no ability for such acts of duty and generosity as are required by his situation and fortune, especially his willingness to defend his country."[23]

The central example of the corruption worked by luxury is indeed the abandonment of war, the citizen's duty, to professionals. From a viewpoint like Jean-Jacques Rousseau's, this is just a special case—one given central importance as the traditional symbol of civic virtue—of a more general effect of the growth of trade: the specialization of function that goes with the division of labor. Gone is the sturdy independence of the model citizen; liberty has vanished with the multiplication of needs satisfiable only by a multitude of others, "since the bonds of servitude are formed merely from the mutual dependence of men and the reciprocal needs that unite them,"[24] which have replaced the fellow feeling of independent equals. "Ancient politicians incessantly talked about morals and virtue, those of our time talk only of business and money."[25] According to Rousseau, the society of the ancient Greeks and Romans decayed when love of country and virtue gave way to vanity and the desire for pleasure, to be satisfied only by luxury and money: "individuals enriched themselves, commerce and the arts flourished, and the state soon perished."[26] The ancient world thus furnishes not only a model to which the present may aspire but also the spectacle of decline to serve as a warning. In the modern world, as well, the death of civic virtue will bring that of liberty, as the field of government is left to tyrants and their hired armies.

A British version of Rousseau's conception held, as Pocock reminds us apropos of Gibbon's treatment of Rome's decline, that after the corrupting mutation of republic into empire in the ancient world, virtue was restored in the north in the form of the communities of armed freeholders established by the Gothic invaders. "But the image of Gothic freedom, like that of primitive Roman virtue, rested on the assumption that the form of property which gave the individual arms and independence, liberty and virtue, must necessarily be land."[27] With the shift of social power away from the landed gentry toward a centralized state

---

23 Hume, "Of Refinement in the Arts," in *Essays*, p. 269; for "commercial humanism," see J. G. A. Pocock, *Virtue, Commerce, and History* (Cambridge: Cambridge University Press, 1985), p. 194.

24 Jean-Jacques Rousseau, *Discourse of the Origin of Inequality*, in *On the Social Contract*, ed. and tr. D. A. Cress (Indianapolis: Hackett, 1983), p. 139.

25 Jean-Jacques Rousseau, *Discourse of the Sciences and Arts*, in *The First and Second Discourses*, ed. and tr. R. D. Masters (New York: St. Martin's, 1964), p. 51.

26 "Quand ces peuples commencèrent à dégénérer, que la vanité et l'amour du plaisir eurent succédé à celui de la patrie et de la vertu, alors le vice et la molesse pénétrèrent de toutes parts, et il ne fut plus question que de Luxe et d'argent pour y satisfaire. Les particuliers s'enrichirent, le commerce et les arts fleurirent, et l'Etat ne tarda pas à périr" (Jean-Jacques Rousseau, *Fragments politiques*, VII ("Le luxe, le commerce et les arts"), in *Oeuvres complètes*, ed. B. Gagnebin and M. Raymond (Paris: Gallimard (Pléïade), 1964), vol. 3, p. 517.

27 Pocock, *Virtue, Commerce, and History*, p. 147. On the eighteenth-century problematic of political virtue, see also *idem*, *The Machiavellian Moment*, Chapter 14.

financed not only by taxation but by newly developing instruments of credit, and so toward the world of high finance, rooted in commerce, civic virtue was doomed to decline.

With this we touch on a central theme in the eighteenth-century discourse of progress and corruption, one that embodied in a different but related way the conflict between "liberal" activity and mercenary motivation visible in the discussion of the arts: the opposition of agriculture and commerce. The national household was still seen as based on farming, though already imbued with a capitalist form. Physiocratic theory, notably, explained that agriculture alone generated new wealth; thus Quesnay distinguished between "luxury in the way of subsistence" and "luxury in the way of ornamentation," arguing that "an opulent nation which indulges in excessive luxury in the way of ornamentation can very quickly be overwhelmed by its sumptuousness." The science of economic administration of which his *Tableau* presented the principles was not to be confused "with the trivial and specious science of financial operations whose subject-matter is only the money-stock of the nation and the monetary movements resulting from traffic in money."[28] But the ideological conflict between landed property and the new order of the market overflowed this boundary; even though the point of economic policy was to foster internal and external trade we find Quesnay rehearsing the old complaint that "those engaged in commerce share in the wealth of nations, but the nations do not share in theirs. The merchant is a stranger in his country."[29]

These ideas, expressed by physiocracy in the form of an economic system, are present throughout the philosophical writing of the time. Rousseau's work, which made such an impact on urban intellectuals throughout Europe, voiced them in the association of the fallen state of humanity with an economically expansive urban culture, in contrast to the healthy virtue of a modest rural existence. In Voltaire's *Candide*, as in the proliferating literature of the garden, georgic pursuits represented both a haven from and a rational reproach to a world of exploitation, bloodthirstiness, and falsehood motivated by greed for gold. In general, the opposition of city to country contrasted both a site of (idle) consumption with one of production, and wealth based on commercial and financial speculation with that derived from the honest cultivation of landed property.

---

28 M. Kuczynski and R. Meek (eds and trs), *Quesnay's Tableau Economique* (London: Macmillan, 1972), pp. i, ii, 21.

29 "Les commerçants participent aux richesses des nations, mais les nations ne participent pas aux richesses des commerçants. Le négociant est étranger dans sa patrie" (F. Quesnay, *Du commerce*, in *François Quesnay et la physiocratie* (Paris, 1958), vol. 2, p. 827; cit. Daniel Roche, "Négoce et culture dans la France du XVIIIe siècle," *Revue d'histoire moderne et contemporaine* 25 (1978), p. 375). Note in the last phrase the Homeric echo; here again classical culture showed the way.

31

Luxury and the fine arts[30]

Ruled by the passions, whose force is swelled by the needs incessantly generated by the progress of the arts and sciences, men grow "effeminate": they cease to be warriors and become devotees of pleasure. Sébastien Mercier's *Tableau de Paris*, far from being a critique of the modern economy, has as clear subtext an argument for laissez-faire and the advantages for civilization of the division of labor. But even he discovers in luxury a source of the incompetence of generals and their lack of discipline:

> Luxury encourages indolence, people busy themselves with all the arts that flatter sensual delicacy: they make a major study of these wretched things, and ignore the theory of combat. Brilliant reviews are organized to provide a spectacle for the ladies. We want a soldier turned out and posed like a dancer.[31]

One result of such a state of affairs is the degeneration of the very arts that have been such a powerful agent of social decline. In Rousseau's dire words, "the dissolution of morals, a necessary consequence of luxury, leads in turn to the corruption of taste." Taste itself is feminized (here again we have a reference to the rococo), sacrificed by men to "the tyrants of their liberty," women, who are governed naturally by passion rather than by the stern dictates of reason and duty.[32] It is clear to Rousseau that under circumstances such as those that characterize modern commercial society, an artist has no choice but to "lower his genius to the level of his time."[33]

This idea of the moral decline of the arts as an aspect of the general corruption of society underlies the discussion of the condition of music in Barthélémy's *Voyages du jeune Anacharsis* of 1788. "[N]ow that music has made such great progress it has lost the noble privilege of instructing and improving men," observes the pupil

---

30 "L'influence du luxe sur les beaux-arts. Vous conviendrez qu'ils ont tous merveilleusement embrouillé cette question" (Diderot, *Salon de 1767*, DPV vol. 16, p. 165).

31 "L'impéritie des généraux, leur peu de discipline sont une suite du luxe. Le luxe favorise l'indolence, on s'occupe de tous les arts qui flattent la délicatesse sensuelle: on se fait une étude capitale de ces misères, & l'on ignore la théorie des combats. On fait des revues brillantes, pour donner un spectacle à des dames. On veut qu'un soldat soit tourné & aligné comme un danseur" ([Sébastien Mercier], *Tableau de Paris*, nouvelle édition (Amsterdam, 1782), vol. 2, pp. 11–15).

32 Typically, Hume, at home as Rousseau was not in the emerging commercial culture, asks, "What better school for manners" there could be "than the company of virtuous women, where the mutual endeavour to please must insensibly polish the mind." In fact, he observes, the ancients' exclusion of "the fair sex" from "the polite world" may be the reason why they "have not left us one piece of pleasantry that is excellent . . . This, therefore, is one considerable improvement which the polite arts have received from gallantry, and from courts where it first arose" ("Of the rise and progress of the arts and sciences," in *Essays*, p. 134.).

33 Rousseau, *Discourse of the Sciences and Arts*, pp. 53, 52.

of Plato with whom the young Scythian is conversing in an Athens prefigurative of eighteenth-century Paris. Music has lost its former social use, the encouragement of virtue, because it "only serves today to give pleasure." Itself corrupted by new melodic and harmonic riches, it is no longer capable of inspiring citizenship. "In our society workmen and mercenaries decide the fate of music. They fill the theatres; they attend the musical competitions and they set themselves up as arbiters of taste . . . No, music will never rise again after its fall."[34]

As Diderot wrote in his commentary on the Salon of 1763, although it is individual genius that makes the arts bloom, "it is the general taste that perfects the artists." Less censorious than Rousseau, he suggested on this occasion that the stimulation of that taste—in France alone among modern nations—by the Salon had postponed the decadence of painting in that country, perhaps by a hundred years. But the art of speech was already gone, for "true eloquence appears only in the context of great public interests . . . To speak well, one must be a tribune of the people . . . After the loss of liberty, there were no more orators in Athens or in Rome."[35]

Four years later Diderot opened his survey of the Salon of 1767 with the sad reflection that the springs of art were being exhausted ("Tout s'épuise"). This he explained in part by the rise of speculation in art by collectors, for whom as individuals, rather than the nation, artists were now painting their best works. Most generally, it is luxury "that degrades great talents, by subjecting them to small works, and that degrades great subjects by reducing them to scenes of revelry." Or, as Diderot was to put it in the *Pensées detachées sur la peinture*, first drafted ten years later, "At the moment when the artist thinks of money, he loses his feeling for beauty."[36]

The *Salon de 1767* goes on to take up this theme in greater (physiocratic) detail, explaining that it is not wealth per se that leads to the downfall of the arts, but the kind of wealth involved. A prince who favors agriculture over usury and

---

34 Jean Jacques Barthélemy, *Voyages du jeune Anacharsis en Grèce* (Paris, 1788), pp. 241–69; tr. in P. le Huray and J. Day (eds), *Music and Aesthetics in the Eighteenth and Early Nineteenth Centuries* (Cambridge: Cambridge University Press, 1988), pp. 121–9.

35 "C'est le génie d'un seul qui fait éclore les arts; c'est le goût général qui perfectionne les artistes" (Diderot, *Salon de 1763*, DPV, vol. 13, p. 340). The meaning of the term *le peuple*, bearers of *le goût général*, used two sentences later is soon clarified. Why were there among the ancients such great musicians? "C'est que la musique faisait partie de l'éducation générale: on présentait une lyre à tout enfant bien né."

36 "N'oubliez pas parmi les obstacles à la perfection et à la durée des beaux-arts, je ne dis pas la richesse d'un peuple, mais ce luxe qui dégrade les grands talents, en les assujettissant à de petits ouvrages, et les grands sujets en les réduisant à la bambochade" (Diderot, *Salon de 1767*, DPV, vol. 16, p. 62); "Au moment où l'artiste pense à l'argent, il perd le sentiment du beau" (*Pensées détachées sur la peinture* [ca. 1776], in *Oeuvres esthétiques*, ed. P. Vernière (Paris: Garnier, 1988), p. 829). For an enlightening discussion of Diderot, "man of the Enlightenment with an acute if not woeful sense of decadence and degradation," see A. Becq, "Diderot, historien de l'art?" *Dix-huitième siècle* 19 (1987), pp. 421–38.

tax farming will lead his nation to luxury indeed, but a luxury meeting the interest of society and not that of the "fantasy, passion, prejudices, opinions" of individuals. "Painters, poets, sculptors, musicians, and all the arts grow from the soil, they are also children of good Ceres; and I answer you that wherever they originate in that sort of luxury they will flourish and will always flourish." But according to Diderot's historical pessimism, this happy condition cannot last. In the fragment of a dialogue on luxury, thematically as well as chronologically related to the 1767 Salon critique, he explains that agriculture itself engenders commerce, industry, and wealth, leading to social and artistic decadence. His only solution to this paradox seems a flimsy one, especially given the social dynamics Diderot believed he saw at work: if the rulers of wealthy nations would strip from gold its character as representation of merit and abolish the venality of public office, then the wealthy could have all the palaces, pictures, statues, fine wines, and beautiful women they want, without claiming the merit of state functions, and citizens would become enlightened and virtuous.[37]

It is luxury based on money, "with which one can buy everything," which "becomes the common measure of everything," and of which one needs ever more, that "degrades and destroys the fine arts, because the fine arts, their progress, and their survival require true opulence, and this luxury is only the fatal mask of a nearly universal poverty, whose development it accelerates and aggravates." The arts under these conditions are either subjected to the caprices of the rich or "abandoned to the mercy of the indigent multitude, which strives, by poor productions of every sort, to give itself the credit and the look of wealth."[38] As Barthélémy decried the invasion of the opera by "workmen and mercenaries," so Diderot laments the disruption of social order that results from the corrosive effect of a money-centered economy:

---

37 Diderot, *Satire contre le luxe, à la manière de Perse* (1767?), DPV, vol. 16, p. 555.

38 "Si l'agriculture est la plus favorisée des conditions, les hommes seront entraînés où leur plus grand intérêt les poussera, et il n'y aura fantaisie, passion, préjugés, opinions qui tiennent . . . Les peintres, les poètes, les sculpteurs, les musiciens et la foule des arts adjacents naissent de la terre, ce sont aussi les enfants de la bonne Cérès; et je vous réponds que partout où ils tireront leur origine de cette sorte de luxe ils fleuriront et fleuriront à jamais . . . L'argent, avec lequel on peut se procurer tout, devint la mesure commune de tout. Il fallut avoir de l'argent, et quoi encore? de l'argent . . . c'est celui-là [cette sorte de luxe] qui dégrade et anéantit les beaux-arts, parce que les beaux-arts, leur progrès et leur durée demandent une opulence réelle, et que ce luxe-ci n'est que le masque fatal d'une misère presque générale, qu'il accélère et qu'il aggrave . . . C'est sous une pareille constitution que les beaux-arts n'ont que le rebut des conditions subalternes; c'est sous un ordre de choses aussi extraordinaire, aussi pervers qu'ils sont subordonnés à la fantaisie et aux caprices d'une poignée d'hommes riches, ennuyés, fastidieux, dont le goût est aussi corrompu que les mœurs, ou abandonnés à la merci de la multitude indigente qui s'efforce, par de mauvaises productions en tout genre, de se donner le crédit et le relief de la richesse" (Diderot, *Salon de 1767*, DPV, vol. 16, pp. 62, 161–8).

When a handful of speculators in public funds possessed fantastic riches, lived in palaces, made a public spectacle of their shameful opulence, all ranks were mixed up; a grievous emulation appeared, a demented and cruel struggle between all the orders of society.[39]

The rise of a money economy displaces both nobility in the arts and that repre-sentative of the social order based on landed property.

Art and commerce

The service to the arts rendered, in Diderot's eyes, by the Salon in France was also that hoped for in Britain by Sir Joshua Reynolds from the institution of the Royal Academy in 1769: "that *the dignity of the dying Art* (to make use of an expres-sion of PLINY) may be revived under the Reign of GEORGE THE THIRD."[40] In 1780 he celebrated the opening of Somerset House as seat of the Academy with the thought that the

> estimation in which we stand in respect to our neighbors, will be in pro-portion to the degrees in which we excel or are inferior to them in the acquisition of intellectual excellence, of which Trade and its consequen-tial riches must be acknowledged to give the means; but a people whose whole attention is absorbed in those means, and who forget the end, can aspire but little above the rank of a barbarous nation.[41]

This conception lay behind Reynolds's low evaluation of Venetian and Dutch painting, which "depart from the great purposes of painting" and aim "at applause by inferior qualities."[42] The attack is complex. The Venetians, says Reynolds, draw attention to their craft skills rather than to the "intellectual dig-nity . . . that ennobles the painter's art" and "lays the line between him and the mere mechanick" who produces not art but mere ornament.[43] As a result, the art of Venice and that of Holland share an emphasis on color, which appeals to the eye and reflects an orientation to sensuality and elegance rather than to the uplifting dignity of subject-matter basic to history painting. In Holland the departure from themes of general ethical interest is carried the farthest, for their history pieces "are so far from giving a general view of human life, that they

---

39 Diderot, *Satire*, DPV, vol. 16, p. 553.
40 Reynolds, *Discourses on Art*, p. 21.
41 Ibid., p. 169.
42 Ibid., p. 63.
43 Ibid., pp. 43, 57. Reynolds's remarks on Dutch (and Flemish) painting in his *Journey to Flanders and Holland* frequently pays homage to their masterly skill, while reminding us that "it is to the eye only that the works of this school are addressed," not to the mind (*The Literary Works of Sir Joshua Reynolds*, ed. H. W. Beechey (London: Bohn, 1851), vol. 2, p. 205).

exhibit all the minute particulars of a nation differing in several respects from the rest of mankind."[44]

In John Barrell's words, "what distinguishes Venice and Holland" for Reynolds "is the single-mindedness of their pursuit of trade as an end in itself."[45] Such a conception was hardly peculiar to Reynolds; Holland in particular was practically a synonym for commerce in the eighteenth century. The brief paragraph devoted to painters in Diderot's survey of the Low Countries in 1774 asks only rhetorically whether it is not "commerce that has narrowed the minds of these marvelous men? However skillful the Dutch painters might have been, they rarely raised themselves to purity of taste and grand ideas and character."[46] Indeed, this was not only an outsider's view, for the topic of the corruption of virtue by commerce was a central one in the Hollanders' discourse about themselves even during the seventeenth-century high point of their prosperity. Commerce directs the mind to concrete matters and to particular interests, and so Dutch art—as Winckelmann tells us—derives its "forms and figures" from observation of particulars rather than from the synthesis of ideal beauty from observations of many objects. Hence "the trifling beauties that make the works of Dutch painters so popular" are at an infinite distance from the noble simplicity and quiet grandeur of Raphael's works.[47]

As Reynolds's text indicates, the political theme opposing art's uplifting capacities to the deleterious effects of modern trade and luxury could also express a more particular interest of artists, the definition of their pursuits as *fine arts* in distinction to "mechanical" crafts or trades. Institutional statement of this conception was one of the motives of the foundation of the Royal Academy, as well as of the exclusion of (largely reproductive) printmakers from membership. Despite the vastly different circumstances, a similar motivation was visible in the rules of the Académie royale de peinture et de sculpture established in Paris in 1648, which

> decided that all members, under penalty of being expelled, would refrain from keeping an open shop for displaying their work, from exhibiting it in windows or outside their place of residence, from posting any commercial sign or inscription, or from doing anything which

---

44 Reynolds, *Discourses on Art*, p. 69.

45 J. Barrell, *The Political Theory of Painting from Reynolds to Hazlitt* (New Haven: Yale University Press, 1986), p. 73.

46 "On connaît suffisamment les grands maîtres de l'école hollandaise. Ne serait-ce pas l'esprit de commerce qui a rétréci la tête de ces hommes merveilleux? Quelque habiles qu'aient été les peintres hollandais, ils se sont rarement élevés à la pureté du goût et à la grandeur des idées et du caractère" (D. Diderot, *Voyage en Hollande*, in *Oeuvres complètes*, ed. J. Assezat and M. Tourneux (Paris: Garnier, 1876), vol. 17, p. 430).

47 Winckelmann, *Reflections*, pp. 21, 43.

might confuse the honorable rank of Academician with the debased and mercenary rank of Guild Master.[48]

Though great gains were made in the effort to counter this confusion, a multitude of texts show that the status of the visual arts remained in question throughout the 1700s.[49] By the end of the century, when art had largely been redefined as a "liberal" occupation, the system of court commissions that had structured the high-prestige end of the profession was giving way to production for a relatively open market. Ideologically as well as practically, the academic system which had served the liberation of the artist from the medieval guild structure came into conflict with the extension of the market as a general model for the linking of production with consumption into cultural fields as well as all others.[50]

This conflict appears, notably, in the lament of many later eighteenth-century writers over the displacement of the *grand* by the *petit goût*, the shift of taste from history painting to portraits, landscapes, and genre works. The portrait, other than that of the monarch or other great noble, naturally suggests the self-love of the individual celebrating his or her wealth and power; often compared to the multiplication of mirrors in the apartments of the wealthy, it was also the bread and butter of a multitude of artists. A 1777 article in the *Journal de Paris* condemned, along with portraiture, the "low and ignoble" subjects of Flemish painting, "unfortunately more fashionable than ever with its scenes of revelry."[51] It might seem that the critical as well as commercial success of Chardin and Greuze, painters of still life and genre scenes, constitutes an exception to this rule of official taste. But these artists, lauded in particular by Diderot himself, are exceptions that prove the rule. Thus Chardin was praised (by Raynal) for the

---

48 A. de Montaiglon (ed.), *Mémoires pour servir à l'histoire de l'Académie royale de peinture et de sculpture depuis 1648 jusqu'en 1664* (Paris, 1853), vol. 1, pp. 61–2; cit. P. Mainardi, *Art and Politics of the Second Empire* (New Haven: Yale University Press, 1987), pp. 1–9. For the seventeenth-century controversy over the painters' attempt to raise their status, see T. Crow, *Painters and Public Life in Eighteenth-Century Paris* (New Haven: Yale University Press, 1985), Chapter 1, esp. pp. 25, 31.

49 A useful as well as entertaining survey is offered in Jean Chatelus, *Peindre à Paris au XVIIIe siècle* (Paris: Jacqueline Chambon, 1991), pp. 125 ff.

50 See the excellent analysis of Annie Becq, "Expositions, peintres et critiques: vers l'image moderne de l'artiste," *Dix-huitième Siècle* 14 (1982), pp. 131–49, esp. pp. 144 ff., which discusses David's experiments, in the first years of the nineteenth century, with the public exhibition of his works for an admission fee, outside the framework of the Salon. It is interesting that David sought to justify this attempt by reference to earlier English practice in his use of the term "exhibition," a word used in France, as opposed to "exposition," to mean commercial, shop-window displays. In this David anticipated Courbet, whose "exhibition" of his works in a pavilion outside the gate of the Exposition universelle of 1855 was another historical pointer toward the coming of the modern gallery-structured art market (see Patricia Mainardi, "Courbet's exhibitionism," *Gazette des beaux-arts*, Dec. 1991, pp. 251–66).

51 Chatelus, *Peindre à Paris*, p. 171.

charm of his images, which "offers a strong criticism of the Flemish painters in general," whereas Greuze, hailed by Diderot as the inventor of a new genre of "moral painting," demonstrated to another commentator that "the least noble style nevertheless has its nobility."[52]

While the "grand taste" seemed to be giving way in France to "little pictures," "noble and sublime" art to "superficial and momentary beauties," history painting to genre pictures,[53] in England painters were still attempting to establish the claims of the great style. In that country, Patricia Crown has argued, in the eyes of its critics the "complexity, variety, multiplicity, nuance, irregularity, and lack of subordination" that characterized the rococo style pertained "to early- and mid-eighteenth century society as well as to art." We thus encounter in the classicizing texts of early eighteenth-century writers on art like Shaftesbury, Richardson, and Webb themes identified above in the discourses of French theorists, notably the illegitimacy of the aesthetic preferences of the lower orders, artisans, tradesmen, and in particular women; what was then called the "modern" style, applied in the making of furniture and decoration as well as pictures, was deemed "effeminate in subject as well as form," for "like women it was little and licentious."[54] These theoretical disputes had a practical equivalent in the quarrels of the 1750s over the choice of pictures and the public to be admitted to the exhibitions mounted by painters under the auspices of the Society for the Encouragement of Arts, Manufactures, and Commerce. The very name of this society suggests the problem posed for artists seeking the encouragement of the *grand goût* in England and the promotion of history painting in place of the portraiture that constituted the basic stock in trade of English artists, a problem ultimately resolved, however temporarily, by the institutional power of the Royal Academy.[55]

It is an irony typical of, and indeed essential to, the ideological relation of art and money that the critique of Dutch painting as the expression of a commercial culture had a specific commercial significance for artists and critics. In both France and England, the growing interest of collectors in Dutch and Flemish painting probably reflected the rise of a new group of collectors with a taste different from that of earlier dominant connoisseurs (the number of French collectors seems to have increased from around 150 during the period 1701–20 to at least 500 during 1751–90). This was part of the background to Diderot's

---

52 Quotations cited in Crow, *Painters and Public Life*, pp. 137, 141; for Diderot on Greuze, see his *Salon de 1763*, DPV, vol. 13, pp. 391–4.

53 K. Pomian, "Marchands, connaisseurs, curieux à Paris au XVIIIe siècle," in *Collectionneurs, amateurs et curieux: Paris, Venise: XVe–XVIIIe siecle* (Paris: Gallimard, 1987), p. 191. This extremely interesting article is the chief source of the information about French collecting cited in the remainder of this section.

54 Patricia Crown, "British Rococo as social and political style," *Eighteenth-Century Studies* 23:3 (1990), p. 281.

55 See Iain Pears, *The Discovery of Painting* (New Haven: Yale University Press, 1988), Chapter 4.

complaint about the rise of speculation in the art market and its deleterious effect on artistic quality. The growth and differentiation of the art public disrupted at once the supremacy in matters of taste of earlier aristocratic collectors, the influence (and paid advisory services) of critic-connoisseurs, and the commercial success of painting in the grand style, while initiating the rise of the art dealer as a key figure in the movement of taste and directing that movement toward the dominance of landscape and genre painting in the later nineteenth century.

Kzrysztof Pomian suggests that the shift in interest from Italian and Italianate painting on grand classical, biblical, and national-historical themes to Dutch and Flemish genre painting involved a change of the focus of judgment from the norms spelled out by such writers as Reynolds and Diderot to questions of attribution, in which picture merchants themselves had the upper hand. However, Pomian stresses, this victory of attribution over art-theoretical judgment was confined to the market, outside which aesthetics managed to maintain its supremacy:

> In these places a victory for neoclassicism and a return in strength of the Italians was gathering force, at the very moment when the "little Flemish and Dutch paintings" triumphed in the market. And it was in these places that the new type of connoisseur, who would dethrone the merchant, was formed: the art critic and art historian.[56]

Illusions of disinterest

Along with art history and criticism, the advent of aesthetics—above all in Germany, where Baumgarten first gave the field its name—both reflected the emerging practice of production and enjoyment of the fine arts as increasingly detached from their earlier functional contexts, and played a role in the definition of this practice as conceptually opposed to trade. This can be seen, for instance, in the "reading debate" carried on by German writers at the century's end, when the growing demand for "light" reading matter—poetry based on popular forms, as well as periodicals and gothic and romance novels, many directed specifically at female readers—rapidly outran that for philosophically uplifting texts. This development was viewed by "serious" writers, themselves increasingly dependent on the market for a living, as a sign of cultural degeneration due to the commercial orientation of literary production. The challenge posed by the appeal of *Trivialliteratur* had an important influence on the formulation of aesthetic theory, strengthening the emphasis on architectonic structure, on aesthetic distance, on originality in composition, and on the

---

56 Pomian, "Marchands, connaisseurs, curieux," p. 194. On English collecting of Dutch pictures after the 1740s, see Louise Lippincott, *Selling Art in Georgian London* (New Haven: Yale University Press, 1983), pp. 61–2, 121–3; and Pears, *The Discovery of Painting*, pp. 161–9.

noncommercial character of the work of true art.[57] Philosophical questions about the function of art resonated with matters of concrete interest to a writer like Friedrich Schiller, seeking to live by the pen. But even for a philosopher like Kant, little concerned with the fine arts as practiced in Paris and London and not competing in the marketplace of belles lettres, the opposition of aesthetic and commercial concerns appears as a simple presupposition.

In Winckelmann's *Reflections on the Imitation of Greek Works* the historical distance between ancient and modern appears intermittently as a fall from grace, in which the corrupting effect of a commercial economy plays a central role. Explaining the special access of the ancient Greeks to "good taste," for instance, Winckelmann emphasizes the role played by the classical gymnasium as a school of art, where (thanks to the absence of "our present-day criteria of respectability") "natural beauty revealed itself naked for the instruction of the artist":

> The nude body in its most beautiful form was exhibited there in so many different, authentic, and noble positions and poses not obtainable today by the hired models in our academies.
>
> Truth springs from inner sentiment, and the draughtsman who wants to impart truth to his academy studies cannot preserve even a shadow of it unless he himself is able to replace that which the unmoved and indifferent soul of his model does not feel or is unable to express by actions appropriate to a given sentiment or passion.[58]

Here authenticity and nobility, embodied (ideally, at least) in the "inner sentiment" of the artist, are opposed to the gracelessness of the hired model, whose movements reflect not the free spirit of his personality but the requirements of his drawing-master employer. But the artist too suffers the distortions of the money-oriented society, for "an artist of our times . . . feels compelled to work more for bread than for honor."[59] Not only is his product at the mercy of its purchaser, who may choose to place it in positions quite unsuitable for proper viewing,[60] but he is more or less required by the pressures of earning a livelihood to depend on the practical techniques he has picked up in his apprenticeship rather than engaging in the rigorous research into the principles of formal truth that allowed Michelangelo to come so near to the achievement of antiquity.

Winckelmann's account of art is, to say the least, philosophically naive in

---

57 See Jochen Schulte-Sasse, *Die Kritik an der Trivialliteratur seit der Aufklärung: Studien zur Geschichte des modernen Kitschbegriffs* (Munich: Fink, 1971); Martha Woodmansee, *The Author, Art, and the Market: Rereading the History of Aesthetics* (New York: Columbia University Press, 1994), especially Chapters 1, 3, 4.

58 Winckelmann, *Reflections*, p. 13 (translation modified).

59 Ibid., p. 55 (translation modified).

60 Ibid., pp. 61–9.

comparison with Kant's, but themes present in his work reappear in the Third Critique. For Kant taste is not just ennobling and art not just an education in natural grace; the experience of beauty is in his system an essential element of the spiritual progress of humankind toward the realization of our rational nature. But the features in Kant's eyes essential to the fine arts (as opposed to the merely "agreeable" arts, like table conversation and games) involve the familiar oppositions, not only to the "mechanical" or manual but also to effort performed for a monetary reward. The basic principle is that "we should not call anything art except a production through freedom, i.e. through a power of choice that bases its acts on reason."[61]

Kant also clearly distinguishes art from science, as it had not been distinguished two and even one hundred years earlier. Freedom implies, on the one hand, the absence of governance by rules, characteristic of science. Art is the product of the creative genius, for whom technical training and the imitation of the ancients serve to shape a soul that will spontaneously generate new forms. For "genius is the exemplary originality of a subject's natural endowment in the *free* use of his cognitive powers."[62] The emphasis on an exercise of reason specific to the arts establishes their autonomy: they are to be guided not by demands external to their own formal natures but by principles internal to the sphere of art (Kant distinguishes "paintings properly so called," which are "there merely to be looked at" from those "intended to teach us, e.g. history or natural science").[63] On the other hand,

> *Art* is likewise to be distinguished from *craft* [Handwerke]. The first is
> also called *free art*, the second could be called *mercenary art* [Lohnkunst].
> We regard free art [as an art] that could only turn out purposive (i.e.
> succeed) if it is play, in other words, an occupation that is agreeable on
> its own account; mercenary art we regard as labor, i.e. as an occupation
> that on its own account is disagreeable (burdensome) and that attracts
> us only through its effect (e.g. pay [*Lohn*]) so that people can be coerced
> into it.[64]

This passage, not unrelated to the status preoccupations of eighteenth-century artists, evokes elements basic to Kant's theory of taste as "the ability to judge an object, or a way of presenting it, by means of liking or disliking *devoid of all interest*."[65] The experience of beauty is the experience of an object as "purposive"—as

---

61 I. Kant, *Critique of Judgement* (1790), tr. W. S. Pluhar (Indianapolis: Hackett, 1987), p. 170.
62 Ibid., p. 186.
63 Ibid., p. 193. Such passages explain Clement Greenberg's tracing of his conception of "modernism" to the Kantian aesthetic (if we allow the transformation of the "autonomous reason" at work in art into the "logic of the medium").
64 Ibid., pp. 170, 171.
65 Ibid., p. 53.

having, we might say, the character of design—but without actually having a defined purpose for the viewer, who is caught up in no relation of action (including that of scientific cognizing) with it. Hence the object is a "free beauty," exemplifying design in the abstract and in principle representing nothing under a determinate concept; given Kant's (inter-) subjective conception of beauty, this reflects the fact that the viewer's judgment of taste can be considered free of any idea of functions which the object might serve for him or her and therefore involves "no concept [as to] what the object is [meant] to represent; our imagination is playing, as it were, while it contemplates the shape, and such a concept would only restrict its freedom."[66]

The concept of "interest" at work here includes both morality (we have an interest in the good) and the common eighteenth-century sense of that word which "centered on economic advantage as its core meaning."[67] The contemplative realm of the aesthetic is contrasted, therefore, with realms of action: that of the good, object of the Practical Reason, and that of the "agreeable" (pleasing to the senses) and of those things answering to "material" needs. (In the case of cooking, "only when their need has been satisfied can we tell who in a multitude of people has taste and who does not."[68]) Freedom, at least of the will, is essential to morality; the freedom of aesthetic play signifies the bracketing of material desire and so of the economic domain to which those desires look for satisfaction. Aesthetic appreciation requires neither ownership nor consumption, but only perception.

Kant's treatment of the nature of art involves a complex drawing together of many conceptual strands in the idea of freedom. The production of beautiful things must have an aristocratic character opposed to *labor*: "anything studied and painstaking must be avoided in art." The idea of "play" is central because it is the opposite of "work." And the concept of labor involved here is that of wage labor: art must be free in a double sense, including that "of not being a mercenary occupation [*Lohngeschäft*] and hence a kind of labor, whose magnitude can be judged, exacted, or paid for according to a determinate standard" and "the sense that, though the mind is occupying itself, yet it feels satisfied and aroused (independently of any pay [*Lohn*]) without looking to some other purpose."[69]

The aristocratic flavor of aesthetic experience is if anything more pronounced in Kant's doctrine of the sublime, the experience of the superiority of the reason to the imagination, bound to the representation of empirical material. Like the

---

66 Ibid., p. 77.
67 A. O. Hirschman, *The Passions and the Interests* (Princeton: Princeton University Press, 1977), p. 32. Hirschman presents a useful chronicle of the evolution of "interest" from a general sense of "concerns, aspirations, and advantage" (p. 32) to Shaftesbury's definition of it as the "desire for those conveniences, by which we are provided for, and maintained" and Hume's use of "interested affection" as synonymous with "love of gain" (p. 37).
68 Kant, *Critique of Judgement*, p. 52.
69 Ibid., p. 190.

experience of the beautiful, that of the sublime presupposes the satisfaction of material needs, in this case that for physical safety: "Just as we cannot pass judgment on the beautiful if we are seized by inclination and appetite, so we cannot pass judgment at all on the sublime in nature if we are afraid." But paradoxically physical safety allows us to respond (aesthetically, not practically) to the thrill of danger viewed and therefore "to regard as small the [objects] of our [natural] concerns: property, health, and life." This appreciation of human response to aestheticized peril reflects the esteem given by society to a person "who does not yield to danger but promptly sets to work with vigor and full deliberation." This character is best exemplified by the warrior, so that "no matter how much people may dispute, when they compare the statesman with the general, as to which one deserves the superior respect, an aesthetic judgment decides in favor of the general." For "even war has something sublime about it," whereas peace, in contrast, "tends to make prevalent a mere[ly] commercial spirit," which brings with it "base selfishness, cowardice, and softness."[70] In such a passage we may recognize, in this student of Hume and Rousseau, the discourse of civic virtue and its decline under the influence of commerce—here to be countered by the transmutation of aristocratic (military) values into a spiritual principle.

Since work, as wage labor, is marked by the anti-artistic character of mercenary culture, it is not surprising that play will appear to incarnate the aesthetic impulse. It was in Schiller's *Aesthetic Education* that this theme received its fullest development at the end of the eighteenth century. For Schiller too "the character of our age" is established by way of "an astonishing contrast between contemporary forms of humanity and earlier ones, especially the Greek." With the development of the division of labor, the unified human personality of the ancients has been split into fragments, so that "we see not merely individuals, but whole classes of men, developing but one part of their potentialities, while of the rest, as in stunted growths, only vestigial traces remain."[71] When a society "insists on special skills being developed with a degree of intensity which is only commensurate with its readiness to absolve the individual citizen from developing himself in extensity—can we wonder that the remaining aptitudes of the psyche are neglected in order to give undivided attention to the one which will bring honor and profit [*welche ehrt und lohnt*]?"[72] It is the task of art, expression of the drive to play, to reconstitute the fragmented human person, "to restore by means of a higher art the totality of our nature which the arts themselves have destroyed."[73]

---

70 Ibid., pp. 121–2.
71 F. Schiller, *On the Aesthetic Education of Man*, ed. and tr. E. M. Wilkinson and L. A. Willoughby (Oxford: Oxford University Press, 1967), p. 31, 33.
72 Ibid., p. 37.
73 Ibid., p. 43.

If art is to be the instrument of humankind's education and elevation to a more advanced order of social being, it must resist the characteristic forces of the present age. The artist must protect himself from the corruption of modernity: "Let him direct his gaze upwards, to the dignity of his calling and the universal Law, not downwards towards Fortune and the needs of daily life." And he must seek an audience among people of similar temperament: "Those who know no other criterion of value than the effort of earning or the tangible profit, how should they be capable of appreciating the unobtrusive effect of taste on the outward appearance and on the mind and character of men?"[74] Taste, by fostering harmony in the individual, will bring harmony to society. Providing a spiritual experience of the physical world, it opens a realm of experience in which the interests of reason are reconciled with the interests of the senses. Art thus holds out the promise of a future happiness for humankind, but even under current conditions it provides "an ideal semblance which ennobles the reality of common day." Taste, that is,

> throws a veil of decorum over those physical desires which, in their naked form, affront the dignity of free beings; and by a delightful illusion of freedom, conceals from us our degrading kinship with matter. On the wings of taste even that art which must cringe for payment can lift itself out of the dust.[75]

With these words, nearly the concluding ones of Schiller's book, a conflict at the heart of the modern practice of art—that the commodity status of artworks hinges on their representation of an interest superior to that of mundane commerce—has achieved frank expression, if only in the form of the wistful hope that it can be overcome. Fundamental to this practice is the idea that art's production differs from all other production in its freedom from the market. Hence art is like play, not work; hence, considered as work, it engages the whole person, not the fragmented laborer of today; hence it is a fully creative effort, not constrained by a mechanical process; hence it is "disinterested," not aiming at the satisfaction of material needs. In reality, however, art's rise to autonomous status itself involved the replacement of artistic work to the order of premodern patronage by production for the market. It is therefore not surprising that the "delightful illusion" of art's separateness from the commercial culture which in fact produced it in its modern form has proved impossible to sustain, and that the history of this institution to the present day has seen artists alternate between claims to a higher calling and complaints of insufficient payment for their practice of it.

From the side of the consumer, the worship of art has expressed the claim of capitalist society's higher orders to rise above the confines of commerce as

74 Ibid., pp. 57, 65.
75 Ibid., pp. 201, 219.

worthy inheritors of the aristocratic culture of the past. Here, involvement with the autonomous artwork represents detachment from the claims of practical life, even while its ownership and enjoyment require both money and the time made possible by money and so signify financial success along with cultural superiority. It is indeed the new uses made of images, music, writing, and the rest—notably for the construction of a mode of sensibility characterized by distance from material necessity and so free to cultivate responsiveness to experience—that appear as the autonomy of art. Essential to this concept is not just the liberation of the arts from their former social functions but their conceptual separation from the everyday life under the sway of economic interest that the bourgeoisie in reality shares with its social inferiors, apart from those moments devoted to the detachment essential to the aesthetic attitude. In fact, the acquisition of the aesthetic attitude derives from and marks a position of privilege in the very realm of economics from which that attitude officially declares its independence. And although the conception of art as transcendent of social reality provides a naturalist disguise for the actual historical process within which it came into existence and for the socio-economic prerequisites—leisure and education—of its enjoyment, the truth, as we have seen, will out. If Baudelaire was moved by the Salon of 1859 to compare poetry and progress to "two ambitious men who hate one another with an instinctive hatred," it was the same poet who had addressed his criticism of the Salon of 1846 "To the Bourgeois": "for as not one of you today can do without power, so not one of you has the right to do without poetry."[76]

76 Charles Baudelaire, *Arts in Paris, 1841–1862*, tr. Jonathan Mayne (Oxford: Phaidon, 1965), pp. 154, 41.

4

BEAUTIFUL AND SUBLIME

Ancient writers described artworks in gender terms: Vitruvius called the Doric order appropriate to honor the "virile strength" of male gods and assigned the ornamented Corinthian to female deities. But such terminology acquired a new, systematic character with the beginning of aesthetics as philosophy of art in the eighteenth century. Texts of this period, for example, categorize forms of painting as "virile" or "effeminate," and celebrate poetry as a peculiarly masculine art. What—and how much—is to be made of such expressions? Does the metaphorical application of gender stereotypes to the domain of art simply reflect the *mentalité* of a sexist society? To look at it this way is to ignore the complexity of metaphor, the extension of a system of concepts from one kind of object to another. Metaphor changes not only the way we think about the new range of objects a concept is applied to, but the meanings of the concept itself.

Anthropologist Judith Shapiro has observed that the qualities a society—such as our own—may think of as distinguishing women and men

> belong to a web of metaphors that have, in fact, to do with many things other than gender *per se*. The opposition between male and female serves as a source of symbolism for a diversity of cultural domains; at the same time, gender differences themselves are defined through categories of the economy, the polity—in brief, of the wider social universe in which they are located.[1]

This social universe includes the arts. Ideas about gender, I will argue, beyond providing a conceptual system for describing artworks, have been deeply involved with the very idea of the fine arts; while in the process by which this system was developed in the eighteenth century, the arts provided a sphere for the modern conceptualization of gender.

1 Judith Shapiro, "Gender totemism," in Richard R. Randolph, David M. Schneider, and May N. Diaz (eds), *Dialectics and Gender: Anthropological Approaches* (Boulder and London: Westview Press, 1988), p. 2.

It is, we must remember, only since the late eighteenth century that people in the West have taken for granted (in P. O. Kristeller's words) "that the five 'major arts' constitute an area all by themselves, clearly separated by common characteristics from the crafts, the sciences, and other human activities."[2] The development of this "modern system of the arts" reflected not the recognition of hitherto overlooked properties shared by the fine arts, but an actual transformation of the social place and significance of writing, painting and sculpture, music, dance, and architecture. This involved, centrally, their increasing autonomy as practices with respect to earlier religious and political functions. New social institutions—the academy, the museum, the public concert—were created around them, in turn transforming them. The objects and performances involved became significant for their properties *as works of art*, expressive of the genius of their producers, which come to life under the gaze or in the hearing of the attentive viewer or auditor. Aesthetics, together with art criticism and art history, came into existence in connection with this emergence of the fine arts, in close intellectual contact with other philosophical, political, and literary discourses as well as with artistic practice.[3]

As the eighteenth-century reconstruction of art was a Europe-wide phenomenon, aesthetic theorizing developed as an international discourse. For example, Edmund Burke's essay on the sublime directly influenced the thinking of such different writers as Denis Diderot, Gotthold Lessing, and Immanuel Kant. The international character of the discussion reflected the scale of the changes—the growth of market economies, urbanization, nation-state formation, and the rise to power of new social classes—that produced modern society. During the later eighteenth century, people experienced the accelerating emergence of capitalism as a continuous series of upheavals in social, political, economic, and cultural relations, which provoked a desire for principles, practical and theoretical, in terms of which order could be imposed on this alternatively or even simultaneously exhilarating and terrifying experience. As the reconfiguring of the arts was an element of this general social transformation, classically based definitions of art as the pursuit of beauty no longer seemed adequate. New times called for new concepts.

Writers responding to the transgression of traditional social and conceptual boundaries, and to the emotionally overwhelming experience of vastness and power the period's changes imposed on whole populations, were especially drawn to the ancient idea of the sublime, reintroduced into European literary criticism at the end of the seventeenth century. Although she does not use the word, this

---

2 Paul Oskar Kristeller, "The modern system of the arts," Chapter 9 in his *Renaissance Thought II* (New York: Harper Torchbook, 1965), p. 165.

3 On the place of aesthetics in this complex development, see the introduction and essays in Paul Mattick (ed.), *Eighteenth-Century Aesthetics and the Reconstruction of Art* (Cambridge: Cambridge University Press, 1993); see especially, for a discussion of gender in early aesthetics, Elizabeth Bohls's "Disinterestedness and the denial of the particular: Locke, Adam Smith, and the subject of aesthetics."

passage from a letter written by Abigail Adams to her son John Quincy Adams on his voyage to France in 1779 almost perfectly characterizes the sublime:

> These are the times in which a genius would wish to live. It is not in the still calm of life, or the repose of a pacific station that great characters are formed. The habits of a vigorous mind are formed in contending with difficulties. Great necessities call out great virtues. When a mind is raised, and animated by scenes that engage the heart, then those qualities which would otherwise lay dormant, wake into life and form the character of the hero and the statesman.[4]

The sublime names an experience; by 1759, when Burke published his *Philosophical Enquiry into the Origin of Our Ideas of the Sublime and Beautiful*, it was common also to define the sublime's sister concept, beauty, by reference to the emotions awakened by natural phenomena or works of art, rather than—as earlier—by characteristics (harmony and proportion) of the thing itself. I say "sister concept," because Burke differentiates the beautiful from the sublime in terms clearly identifying them with the feminine and masculine poles of the modern gender system; in this he only states more explicitly than usual the consensus of his period.

The features that, according to Burke, give rise to the experience of beauty would still today likely be typed as "feminine": smallness, smoothness, curviness, delicacy, cleanliness, soft coloration, lack of resistance, quietness.[5] Similarly, the properties of objects said to induce the sensation of sublimity are conventionally "masculine"—vastness, roughness, jaggedness, heaviness, strong coloration, hardness, loudness.[6] These two sets of characteristics are associated, respectively, with the emotions of love and fear, which for Burke are responses to weakness and to

---

4 Quoted in David McCullough, *John Adams* (New York: Simon and Schuster, 2001), p. 226.

5 Interestingly enough, "beauty" is a development from Latin *bellum*, which replaced *pulchrum* during the Renaissance. This derives from *bonellum*, a diminutive of *bonum* applied originally only to women and children. See Wladislaw Tatarkiewicz, *A History of Six Ideas* (The Hague: Nijhoff, 1980), p. 121.

6 Had Burke himself not unequivocally identified the sublime as masculine in nature, we could cite John Cleland's description of "the essential object of enjoyment," as seen through the eyes of Fanny Hill:

> its prodigious size made me shrink again; yet I could not, without pleasure, behold, and even ventur'd to feel, such a length, such a breadth of animated ivory! . . . then the broad and bluish-casted incarnate of the head, and blue serpentines of its veins, altogether composed the most striking assemblage of figure and colours in nature. In short, it stood an object of terror and delight.
>
> *Memoirs of a Woman of Pleasure* [1749] (New York: Putnam, 1963), p. 85

To this may be compared not only Kant's discovery of the sublime in the *monstrous* and the *colossal*, but also his analysis of our feeling of the sublime as "a pleasure . . . produced by the feeling of a momentary inhibition of the vital forces followed immediately by an outpouring of them that is all the stronger." Immanuel Kant, *Critique of Judgment*, tr. Werner Pluhar (Indianapolis: Hackett, 1987), pp. 109, 98.

strength. Criticizing the (once standard) view that some formal "perfection" of an object causes us to experience it as beautiful, he states that beauty,

> where it is highest in the female sex, almost always carries with it an idea of weakness and imperfection. Women are very sensible of this; for which reason, they learn to lisp, to totter in their walk, to counterfeit weakness and even sickness. In all this, they are guided by nature. Beauty in distress is the most affecting beauty.[7]

The sublime, in contrast, causes not love but admiration. It "always dwells on great objects" while the beautiful is found in "small ones, and pleasing; we submit to what we admire, but we love what submits to us." Sublimity is to be found, for example, in "the authority of a father," which "hinders us from having that entire love for him that we have for our mothers, where the parental authority is almost melted down into the mother's fondness and indulgence."[8] Fundamentally, the source of the sublime is to be found in "whatever is fitted in any sort to excite the ideas of pain and danger, that is to say, whatever is in any sort terrible, or is conversant about terrible objects, or operates in a manner analogous to terror"—at any rate, "at certain distances" from danger, when fear gives way to the delightful *frisson* of an aesthetic experience.[9]

There is a deeper significance to the dual grouping of properties and the emotions they arouse than simple sexual difference. The distinction between terror and love corresponds for Burke to the division of the human passions under the two familiar headings of pains and pleasures. And the experiences classed under these headings "may be reduced very nearly to these two heads, *self-preservation* and *society*; to the ends of one or the other of which all our passions are calculated to answer." The former, "the most powerful of all the passions," are those "which are conversant about the preservation of the individual." The latter in its turn has two subdivisions: "1. the society of the *sexes*, which answers the purpose of propagation" and, second, "the more *general society*, which we have with men and with other animals." The paradigm of the pleasures derived from "the society of the sexes" is that of orgasm, a pleasure "of a lively character, rapturous and violent, and confessedly the highest pleasure of sense." While coupling gives pleasure, deprivation of it gives no great pain; this frees us from obsession with orgasm, and allows us, as rational creatures, to integrate sexual pleasure into our social existence generally. This takes the concrete form—or so Burke appears to suggest—of our choice of a single partner, in our feeling for whom sexual passion

---

7 Edmund Burke, *A Philosophical Enquiry into the Origin of Our Ideas of the Sublime and the Beautiful*, ed. J. T. Boulton (Notre Dame: University of Notre Dame Press, 1968), p. 110.

8 Ibid., pp. 110, 113, 111.

9 Ibid., pp. 39, 40; see also p. 46: "for terror is a passion which always produces delight when it does not press too close."

is connected with and heightened by "the idea of some *social* qualities." This "mixed passion" is love, and its general object "is the *general beauty* of the *sex*," just as "men . . . are attached to particulars by personal *beauty*."[10]

There is a slippage in Burke's language here that seems unconscious: from "man" as subject of analysis to "men." Even though the passage continues with the observation that "women and men, and not only they, but . . . other animals give us a sense of joy and pleasure in beholding them," the "we" is the masculine "we" who "love what submits to us."[11] This is made clearer in a later passage, where Burke describes the object of sexual love as "the beauty of women" while that of its extension into love for "the great society with man and all other animals" is beauty *tout court*, "a name I shall apply to all such qualities in things as induce in us a sense of affection and tenderness."[12] It is from the male point of view that beauty lines up with femininity and love, the sublime with masculinity and fear.

Sex and society

Burke's association of sociality and sexuality was no novelty. Pope's *Essay on Man* (1734), for instance, sees the latter as the foundation of the former: with man as with all creatures, he explains in Epistle III,

> Each loves itself, but not itself alone,
> Each sex desires alike, till two are one.
> Nor ends the pleasure with the fierce embrace;
> They love themselves, a third time in their race.

Generation leads to social complexity:

> A longer care man's helpless kind demands;
> That longer care contracts more lasting bands:
> Reflection, reason, still the ties improve,
> At once extend the interest, and the love.

Pope imagines no conflict between self-preservation and the social passions: both God and Nature bid "self-love and social be the same." He seems also to experience no difficulty in leaping from finding the source of "mutual happiness" in "mutual wants" to discovering the principle of political order in the rule of the father over his family:

> The same which in a sire the sons obeyed,
> A prince the father of a people made.

10 Ibid., pp. 38, 40, 42.
11 Ibid., p. 43.
12 Ibid., p. 51.

In Rousseau's version of the story, published twenty years later, the birth of society as byproduct of sexual passion leads to the fall of man from the state of freedom in which he was born to the chains he lives in now. While "man's first sentiment was that of his own existence; his first concern was that of his preservation," things changed radically with the gradual formation of family groups:

> The first developments of the heart were the effect of a new situation that united the husbands and wives, fathers and children in one common habitation. The habit of living together gave rise to the sweetest sentiments known to men: conjugal love and paternal love . . . [I]t was then that the first difference was established in the lifestyle of the two sexes . . . Women became more sedentary and grew accustomed to watch over the hut and the children, while the man went to seek their common subsistence.[13]

In this situation, male competition for women leads to the birth of *amour-propre*—"this is the source of emulation, rivalries, and jealousy"[14]—contrasted by Rousseau in *Emile* (1755) with "the gentle and affectionate passions born of self-love," which "is always good and always in conformity with order." It is after the birth of *amour-propre* "that man finds himself outside of nature and sets himself in contradiction with himself."[15] Sociality is thus double-edged. While it makes possible a higher, self-conscious moral state, perhaps to be achieved in the future, it also means the loss of the primal innocent freedom of the individual in the state of nature.

Given sociality's roots in sexuality, regeneration demands, among other things, the correct ordering of relations between the sexes. According to Rousseau, the two sexes are—given the institution of society—radically different. "One ought to be active and strong, the other passive and weak." Woman "is made to please and to be subjugated," while man's "merit is in his power; he pleases by the sole fact of his strength. This is not the law of love."[16] Indeed it is not; it is the law of terror, for what have we here but the figures of the beautiful and the sublime?

Only "a strange depravity of judgment," insists Rousseau, could think it appropriate for men and women to behave as equals in the expression of sexual desire:

> how can one fail to see that if reserve did not impose on one sex [the female] the moderation which nature imposes on the other, the result would soon be the ruin of both, and mankind would perish by the

---

13 Jean-Jacques Rousseau, "Discourse on the origin of inequality" [1754], in *On the Social Contract*, tr. D. A.Cress (Indianapolis: Hackett, 1983), pp. 140, 141–3.

14 Jean-Jacques Rousseau, *Emile, or On Education* [1755], tr. A. Bloom (New York: Basic Books, 1979), p. 214.

15 Ibid., pp. 214, 213.

16 Ibid., p. 358.

means established for preserving it? If there were some unfortunate region on earth where philosophy had introduced this practice— especially in hot countries, where more women are born than men— men would be tyrannized by women . . . [Men] would finally be their victims and would see themselves dragged to death without ever being able to defend themselves.[17]

Instead of tempting men to physical destruction by endless intercourse, women must be encouraged to take their natural place at the center of the family, as bearers, sucklers, and caretakers of children. In this position they mediate nature and culture. But just as procreation and the pleasing of men are women's chief functions, so the cultural realm is preeminently men's:

> The quest for abstract and speculative truths, principles, and axioms in the sciences, for everything that tends to generalize ideas, is not within the competence of women. All their studies ought to be related to prac- tice . . . [All] the reflections of women ought to be directed to the study of men or to the pleasing kinds of knowledge that have only taste as their aim; for, as regards works of genius, they are out of the reach of women.[18]

Given mankind's emergence from the state of nature, which has led to the birth of gender distinction, culture must take clear precedence over nature. The reintegration of the two principles, now set in opposition, requires patriarchy, so that woman's "first and most important quality" is "gentleness."[19]

Despite the dissimilarity between their accounts of social experience, the common elements in Rousseau's conception of relations between the sexes and Burke's theory of the sublime and beautiful are striking. More is at work here than an association of the beautiful with the pleasurable subservience assigned to women, and of the sublime with the dominating power of the male. For both writers, feminine nature must be subordinated to masculine culture. In the course of his discussion of the sublime and beautiful, for example, when Burke compares the powers of poetry and painting to move the auditor or spectator, he attributes the superiority of poetry to the artificial, nonmimetic character of its medium, language, contrasted with the natural character of the painted sign.

This is a reversal of the terms in which, for instance, Leonardo da Vinci had

17 Ibid., pp. 351–9.
18 Ibid., p. 386.
19 Hence a proper education for females must incorporate "habitual restraint" which will produce "a docility which women need all their lives, since they never cease to be subjected either to a man or to the judgments of men and they are never permitted to put themselves above these judgments" (*Emile*, p. 370).

two centuries earlier compared painting and poetry in his *Paragone*. He argued
for the superiority of painting, founded on the mathematical science of perspective and the evidence of the senses, from its natural system of representation:
"The poet is not able to present in words the true configuration of the elements
which make up the whole [figure represented], unlike the painter, who can set
them before you with the same truth as is possible with nature."[20] For Burke, in
contrast, painting, transcribing what is given to the senses, must be weaker in its
effect on us than the thing pictured itself, while poetry, which does not operate
by way of an image, produces a stronger emotion than painting can. The
strength of this emotion is due precisely to the absence of image. We know things
by seeing them, but "it is our ignorance of things that causes all our admiration,
and chiefly excites our passions."[21] This "ignorance of things," from the hidden
mechanism of natural forces to the secret councils of government, is a source of
the sublime, a middle term between the masculine and the cultural. Painting,
when it reaches for the higher power of the sublime, must imitate the techniques
of poetry. The heights of art—the territory of genius, one might say (though
Burke does not speak of it this way)—are reserved for the male principle.

Painting and poetry

The contrast of natural with artificial signs is fundamental also to Gotthold Lessing's argument, in the *Laocoön*, about "the limits of painting and poetry." The
former makes use of the natural signs of "figures and colours in space" to "imitate physical beauty." In contrast, speech, the poet's medium, consists of
"arbitrary signs."[22] This means that poetry cannot very successfully imitate physical beauty; whatever the skill of Ariosto's word-portrait of Alcina, "What good
is all this erudition and insight to us his readers who want to have the picture of
a beautiful woman, who want to feel something of the soft excitement of the
blood which accompanies the actual sight of beauty?"[23] The special dignity of

20 Martin Kemp (ed.), *Leonardo on Painting* (New Haven: Yale University Press, 1989), p. 37.
21 Burke, *Philosophical Enquiry*, pp. 60, 61.
22 G. E. Lessing, *Laocoön, or On the Limits of Painting and Poetry* [1766], tr. W. A. Steel, in H. Nisbet
    (ed.), *German Aesthetic and Literary Criticism: Winckelmann, Lessing, Hamann, Herder, Schiller, Goethe*
    (Cambridge: Cambridge University Press, 1985), pp. 99, 114, 105.
23 Ibid., pp. 111–17. In his important letter to Nicolai of May 26, 1769, Lessing clarifies his
    position:

> it is not true that painting uses only natural signs, just as it is not true that poetry uses
> only arbitrary signs. But one thing is certain: the more painting departs from natural
> signs, or employs natural and arbitrary signs mixed together, the further it departs
> from its true perfection, just as conversely poetry draws all the closer to its true per-
> fection, the closer it makes its arbitrary signs approach the natural.

—i.e. in drama, which represents speech, culture as human nature in action (p. 133).

poetry lies elsewhere, in its appeal to the reader's or listener's imagination, which must create an image not from "sensuous impressions" but "from weak and wavering descriptions of arbitrary signs."[24]

From this difference between two types of sign Lessing draws his central conclusion:

> If it is true that painting employs in its imitations quite other means or signs than poetry employs, the former [using] figures and colors in space [and] the latter articulate sounds in time; as, unquestionably, [!] the signs used must have a definite relation to the thing signified, it follows that signs arranged together side by side can express only subjects which, or the various parts of which, exist thus side by side, whilst signs which succeed each other can express only subjects which, or the various parts of which, succeed one another . . . Consequently, bodies with their visible properties form the proper subjects of painting . . . [and] actions form the proper subjects of poetry.[25]

The presence here of the gender categories we have been examining is visible in the opposition of the body as aesthetic object, passive and still—the exemplar of the beautiful—to action, allied in eighteenth-century aesthetics with the experience of the sublime.

Lessing's view implies that neither historical nor allegorical painting can exemplify the best of that art, "because they can be understood only by means of their additional arbitrary signs." Such pictures, that is, are fully comprehensible only to someone who knows the classical legend depicted or who is able to recognize allegorical subjects from emblematic signs. Lessing thus argues against illustration, the production of images whose comprehension requires an accompanying text. It is an early form of argument in favor of what would later be thought of as the autonomy of visual art, criticizing the use of painting in religious ritual as "an outward compulsion" on the work of the creative artist, forced to look "more to the significant than to the beautiful."[26]

This conception reappears in the contrast made in Kant's *Critique of Judgment* between "paintings properly so called" and "those intended to *teach* us, e.g. history or natural science." Visual images ideally are "there merely to be looked at, using ideas to entertain the imagination in free play, and occupying the aesthetic power of judgment without a determinate purpose."[27] Kant, of course, develops this conception far beyond Lessing's version, to the idea of visual beauty as

---

24 Ibid., p. 91; the passage contrasts a painter working after nature with one inspired by nature poetry.
25 Ibid., p. 99.
26 Ibid., pp. 133, 87.
27 Kant, *Critique of Judgment*, p. 193.

exemplified by pure forms that "represent nothing, no object under a determinate concept, and are free beauties." Lest the modern reader be misled by Kant's language, which for us points toward "high art" non-representational painting, it is important to remember that for him "painting" included "the decoration of rooms with tapestries, bric-a-brac, and all the beautiful furnishings whose sole function is to be *looked at*, as well as the art of dressing carefully" and "a room with all sorts of ornaments (including even ladies' attire)."[28] For Kant as for Lessing, among the arts *"poetry* holds the highest rank," because it leads us beyond the world of sensory appearance to the "supersensible" and so "fortifies the mind."[29] But poetry itself, as a fine (*schön*) art has the form of "free play"; writing, in Kant's version of the dichotomy, is a beautiful action. As he explained it in his early *Observations on the Feeling of the Beautiful and Sublime*, to such actions "belongs above all the mark that they display facility, and appear to be accomplished without painful toil," while "strivings and surmounted difficulties belong to the sublime."[30] Whatever the limitations of poetry, however, painting lies farther from sublimity, for the sublime "cannot be contained in any sensible form but concerns only ideas of reason." Indeed, "perhaps the most sublime passage in the Jewish Law is the commandment: Thou shalt not make unto thee any graven image, or any likeness of any thing that is in heaven or on earth, or under the earth, etc."[31]

The rejection of pictorial imagery by the "people of the book" can be related to a further dimension of Lessing's separation of the literary from the visual, beyond the attack on illustration and symbolism: a critique of realism, more specifically of genre painting. While language is the medium of *truth*, painting's specialty is, as we have seen, the "imitation of beautiful bodies." Although freedom of speech is required for the sciences, restrictions should be placed on the arts, whose ultimate purpose is to give pleasure. Language is free to represent the ugly and the laughable, precisely because it is not a physically imitative art; whereas a picture of an ugly object is itself ugly, a poetic description of an ugly

28 Ibid., p. 77.

29 Ibid., p. 196.

30 Immanuel Kant, *Observations on the Feeling of the Beautiful and Sublime* [1763], tr. John T. Goldthwait (Berkeley: University of California Press, 1960), p. 78. Section Three of this text, "Of the distinction of the beautiful and sublime in the interrelations of the two sexes," is devoted to an analysis of gender in terms of the two aesthetic categories. Thus it begins with the statement that "certain specific traits lie especially in the personality of [woman's] sex which distinguish it clearly from ours [*sic*] and chiefly result in making her known by the mark of the beautiful. On the other side, we could make a claim on the title of the *noble* sex," with nobility previously identified with sublimity (p. 76). "Women have a strong inborn feeling for all that is beautiful, elegant, and decorated" (p. 77) and their "philosophy is not to reason, but to sense" (p. 79). This philosophy expresses their inner nature; though in polite conversation one should not acknowledge it with obscenities, only a prude will bridle at the truth that "the sexual inclination ultimately underlies all her remaining charms" (p. 85).

31 Kant, *Critique of Judgment*, p. 135.

scene need not be, and can be used "as an ingredient in order to produce or intensify certain mixed states of feeling with which [the poet] must entertain us in default of feelings purely pleasurable."[32] In visual art, truth must be sacrificed in the interest of the harmony that is its essence; the wise Greeks saw that "this veiling was a sacrifice which the artist offered to Beauty."[33]

The gendered character of the antithesis between truth and beauty is apparent; we need only remember the differing educational programs prescribed by Rousseau to Emile and to his Sophie, or Kant's advice, in the *Observations*, that "deep meditation and long-sustained reflection are noble but difficult, and do not well befit a person in whom unconstrained charms should show nothing else than a beautiful nature."[34] Joseph Wright's *An Experiment on a Bird in the Air Pump* of 1768 (painted, thus, two years after the publication of *Laocoön*; Figure 4.1), while far from expressing a Kantian disdain for women, provides an illustration of the relation of truth to beauty. A mixed company has gathered around a table to view a demonstration of the effects of a vacuum on a living thing. While two girls manifest apprehension and distress, a boy participates eagerly in the experiment. Understanding that the bird, temporarily deprived of air, will soon be revived, he lowers the cage to which the beautiful creature will be returned. The light that shines full on the girls makes them into aesthetic objects for the picture's viewer; while one of them hides her face, a man with his protective arm around them points upward to the sight of the unfortunate cockatoo, a thing of beauty here transformed into an object of rational investigation. The other men in the room are absorbed, each in his own way, in the experiment, except for the male of the couple to the left who, gazing into his betrothed's eyes, in spirit has left his fellows to join her in domestic bliss.[35]

Truth is difficult and painful, and so opposed to the pleasure served by art.

---

32 Lessing, *Laocoön*, p. 124; and see p. 86: "to the poet alone belongs the art of depicting with negative traits, and by mixing them with positive to bring two images into one."

33 Lessing, *Laocoön*, p. 65.

34 Kant, *Observations*, p. 78.

> A woman is embarrassed little that she does not possess certain high insights, that she is timid, and not fit for serious employments, and so forth; she is beautiful and captivates, and that is enough. On the other hand, she demands all these qualities in a man, and the sublimity of her soul shows itself only in that she knows to treasure these noble qualities so far as they are found in him.

> He, meanwhile, "by [her] fine figure, merry naivety, and charming friendliness . . . is sufficiently repaid for the lack of book learning and for other deficiencies that he must supply by his own talents" (pp. 91–4).

35 For a different take on gender in Wright's painting, see David Solkin, "Re-Wrighting Shaftesbury: The air pump and the limits of commercial humanism," in John Barrell (ed.), *Painting and the Politics of Culture: New Essays on British Art, 1701–1850* (Oxford: Oxford University Press, 1992), esp. pp. 91–5. Thomas Eakins's *The Gross Clinic* (1875) demonstrates the longevity of the themes of Wright's painting. Here the bird as object of experimentation is replaced by the human body as a field for dissection; the scientific passion of the medical men contrasts sharply

Figure 4.1 Joseph Wright, *An Experiment on a Bird in the Air Pump* (© National Gallery, London)

This gives truth an aesthetic character of its own: the scientific attitude involves the unflinching contemplation of ugliness, while the voice of the artist faced with a "misshapen" reality should wonder, according to Lessing, "Who will wish to paint you, when no one wishes to see you?" Unfortunately, Lessing continues, many modern artists do wish to paint the ugly, seeking to imitate all of Nature, who "herself at all times sacrifices beauty to higher purposes."[36]

The modern artists with whom eighteenth-century writers associated such themes were, as Lessing says, the Dutch, for whose genre scenes he finds a classical predecessor in Pyreicus, the "rhyparograph, the dirt-painter," whose charmless subjects are elements of *social* nature—"barbers' shops, filthy factories, donkeys and cabbages."[37] These are images of low class and labor: the peasant's

with the inability of the one woman in the scene to face the truth before her: like the older girl in the *Experiment*, she hides her face. Dr. Gross, like the scientist in Wright's picture, is a hero of modern times; successor to the warriors of old, he embodies what a hundred years before was called the sublime. This is not to say that times do not change. Eakins's *Agnew Clinic*, painted fourteen years later, features a woman who has herself entered the territory of the sublime: the assisting nurse, present not for aesthetic enjoyment but as a participant in men's work.

36   Lessing, *Laocoön*, pp. 63, 66.
37   Ibid., p. 63.

draught animal and dinner, urban sites of service and production. That Dutch art followed this tradition was a conventional view. To take a notable instance, Sir Joshua Reynolds judged that Dutch artists wasted their skills "on vulgar and mean subjects."[38] According to Reynolds, the merit of Dutch pictures "often consists in the truth of representation alone,"[39] a mode of truth not equal to the heights of which art is capable.

Lessing's desire to restrict the practice of painting to the representation of beauty betrays a striking conception of the power of visual images. Since beauty, unlike truth, is a matter of pleasure, not necessity, it is legitimate to censor the visual arts; and the plastic arts require "the close supervision of the law" because of "the unfailing influence they exert on the character of a nation" and even on the physical form of its citizens.

> When beautiful men fashioned beautiful statues, those in their turn affected them, and the State had beautiful statues in part to thank for beautiful citizens. With us [moderns] the tender, imaginative power of mothers appears to express itself only in monsters.[40]

Here Lessing equates visual beauty with moral or civic beauty, and credits the plastic arts with the power to affect both. The example Lessing gives, suggested by the "monsters" to which modern mothers' physiological susceptibility to imagery gives rise, is of the "ancient legends" of the birth of warrior heroes to women impregnated by intercourse with a serpent. The true explanation, according to Lessing, is that "honest women" by day "feasted their eyes" on the

---

38 J. Reynolds, *Discourses on Art* [1797], ed. Robert R. Wark (New Haven: Yale University Press, 1975), p. 109, where Reynolds remarks of "Jean Stein" that

> if this extraordinary man had had the good fortune to have been born in Italy, instead of Holland, . . . the same sagacity and penetration which distinguished so accurately the different characters and expression in his vulgar figures, would, when exerted in the selection and imitation of what was great and elevated in nature, have been equally successful; and he would now be ranged with the great pillars and supporters of our Art.

As a painter Reynolds is quite naturally a defender of the claims of that art. "The terms beauty, or nature, which are general ideas, are but different modes of expressing the same thing, whether we apply these terms to statues, poetry, or picture" (p. 124). But his claim that art should satisfy "the natural appetite or taste of the human mind" for Truth (p. 122) proves finally to fit the same conceptual structure as Lessing's, since *nature* for Reynolds signifies not the particular but the general—the ideal form, imperfectly realized in the concrete individual. Thus "deformity is not nature, but an accidental deviation from her accustomed practice" (p. 124). For Reynolds too the highest levels of art must shun the vulgar, the grotesque, and the ugly, though (as we will see) he claimed for painting, beyond the beautiful, the realm of the sublime.

39 Joshua Reynolds, *A Journey in Flanders and Holland*, vol. 2 in *Works* (London, 1809), p. 369.

40 Lessing, *Laocoön*, pp. 61–4.

"beautiful statues and pictures" of the gods, seldom represented without an accompanying serpent; at night, "the bewildering dream called up the image of the reptile," and it was this "adulterous phantasy" that affected the child to be.[41]

The idea that visual imagery can have a formative effect on the unborn[42] expresses a concern about the confusion of genres, here explicitly linked to the confusion of genders. As W. J. T. Mitchell has pointed out, the joining of serpent and beautiful god in a statue is a grotesque mingling of forms that Lessing considered antithetical: of the emblematic, proper to poetry, with the mimetic, proper to the visual arts.[43] The monstrous coupling of artistic genres can be described as a confusion of the beautiful and the sublime. In Lessing's eyes, "Art in these later days has been assigned far wider boundaries" than the ancients allowed. "Let her imitative hand, folks say, stretch out to the whole of visible nature, of which the Beautiful is only a small part."[44] Confusion of forms is possible, because painting can suggest action, as poetry can suggest the experience of physical beauty. But it is essential, if both forms are to achieve their highest possibilities, to keep each within its allotted domain. Furthermore, distinction, as usual, is also hierarchy. For Burke, as we saw, while "poetry and rhetoric do not succeed in exact description as well as painting does," they "are more capable of making deep and lively impressions than any other arts, and even than nature itself in very many cases."[45] Lessing decried the modern critics' tendency to ignore this hierarchy of genre power as a mode of aesthetic violence: "Now they force poetry into the narrower bounds of painting; and again, they propose to painting to fill the whole wide sphere of poetry."[46]

There is more involved in these thematics than some writers' defense of the traditional supremacy of their art in the face of the rising social status of painting. Given the gendered charge carried by poetry and painting, as the arts of the

---

41 Ibid., p. 64.
42 Curiously, Lessing fails to note that the eponymous sculpture his book takes as exemplar of the true powers of the visual arts is itself an image combining beautiful bodies and serpent emissaries of the divine.

Although it was challenged by Enlightenment science, "the belief in a woman's power to imprint upon her baby whatever was in her imagination at the moment of conception or during pregnancy was widely accepted within both regular medicine and popular culture." Roy Porter, "'The secrets of generation display'd': *Aristotle's Master Piece* in eighteenth-century England," in Robert P. Maccubbin (ed.), *'Tis Nature's Fault: Unauthorized Sexuality During the Enlightenment* (Cambridge: Cambridge University Press, 1997), p. 11. Porter mentions also the idea that "monsters"—severely malformed children—may be products of the mother's copulation with an animal or even with a demon. The idea that the mother's imagination can affect the form of her child is still to be found in Professor T. W. Shannon's *Self Knowledge and Guide to Sex Instruction* (Marietta, Ohio: Mulliken, 1913), primarily a tract against masturbation, under the heading of "Prenatal training."

43 W. J. T. Mitchell, *Iconology* (Chicago: University of Chicago Press, 1986), p. 109.
44 Lessing, *Laocoön*, p. 66.
45 Burke, *Philosophical Enquiry*, pp. 172, 173.
46 Lessing, *Laocoön*, p. 59.

sublime and the beautiful, it is not hard to read the passages in Lessing and Burke protesting incursions by the visual arts into the domain of poetry as art-theoretical analogues to the anxiety about female transgression into the sphere of the male exemplified by Rousseau's strictures on women's morals and education. It is not by accident that Lessing's text illustrates the danger to social order posed by visual art's overrunning the limits proper to it by women's adulterous fantasies and their production of monsters.

Sexual disorder

The gender metaphors we have been tracking in aesthetics, that is, seem related to ideas about social disorder that preoccupied many eighteenth-century thinkers, who drew on earlier images of female sexuality to express general social concerns. In Natalie Zemon Davis's words, "the female sex was thought the disorderly one par excellence in early modern Europe." Woman's

> disorderliness was founded in physiology . . . Her womb was like a hungry animal; when not amply fed by sexual intercourse or repro-duction, it was likely to wander about her body, overpowering her speech and senses . . . The lower rules the higher within the woman, then, and if she were given her way, she would want to rule over those above her outside.[47]

Though such ideas are certainly to be found in premodern societies, the acceler-ated development of a secular, urban culture and national state formation from the fourteenth century on seems to have brought with it a "sharp turn toward misogyny." This accompanied a redefinition of male and female gender roles integral to modernization, notably involving an important loss of power by upper-status women and the redefinition of woman's sphere as a domestic one in a restructured patriarchal household, while "the military, financial, and juridical powers of feudal families became 'public,' that is, state functions" and "men moved into the new positions of state control."[48]

These developments intensified in the course of the seventeenth century. By the eighteenth century married women had lost many of their earlier legal, economic,

---

47 Natalie Zemon Davis, "Women on top," in *idem, Society and Culture in Early Modern France* (Stan-ford: Stanford University Press, 1975), pp. 121–5. In the eighteenth century this tradition takes the form of "an archetypal conception of woman as a sexually insatiable creature when her desire is aroused . . . one of the major sexual myths traceable in many medical handbooks, and certainly underlying much eighteenth-century fiction." See Paul-Gabriel Boucé, "Some sexual beliefs and myths in eighteenth-century Britain," in P.-G. Boucé (ed.), *Sexuality in Eighteenth-Century Britain* (Manchester: Manchester University Press, 1982), pp. 41–2.

48 Joan Kelly, "Early feminist theory and the *Querelle des femmes*, 1401–1789," in *idem, Women, His-tory, and Theory* (Chicago: University of Chicago Press, 1984), pp. 70, 85.

and political rights. Of course, the emerging situation could be represented as one of their acquisition of a new dominion of absolute power, within the family, but Rousseau's prescription reveals the basic system of power relations:

> The woman ought to have sole command within the home, and it is even indecent for her husband to know what's going on there. But in turn she ought to limit herself to domestic governance, not meddling with anything outside it, and shut up in her home; mistress of everything around her she ought always to submit her person to the absolute law of her husband.[49]

Nature reconstituted as the domestic sphere called for enclosure.

Formulations like Rousseau's testify that the transformation of gender relations did not happen without resistance on the part of women. From the seventeenth century on we find women "telling off priests and pastors, being central actors in grain and bread riots in town and country, and participating in tax revolts and other rural disturbances."[50] Given the role of the patriarchal family as model for the social order as a whole (visible, to take two examples, in the conception of the king as "father of his country" and in the very name of the new science of "political oeconomy") it is not surprising that "the relation of the wife—of the potentially disorderly woman—to her husband was especially useful for expressing the relation of all subordinates to their superiors."[51] The male–female relationship could, that is, be used to figure both the hierarchical order required for social health, and the threat to or actual disruption of that order. We cannot be surprised when we discover this relationship reappearing, on a more abstract level of representation, in the use in political discourse of the aesthetic categories of the beautiful and sublime.

Aesthetics and politics

Burke emphasizes the connection between aesthetic and political categories in the *Philosophical Enquiry* itself, listing as exemplars of the sublime not just stern fatherhood but "those despotic governments, which are founded on the passions of men, and principally on the passion of fear," who "keep their chief as much as may be from the public eye," thus creating the effect of obscurity basic to the

---

49 J.-J. Rousseau, "Fragments pour *Emile*," in *Oeuvres complètes*, vol. 4 (Paris: Gallimard [Pléïade], 1969), p. 872. For a detailed study of the redefinition of social and economic gender roles in England around 1800, see Leonore Davidoff and Catherine Hall, *Family Fortunes: Men and Women of the English Middle Class, 1781–1850* (London: Hutchinson, 1987).
50 Davis, "Women on top," p. 126.
51 Ibid., p. 127. During the same period—and well into the nineteenth century—we also find male rioters and resisters to oppression dressing as women or taking women's names.

sublime. In praising Milton's poetry for the sublimity of its images, he mentions as themes "the ruin of monarchs, and the revolutions of kingdoms."[52] John Baillie's *Essay on the Sublime*, published ten years before Burke's, finds sublimity of passion in "*Heroism*, or Desire of Conquest, such as in an *Alexander* or a *Caesar*," which "generally arises either from a Desire of *Power*, or Passion for *Fame*; or from both." The sublime is also associated here with love of country, or even the "Universal Benevolence" which loves all mankind.

> But how would the *Sublime* sink, if . . . the *Imagination* should fix upon a narrow Object, a *Child*, a *Parent*, or a *Mistress*! Indeed, *Love* to any of the *Individuals*, nay to *all* of them, when considered as *Individuals*, and one by one, has nothing of Exalted; it is when we love them *collectively*, when we love them in vast Bodies stretching over large Countries, that we feel the *Sublime* rise.[53]

Despite Lessing's insistence on the radical separation of powers between poetry and painting, history painters as well as poets reached for the sublime, giving visible form to the contrasts developed in the texts we have been discussing. To take a well-known example, the first commentators on Jacques-Louis David's *Oath of the Horatii* (1785, Musée du Louvre) stressed the artist's "departures from accepted practice, his defiance of rules and tradition . . . Gorsas [*Promenades de Crites au Salon de l'année 1785*] suggests that the 'sublime' expression of Horatius 'would have escaped any other but M. David.'"[54] The *Horatii*, along with *The Lictors Returning to Brutus the Bodies of his Sons* (1789, Musée du Louvre) and other works of this period, was history painting of a scale and seriousness denied to English artists by the lack of royal and aristocratic patronage for such works, despite the efforts of Reynolds, Dance, West, and (above all) Burke's protégé James Barry. These were sublime works in the classical (Longinian) sense of treating noble subjects, in a manner calculated not to attract the taste for decorative prettiness but, through the idealizing of natural forms, to inspire the viewer to high and profound thoughts. They were also sublime in the newer, Burkean, sense of presenting images of fearsome moments, expressive of the artist's powerful imagination and inspiring strong feeling in the spectator. David himself spoke of Michelangelo as his master, and declared, "there is something Florentine in the rendering of my Brutus," while a review of the 1789 Salon described this painting as "male, severe, terrifying."[55]

---

52 Burke, *Philosophical Enquiry*, pp. 59, 62.
53 John Baillie, *An Essay on the Sublime* (Los Angeles: The Augustan Reprint Society, Clark Memorial Library, University of California, 1953), pp. 11–20, 23.
54 Crow, *Painters*, pp. 211–17.
55 J. L. David, letters to Wicar, in Robert L. Herbert, *David, Voltaire, Brutus, and the French Revolution: An Essay on Art and Politics* (New York: Viking, 1973), pp. 123, 124; review in *Mercure de France*, October 24, 1789, in ibid., p. 126. See the reviews in the *Journal de Paris* and the *Supplément aux remarques sur les ouvrages exposés au Salon*, tr. in ibid., pp. 126, 127, which state (respectively) that in

The paintings themselves reveal the gendered aspect of the aesthetic categories. Both the *Horatii* and the *Brutus* picture the conflict between the claims of
the national polity and those of familial love, and are structured in terms of male
and female embodiments of these claims. The former places the Roman father
in the center; his sons face him on the left, their taut bodies testifying to the
strength of their resolve to use the power of death he holds out to them in the
shape of the three swords. At the right sit three women—one of them a sister of
the men the Horatii are setting out to kill, another a sister of the Roman triplets,
pledged in marriage to one of their opponents—with their children. Though the
picture is strongly divided by the three open spaces that frame the figures, the
twofold division of its subject between masculine and feminine is equally pronounced. The central action is indeed the transmission of power from father to
sons, who at the same moment abandon their marriage-formed family alliances.
To this moment the group of women is linked only by implication: their grief
reflects the fact that they are faced with loss whoever wins the coming fight.
Everything is stronger on the men's side than in the women's: the color of their
clothing, the shadows behind them, and their tense, muscled bodies in contrast
with the soft, smooth skin of the women, who seem not agitated by despair but
sunk in a deep, sleeplike passivity.[56]

The *Brutus* reverses the distribution of action between the sexes. Here the
father sits brooding as the bodies of his sons, executed at his orders for treason,
are carried in, while the women of the house rise in anguish, gesturing toward
the bier. The women are experiencing horror and fear (one has fainted and one
hides her face), but they themselves are beautiful, objects of pity. They are
brightly illuminated, made for the sense of sight, while Brutus sits in obscurity,
awesome, strong, interiorizing his grief rather than acting it out in womanly
rhetoric. The women here are not the female citizens of Sparta whom
Rousseau held up as models, happy to lose their sons for the military good of

---

this work "history belongs in the same manner to painter and to poet" and that David's "production is more of a great poet than of a painter." Joshua Reynolds similarly contrasted the
"grandeur and severity of Michael Angelo" with the "effeminacy" of modern painting. Comparing him to Raphael, he asserts that the latter "had more Taste and Fancy, Michael Angelo more
Genius and Imagination. The one excelled in beauty, the other in energy. Michael Angelo has
more of the Poetical Inspiration; his ideas are vast and sublime" (p. 83).

56 Tischbein's contemporary description shows that this is not simply a present-day commentator's
projection of the categories of beautiful and sublime onto David's picture: "Determination,
courage, strength, reverence for the gods, love of freedom and of the fatherland show themselves in the men; in the women inconsolable dejection, weak and numb collapse, tenderness for
the spouse, the bridegroom, the children, the brothers; in the children playful innocence and
naiveté"; see J. H. W. Tischbein, "Letters from Rome," *Derteutsche Merkur* (February 1786), tr. in
Elizabeth G. Holt (ed.), *The Triumph of Art for the Public, 1781–1848* (Princeton: Princeton University Press, 1983), p. 19. Other contemporary accounts make the same point.

the city, but Brutus is the citizen who "was neither Caius nor Lucius; he was a Roman."[57]

If we turn to a literary depiction of woman in a political context, in Burke's description of the French Revolution, we find the gendered character of the categories of beautiful and sublime demonstrated by the very failure of the women of Paris to play their allotted role. The Queen of France exemplifies the beautiful—lovely, passive, weak, she arouses Burke's pity as she is forced by the "swinish multitude" to flee her palace. Such a scene, one would expect, would have its sublime aspect: here is that ruin of monarchs whose description Burke praised in Milton. But in fact this experience seems so frightful as to lie outside the bounds of artistic representation, which must be a cause of delight even in horror.[58] The overthrow of an actual monarch, and that in a series of acts with serious repercussions for the stability of the British political and social system, could not be kept within the frame of aesthetic experience. After all, for terror to produce delight it must "not press too close"; as Kant was to echo this, "we must find ourselves safe in order to feel this exciting liking" that is the experience of the sublime.[59] And one manifestation of the passing of the scene of the overthrow of the French monarchy beyond the bounds of aesthetic contemplation is women's role, for the king and queen are led from their palace "amidst the horrid yells, and shrilling screams, and frantic dances, and infamous contumelies, and all the unutterable abominations of the furies of hell, in the abused shape of the vilest of women."[60]

---

57 Rousseau, *Emile*, p. 40. Grimm's account of the 1789 Salon noted the familiar duality: "This mature figure [Brutus], isolated and as it were enshrouded in shadows, forms an admirable contrast with this group of women, illuminated with a light that is rather bright, but gentle and tranquil" (tr. in Herbert, *David*, p. 128). A gender-structured contrast similar to that made in David's two paintings on Roman themes can be identified also in his *Death of Socrates* and *Paris and Helen*, produced in 1787 and 1789 respectively, but apparently intended for presentation as a contrasting pair. The first represents the sublime theme of the death of a hero of intellectual and patriotic virtue; the second is a depiction of sexual desire, pursued at whatever cost to national or personal honor.

58 See the passage of Burke quoted by Ronald Paulson in his interesting discussion:

> The condition of France at this moment was so frightful and horrible, that if a painter wished to portray a description of hell, he could not find so terrible a model, or a subject so pregnant with horror, and fit for his purpose. Milton, with all that genius which enabled him to excel in descriptions of this nature, would have been ashamed to have presented to his readers such a hell as France now has . . . he would have thought his design revolting to the most unlimited imagination, and his colouring overcharged beyond all allowance for the license even of poetical painting.
>
> Speech in Commons, April 11, 1794, cit. R Paulson, *Representations of Revolution (1781–1820)* (New Haven: Yale University Press, 1983), p. 66

59 Burke, *Philosophical Enquiry*, p. 46; Kant, *Critique of Judgment*, p. 121.

60 E. Burke, *Reflections on the Revolution in France* [1790], ed. J. G. A. Pocock (Indianapolis: Hackett, 1987), p. 63.

In this picture of the revolutionary mob we can recognize the traditional association of the female—and in particular the woman of the lower classes—with the danger of social disorder. Here this reaches its ultimate point, an attack on the king himself, the paternal keystone of political order. The violation of the queen, embodiment of beauty, is equally terrible, not only in itself but because it mirrors the refusal by the women of the mob to accept their place in the social cosmos. They inspire Burke with horror by their negation of womanly beauty, but this horror is not one that can lead to delight and the sublime. These women are by social nature ugly—"swinish" and "vile."[61] Their action spells the abolition of the social differentiation both exemplified and symbolized by the male privilege implicated in the category system of sublime and beautiful.

We might call this radical undermining of the aesthetic system the Female Sublime or—from the dominant point of view—the Bad Sublime. The whole cast of aesthetic characters can be seen at play in Mozart's *Magic Flute* of 1791. Sarastro, of course, incarnates the sublime: mysterious, deep-voiced, his is the fatherly power whose victory over rebellious femininity the opera celebrates as the triumph of the light of reason over darkness. The Queen of the Night, risen against him, seeks to seduce the young Tamino with her daughter's beauty, as an ally against her husband. Inevitably, social harmony (modeled by that of music) is reestablished: under Sarastro's dominion, Tamino and Pamina take their places as domestic master and wife, while the queen (with her black ally) is "demolished, extinguished, defeated."[62] But Mozart's genius—concretely, his responsiveness to the needs of opera and the demands of singers—makes him give her the great, wild "revenge" aria, in which she achieves true sublimity, if only as prelude to her end.

In a radical woman's treatment of the female sublime the inherent conflict of categories becomes more interestingly apparent: Mary Wollstonecraft's *Vindication of the Rights of Woman* (1792) is an explicit attempt "to convince the world that the poisoned source of female vices and follies," as well as of women's oppression by men, "has been the sensual homage paid to beauty." She contrasts "beauty of features" or "a pretty woman, as an object of desire" with "a fine woman, who inspires more sublime emotions by displaying intellectual beauty." The juncture of aesthetics and politics is as clear here as in the writings of her great antagonist, Burke. Wollstonecraft's enemies are "tyrants of every denomination, from the weak king to the weak father of a family;" she wishes to move "the civilized women of the present century" who, "with a few exceptions, are only anxious to

---

61 Burke complains that the mob's action expresses a scheme of things in which "a king is but a man; a queen is but a woman; a woman is but an animal; and an animal not of the highest order" (*Reflections*, p. 67)—that is, queen and woman of the "swinish multitude" are equalized.

62 "Zerschmettert, zernichtet ist unsere Macht,/ Wir alle gesturzet in ewige Nacht."

inspire love, when they ought to cherish a nobler ambition, and by their abilities and virtues exact respect."[63]

Wollstonecraft's argument is based on a set of reversals of the standard discourse of the beautiful and sublime. For her it is the sacrifice of "strength of body and mind . . . to libertine notions of beauty" with the goal of establishing themselves in the world by marriage that makes "mere animals" of women. She points to the contradiction inherent in the idea of the family as woman's sphere within a patriarchal order: can women educated to be "weak beings . . . only fit for a seraglio . . . be expected to govern a family with judgment . . .?" In fact, she observes, this situation creates the apparent paradox which forms a staple of misogynist literature, that women's "artificial weakness produces a propensity to tyrannize, and gives birth to cunning, the natural opponent of strength." The fiction of complementary roles reveals the truth it obscures: the struggle for power, within the family, of women against men. And this is a struggle that cannot be limited to the household. "Women cannot by force be confined to domestic concerns; for they will, however ignorant, intermeddle with more weighty affairs, neglecting private duties only to disturb, by cunning tricks, the orderly plans of reason which rise above their comprehension."[64]

Having compared beautiful women to animals (and children), Wollstonecraft reverses a fundamental archetype pair of beauty and sublimity by comparing degraded womankind to military men who, like women, "become a prey to prejudices, and taking all their opinions on credit, . . . blindly submit to authority." Soldiers, like women, are "attentive to their persons, fond of dancing, crowded rooms, adventures, and ridicule."[65] No more than soldiers are monarchs and aristocrats generally exemplars of sublimity. We have already seen the propensity to tyranny inherent in beauty. As Wollstonecraft observes, her

> argument branches into various ramifications. Birth, riches, and every extrinsic advantage that exalt a man above his fellows, without any mental exertion, sink him in reality below them. In proportion to his weakness, he is played upon by designing men [as husbands are by their designing wives—P. M.], till the bloated monster has lost all traces of humanity. And that tribes of men, like flocks of sheep, should quietly follow such a leader, is a solecism that only a desire of present enjoyment and narrowness of understanding can solve. Educated in slavish dependence, and enervated by luxury and sloth, where shall we find men who will stand forth to assert the rights of man, or claim the privilege of moral beings? Slavery to monarchs and ministers, which the

63 Mary Wollstonecraft, *Vindication of the Rights of Woman*, ed. M. H. Kramnick (Harmondsworth: Penguin, 1975), pp. 134, 87, 79.
64 Ibid., pp. 83, 88.
65 Ibid., p. 106.

world will be long in freeing itself from, and whose deadly grasp stops the progress of the human mind, is not yet abolished.[66]

Where, then, are heroes to be found? In her basic reversal, Wollstonecraft calls on women to exemplify the sublimity absent from patriarchal society. "It is time to effect a revolution in female manners—time to restore to them their lost dignity—and make them, as a part of the human species, labour by reforming themselves to reform the world."[67] The overthrow at once of the divine right of husbands and the divine right of kings will abolish a corrupt social order, in which "wealth and female softness equally tend to debase mankind."[68] Beauty may be, as Burke proclaimed, the virtue of subordinates, but if the great end of human beings is "to unfold their own faculties, and acquire the dignity of conscious virtue,"[69] then the beautiful must be recognized as itself an image of deformed nature, whose true shape is visible only in the sublime.

Sublimity for Wollstonecraft remains a masculine attribute, although one that men themselves have lost. Taken up by women, it is desexualized, and her ideal woman seems to be a widowed mother. The embodiment of republican virtue in a world without men,

> she subdues every wayward passion to fulfill the double duty of being the father as well as the mother of her children. Raised to heroism by misfortunes, she represses the first faint dawning of a natural inclination, before it ripens into love, and in the bloom of life forgets her sex.[70]

The categories are strained to the breaking point in the effort to figure a radical alteration of society.

Given the aesthetic character of these categories, it is no wonder that Wollstonecraft steps with ease from a critical analysis of Rousseau's fantasy of family life in *Emile* to a critique of "Milton's pleasing picture of paradisaical happiness." The picture of Adam and Eve in Paradise evoked by Milton's verse is indeed a beautiful one; "yet, instead of envying the lovely pair, I have with conscious dignity or satanic pride turned to hell for sublimer objects." Similarly, "when viewing some noble monument of human art," her mind looked for "the grandest of all human sights; for fancy quickly placed in some solitary recess an outcast of human fortune, rising superior to passion and discontent."[71] She must be thinking here of an image like Reynolds's *Count Hugolino*, exhibited in 1773, when it attracted much interest, and published as a mezzotint the following

---

66 Ibid., pp. 131–2.
67 Ibid., p. 132.
68 Ibid., p. 140.
69 Ibid., p. 109.
70 Ibid., p. 138.
71 Ibid., p. 108 n.

year.[72] A reader familiar with the later history of the sublime may also be put in mind of Turner's Academy diploma picture, *Dolbadern Castle* (1800), with its mists, rocks, and tower "Where [in Turner's own verses] hopeless OWEN, long imprison'd, pin'd, / And wrung his hands for liberty, in vain." And Wollstonecraft's own writing follows a style consistent with her aim, "to show that elegance is inferior to virtue":

> Animated by this important object, I shall disdain to cull my phrases or polish my style. I aim at being useful, and sincerity will render me unaffected; for wishing rather to persuade by the force of my arguments than dazzle by the elegance of my language, I shall not waste my time in rounding periods, or in fabricating the turgid bombast of artificial feelings, which, coming from the head, never reach the heart.[73]

Wollstonecraft's critique of beauty as degraded state is confirmed by the evidence of turn-of-the-century salon art. In general, woman, if beautiful, is passive, grief-stricken, asleep, or dead. Woman represented as active and powerful reflects the fear voiced by Burke and Rousseau: she is a killer of children or husband (Medea, Clytemnestra, Phaedra). The former type appears over and over in the nineteenth century as Juliet, Ophelia, or harem girl (and strikingly in Jean-Baptiste Clésinger's *Woman Bitten by a Serpent* (1847, Musée d'Orsay), in which the image of death is nearly completely displaced by that of the sexual pleasure with which it is conjoined or equated). The latter type—the Bad Sublime—takes fin-de-siècle form as Salome, sphinx, and vampire (she makes a notable twentieth-century entrance, as we have seen, among the Demoiselles d'Avignon).

Perhaps the most perfect painted embodiments of the beautiful are the dying women in Delacroix's *Death of Sardanapalus* (Figure 4.2), who have their place within a sublime image, of a kingdom fallen and a monarch overthrown. Sardanapalus lies in shadow as the smoke of his burning city billows behind him. Light falls on the women who are being killed or choosing death; three of these beautiful bodies form the center of the image. Shifts in perspective, by destroying a stable pictured space, dematerialize this image filled with precious objects and making it, not a space we are looking into, but an evocation of the monarch's last vision. Subordinate to his will, at this moment of their destruction they are objects only for his sight. Of one this is not true: the dark-skinned woman at the center below the bed looks straight out at us. She is perhaps not unrelated to the female center of another painting by Delacroix. In *Liberty Leading the People* (Musée du Louvre), we have the transformation of the Burkean mob of the "vilest of women" into a revolutionary avatar of Mary Wollstonecraft's

---

72 See Nicholas Penny (ed.), *Reynolds* (London: Royal Academy of Arts, 1986), pp. 251 ff.
73 Ibid., p. 82.

Figure 4.2 Eugène Delacroix, *Death of Sardanapalus*, 1827. Courtesy of Réunion des Musées Nationaux/Art Resource, NY.

female sublime. Gun in one hand, tricolor in the other, her bare breasts demonstrating her continued sexual presence, she appears at the barricade not as destroyer of order but as incarnation of a new order in which the bourgeois and laboring classes will create a common destiny. Republican men here stand with her, not against her. Perhaps it is not just the difference between France and Britain but the actuality of revolution—the picture was made in 1830—that saved her from restriction to sublime widowhood and allowed her the sexuality of the "woman of the people" crowned as Liberty in 1789.[74]

But of course the new order was a chimera, and this image had no immediate successor. It might be said to have reappeared in the late 1960s, in the form of the heroine of Third World revolutionary struggle—Asian, African, or Native American—with a rifle in her hand or on her back. Its provenance in modernizing movements suggest what might be called its early nineteenth-century nature—and also the centrality of gender issues to social transformation. Here again the difficulty of imagining the feminine sublime in terms other than those of uneasy compromise between masculine attributes and rejection of the patriarchal order is further testimony to the gendered character of the categories of beautiful and sublime.

Abstraction and the sublime

In 1805 Goethe could still write, "To make the transition from the world of letters, and even from the highest manifestations of words and language, namely poetry and rhetoric, to the visual arts, is difficult and well-nigh impossible: for between them lies an enormous gulf which only a special natural aptitude can bridge."[75] On the other hand, in 1795 Schiller demanded that "the plastic arts . . . must become sheer form," though only because "it is an inevitable and natural consequence of their approach to perfection that the various arts, without any displacement of their objective frontiers, tend to become ever more like each other in their effect upon the psyche." In any and every art, "subject-matter . . .

---

74 See the related mythology sketched by Victor Hugo, reporting the June Days of 1848 in his *Choses Vues*:

> At that moment a young woman appeared on the crest of the barricade, a young woman, beautiful, disheveled, terrifying. This woman, who was a public whore, pulled her dress up to the waist and cried to the guardsmen, in that dreadful brothel language that one is always obliged to translate: "Cowards! Fire, if you dare, at the belly of a woman!" . . . It's a hideous thing, this heroism of abjection, when all that weakness contains of strength bursts out.
>
> Victor Hugo, *Oeuvres complètes* (Paris, 1955) vol. 31, pp. 361–6; cit. Neil Hertz, "Medusa's head: male hysteria under political pressure," *Representations* 4 (1983), p. 29

75 J. W. von Goethe, "Winckelmann," tr. H. B. Nisbet, in Nisbet, *German Aesthetic and Literary Criticism*, p. 243.

always has a limiting effect upon the spirit, and it is only from form that true aesthetic freedom can be looked for."[76] To say this is to abandon the claims of Lessing and Burke for the superiority of poetry over painting, but only by abandoning the "feminine" nature of the visual arts, as clearly defined images of beautiful bodies, as in Delacroix's claim that painting and music are "above thought" and hence superior to literature precisely "through their very vagueness."[77] By freeing itself from clarity of image, and moving in the direction of "abstraction," painting moves in the direction of sublimity, or masculinity.

The goals of art—literary and visual—were radically reformulated in the later nineteenth century, with the rise of Realism. At this time, music continued to be the home of the Romanticism into which the ideal of sublimity had metamorphosed. Music took the place of poetry as the exemplary art; as Carl Dahlhaus says, "music increased its influence because it was almost alone in bearing the burden of providing an alternative to the realities of the world following the Industrial Revolution."[78] Central to at least one important line of the modernist painting of the twentieth century has been a tendency in this art too for the demands of mimesis to be overwhelmed by the reduction of the image to the elements of line, pictorial space, and color. Such versions of modernism identify so-called content, as in Lessing, with literature, while inverting Lessing's critique of history painting to make so-called form a carrier of spiritual truth, free to represent universal structures of meaning and expression. The body of nature is abandoned as inessential; the spirit or soul of nature is identified with the artist's creative act (think of Jackson Pollock's pronouncement, "I am nature").

Barnett Newman is notable for explicitly calling on the categories of the beautiful and the sublime for the statement of a modernist program:

> The failure of European art to achieve the sublime is due to [the] blind desire to exist inside the reality of sensation (the object world) and to build an art within the framework of pure plasticity (the Greek ideal of beauty) . . . In other words, modern art, caught without a sublime content, was incapable of creating a new sublime image . . . [S]ome of us . . . are finding the answer, by completely denying that art has any connection with the problem of beauty . . . We are reasserting man's natural desire for the exalted.

It is hardly surprising that Newman, seeking an ancestry for his art in that of the original inhabitants of the American Northwest, finds it in "an abstract symbolic

---

76 Friedrich Schiller, *On the Aesthetic Education of Man*, tr. E. M. Wilkenson and L. A. Willoughby (Oxford: Clarendon Press, 1967), p. 155.

77 *The Journal of Eugène Delacroix*, tr. Walter Pach (New York: Grove, 1961), p. 61.

78 Carl Dahlhaus, *Between Romanticism and Modernism* (Berkeley and Los Angeles: University of California Press, 1980), p. 8.

art . . . not to be confused with the geometric designs of its decorative arts, which were a separate realm practiced by the women of the tribes. The serious art of these tribes, practiced by the men, took the form of a highly abstract concept."[79] In the preeminence it gives the sublime over the beautiful and in the gender associations of the terms, Newman's conception is more continuous with tradition than he suspected.

"Already in the late nineteenth century," Carol Duncan has written, "European high culture was disposed to regard the male–female relationship as the central problem of human existence." As Duncan suggests, we can understand this focus as due at least in part to the ability of sexual difference to carry meanings of the conflict of the free, creative individual with social convention. For the early twentieth-century avant-garde artist,

> to exercise and express one's unfettered instinctual powers was to strike a blow against, to subvert, the established [social] order . . . The artist . . . exemplified the liberated individual *par excellence*, and the content of his art defined the nature of liberated experience itself.[80]

In this attitude the modern artist took a stance at variance with that of Reynolds, Lessing, Burke, or Rousseau. And yet its ancestry can be traced to the eighteenth century's use of gender metaphors. Already then, as we have seen, woman, even while emblematic of nature, served to incarnate the sphere of sociality, seen as not only the ground of civilization and higher pleasures but also as the domestic sphere from which the male hero must venture forth to do great deeds. In Kant's analysis of the twin categories, the beautiful is our experience of the harmony of the imagination—fed by the senses—with the understanding; the sublime, with its disparity between the imagination and the reason, allows us to feel our non-natural power, our freedom from physical determinism. Although Kant conceives of the sense of freedom connected with the sublime fundamentally as an intimation of our moral nature, its incarnation as a human type is "the warrior" for whom even "a fully civilized society" retains a "superior esteem." Though the hero must embody the virtues of peace as well as those of war, in a comparison between "the statesman" (incarnating the social virtues) and "the general . . . an aesthetic judgment decides in favor of the general." For "war has something sublime about it."[81]

In his development of Kant's aesthetics, Schiller explicitly ties the concepts of

---

79 Barnett Newman, "The sublime is now," [1948] in *Selected Writings and Interviews*, ed. John P. O'Neill (New York: Knopf, 1990), p. 173; *idem*, "The painting of Tamayo and Gottlieb," [1945] in ibid., p. 75.

80 Carol Duncan, "Virility and domination in early twentieth-century vanguard painting," in Norma Broude and Mary D. Garrard (eds), *Feminism and Art History* (New York: Harper and Row, 1982), pp. 294, 309.

81 Kant, *Critique of Judgment*, pp. 121, 122.

the sublime and the beautiful—called by him the "energizing" and "melting" types of beauty—both to gender attributes and to society's control over individual energy. He links energizing beauty to "savagery and hardness," melting beauty to "effeminacy and enervation."

> That is why in periods of vigor and exuberance we find true grandeur of conception coupled with the gigantic and the extravagant, sublimity of thought with the most frightening explosions of passion; and that is why in epochs of discipline and form we find nature as often suppressed as mastered, as often outraged as transcended . . . [E]nergy of feeling is stifled along with violence of appetite, and that character too shares the loss of power which should only overtake passion.[82]

It is art, in Schiller's view, that will make possible resolution of "the eternal antagonism of the sexes"—the "simplest and clearest paradigm" of all the psychological and social divisions experienced by modern humanity—and so more generally of those divisions "in the complex whole of society, endeavoring to reconcile the gentle with the violent in the moral world after the pattern of the free union it there contrives between the strength of man and the gentleness of woman."[83]

Such passages seek reconciliation and harmony, not the conquest of one principle by another. In the Aesthetic State which represents Schiller's ideal, "a-social appetite," the male principle, "must renounce its self-seeking" while "the Agreeable, whose normal function is to seduce the senses, must cast toils of Grace over the mind as well." The terms in which he poses the problem, however, taking for granted the contrast of "strength" and "gentleness," spell the impossibility of a solution. Schiller himself expected modern society to fail to achieve personal and social harmony and therefore located the Aesthetic State "only in some few chosen circles, where conduct is governed, not by some soulless imitation of the manners and morals of others, but by the aesthetic nature we have made our own."[84] But "aesthetic education," as Schiller conceived it, could operate only within the self-divided social world it promised ideally to reform, a bourgeois culture still caught in the toils of gender totemism. In this culture, it was only by taking form in the activity of the heroic male that art could claim to embody both the supposedly elemental, natural force of self-love and the highest development of universal civilization.

82 Schiller, *Aesthetic Education*, p. 113.
83 Ibid., p. 213.
84 Ibid., pp. 217, 219.

5

THE RATIONALIZATION
OF ART

"We are in the presence of a work of art only when it has no preponderant instrumental use, and when its technical and rational organization are not preeminent."[1] These words seem self-evident to their author, George Kubler, because they constitute a restatement of a fundamental conception of modern aesthetics. The most celebrated early appearance of this conception is Kant's, in the *Critique of Judgment* of 1791. By tying the idea of "aesthetic experience" to "disinterestedness" Kant set aesthetic value in opposition both to morality and to instrumental rationality. The aesthetic enjoyment of art (as of nature) is an end in itself, requiring no justification by reference to further purposes. For Kant, similarly, artistic production is "play, in other words, an occupation that is agreeable on its own account."[2] It represents an exercise of personal autonomy, unconstrained by any external goal such as those enforced on the general run of producers by the discipline of wage labor, or on their masters by other commercial interests.

This view was not only distant from the reality of artistic production, which if not "paid for according to a definite standard" was (as it remains) a "mercenary occupation" to the extent that the artist could make it one. It was in contradiction with the actual use of art for a variety of moral, political, and commercial purposes from the Renaissance to the present day. What Kant's writing expressed, however—and this is one of the reasons for its continuing centrality to the discourse of aesthetics—was the idea of art as the embodiment of "spirit," in contrast to the "material," that is, economic, orientation dominant in modern life. In Hegel's characteristic terms, art is a way "of bringing to our minds and expressing the *Divine*, the deepest interests of mankind, and the most comprehensive truths of the spirit."[3]

---

1 George Kubler, *The Shape of Time: Remarks on the History of Things* (New Haven: Yale University Press, 1962), p. 16. The text continues by associating with this idea another essential element of the modern idea of art: "In short, a work of art is as useless as a tool is useful. Works of art are as unique and irreplaceable as tools are common and expendable."
2 Immanuel Kant, *Critique of Judgment*, tr. Werner S. Pluhar (Indianapolis: Hackett, 1987), p. 170.
3 G. W. F. Hegel, *Aesthetics. Lectures on Fine Art*, tr. T. M. Knox (Oxford: Clarendon Press, 1975), vol. 1, p. 7.

"Spirit" in its modern philosophical use refers, roughly, to the human capacities realized in "culture," a term that in the course of the nineteenth century came to signify activities and products invested with value in virtue of the place occupied by similar activities and objects in earlier periods of social history. Devotion to culture, the material embodiment of "the deepest interests of mankind," served those seeking to establish themselves as members of a social elite both to assert a connection to the aristocratic elite of the past and to stake out positions in the newly emerging commercial and industrial society. Art, in particular, could symbolize a number of competing interests in the new social order. As a concentrate of "spirit," art could play roles as varied as the ideal representation of the state (for example, in museum construction or public art programs) and the self-expression of the alienated individual.

If art serves as a mark of social superiority, it can also seem to challenge the basis of that superiority, preserving as it does features of pre-capitalist society—notably the handmade and ideally unique character of paintings and sculptures (or the origin in unique acts of composition of arts like poetry and music) within a social order increasingly based on mechanized mass production. The peculiarity, under modern conditions, of artistic production, and of the artist as producer, has allowed (as Raymond Williams pointed out) for "an emphasis on the embodiment in art of certain human values, capacities, energies, which the development of society towards an industrial civilization was felt to be threatening or even destroying."[4] Thus, writing 44 years after the *Critique of Judgment*, Théophile Gautier employed a variant of the Kantian conception of art when, in opposition to the dominant aesthetic of his day, he attacked "utility" as a criterion of aesthetic judgment and asserted in the preface to *Mademoiselle de Maupin* that nothing "is really beautiful unless it is useless; everything useful is ugly, for it expresses a need."[5]

In an influential image developed in the course of the nineteenth century, the artist's life, freed from the discipline of mass production and consumption, exhibits the costs of this freedom—and so a disturbing aspect of economic rationality itself—in poverty, obscurity, and madness. The position is indicated clearly by Charles Baudelaire in his essay on Edgar Allen Poe. Explaining his conviction that "Poe and [the United States] were not on a level," the poet observes, "Time and money have so great a value over there!"[6] The result was the neglect and early death of the writer, a "natural aristocrat" in a bourgeois

---

4 Raymond Williams, *Culture and Society, 1781–1950* (Garden City: Doubleday Anchor, 1960), p. 39.
5 Théophile Gautier, *Mademoiselle de Maupin* [1835], tr. Joanna Richardson (Harmondsworth: Penguin, 1981), p. 39.
6 Charles Baudelaire, *The Painter of Modern Life and Other Essays*, tr. Jonathan Mayne (London: Phaidon, 1964), pp. 71–3. Only in the efficiency of his pursuit of drunkenness does Baudelaire discover an American element in Poe, described as drinking "with an altogether American energy and a fear of wasting a minute" (p. 88).

culture. Baudelaire's celebration of the *flâneur* expresses the same idea of opposition to the efficiency demanded of modern movement, driven by economic imperatives. The "painter of modern life," as Baudelaire imagines him, strolls through the crowd, a spectator of the social machinery of modernity; producing beauty from its evil, he marvels, as Baudelaire puts it with an ironic evocation of laissez-faire economic theory, at "the amazing harmony of life in the capital cities, a harmony so providentially maintained against the turmoil of human freedom."[7]

Given the antiquity of the association, within European culture, of rationality with masculinity, it is not surprising that the artist, at odds with the spirit of *Homo economicus*, should be a complexly gendered figure. As shaper of matter into form, the artist is essentially masculine. On the other hand, as concerned with the visually pleasing and—especially from the early 1800s on—with the expression of emotion, he bears feminine traits. Similarly, as things of beauty—that is, made for pleasurable consumption via various senses—the products of artistic labor were typed as feminine. On the other hand, considered as contributions to culture, bearing important meanings and spiritual values, they were masculine in character. In the later eighteenth and earlier nineteenth centuries, as we saw in Chapter 4, the idea of the sublime, contrasted with the beautiful, and the recurrent orientation to neoclassicism were conceptualized as stylistically manly; similarly, the feminine aspect of art is the target, for example, of modernist opposition to the "merely decorative."

It is not surprising that some twentieth-century artists should attempt to incorporate signifiers of "rationalization" into artistic practice as a way of overcoming the conflict between art—conceived as the embodiment of a non-instrumental rationality, or of a positively valued irrationality—and the rationalizing orientation of the capitalist order which produced that conception of art. Such attempts were especially significant in the period around the First World War, itself a demonstration both of the irrationality inherent in the social order and of the powers of scientific and technological reason. "The War over," Amédée Ozenfant and Charles-Édouard Jeanneret (soon to adopt the name Le Corbusier) proclaimed in their 1918 manifesto, *After Cubism,*

> Everything organizes, everything is clarified and purified; factories rise, already nothing remains as it was before the War: the great Competition has tested everything and everyone, it has gotten rid of aging methods and imposed in their place others that the struggle has proven their betters.

Cubism is a purely ornamental art, they argue; what is needed is art geared "toward rigor, toward precision, toward the best utilization of forces and materi-

7 Ibid., p. 11.

als, with the least waste, in sum a tendency toward purity." They do not hesitate to claim the spirit of "Taylorism"—the time-saving system of "Scientific Management" promoted by Frederick Winslow Taylor—for the art in tune with the modern spirit they called Purism.[8]

The first decades of the twentieth century saw international enthusiasm for the speedup techniques and, even more, the ideology of Taylorism, as well as for the technology of mass production identified with Henry Ford, among people as varied as French industrialists, the Italian Communist leader Antonio Gramsci, and the Russian theater director Meyerhold.[9] In numerous countries avant-garde artists created styles of representation, abstraction, and even product design intended to embody the spirit of efficiency associated with machine-based production. As Meyer Schapiro has observed, these stylistic developments cannot be explained simply as a reflection of the increasing role of machine production: "Mechanical abstract forms arise in modern art not because modern production is mechanical, but because of the values assigned to the human being and the machine in the ideologies projected by the conflicting interests and situation in society, which vary from country to country."[10] A German critic made a similar observation in response to the Erste russische Kunstausstellung that opened in Berlin in 1922: "A naive striving towards building and constructing objects, which we have, but which are still lacking in Russian technology, has led the Russians to a primitive imitation of machines and architecture in their fine art."[11] Similarly, Futurism arose in Italy, a technologically underdeveloped country, although it was rapidly influential in artistic circles throughout Europe. The development of such styles is to be explained, therefore, by reference to felt pressures to modernize, and the varying relations of groups of artists to modernizing elites, or ones unwilling to abandon obsolete technical and managerial methods.

The complex relation between the idea of rationalization and the idea of art as the domain of free expression of spirit is particularly striking in architecture, included, despite its obvious functional aspects, in the modern system of the fine arts. Classified since the sixteenth century along with painting and sculpture as one of the *arti di disegno*, based on drawing, architecture came with the other arts to be seen as a product of an artist's inventive genius, to be judged on the basis

8 A. Ozenfant and C.-E. Jeanneret, "After Cubism," tr. John Goodman, in Carol S. Eliel (ed.), *L'Esprit Nouveau: Purism in Paris, 1911–1925* (Los Angeles: Los Angeles County Museum of Art, 2001), pp. 132, 147, 142.

9 See Traute Rafalski, "Social planning and corporatism: modernization tendencies in Italian fascism," *International Journal of Political Economy* 18:1 (1988), pp. 11–64, for the common interest of Gramsci and fascist thinkers in Fordist rationalization.

10 Meyer Schapiro, "Nature of Abstract Art" [1937] in *idem. Modern Art: 19th and 20th Centuries* (New York: Braziller, 1978), p. 207.

11 Cit. (without author or original publication) Christina Lodder, *Russian Constructivism* (New Haven: Yale University Press, 1983), p. 133.

of formal, aesthetic considerations. This explains its nineteenth-century definition as "frozen music," an otherwise odd equation with an art that by this time
was the paragon of the non-functional and non-mimetic. According to Hegel,
architecture as art is first to be recognized not in the earliest human-made structures but in "buildings which stand there independently in themselves, as it were
like works of sculpture," such as Egyptian obelisks and temples; in the modern
period, despite their utilitarian functions, buildings remain works of art in being
"undisturbed as it were by this purpose."[12]

I am unaware of any great interest in Hegel on the part of Le Corbusier;[13] this
makes it all the more striking to find an echo of the philosopher's thinking in the
first pages of *Vers une Architecture* of 1923, perhaps the most influential architectural text of the twentieth century:

> The Engineer, inspired by the law of Economy and governed by math-
> ematical calculation, puts us in accord with universal law. He achieves
> harmony.
>
> The Architect, by his arrangement of forms, realizes an order which is a
> pure creation of his spirit; by forms and shapes he affects our senses to an
> acute degree and provokes plastic emotions; by the relationships which he
> creates he wakes profound echoes in us, he gives us the measure of an order
> which we feel to be in accordance with that of our world, he determines the
> various movements of our heart and of our understanding; it is then that we
> experience the sense of beauty.[14]

---

12 Hegel, *Aesthetics*, vol. 2, pp. 633, 634.

13 Unlike the other major modernist architects, Le Corbusier was largely self-educated in his profession. As a result his exposure to the writing of Hyppolite Taine, a common academic conduit
of Hegelian aesthetics, seems to have been limited to Taine's *Voyage en Italie*, read while the
young Jeanneret was making his own Grand Tour. According to Paul Turner's study of the
Swiss architect's reading, "Victor Cousin's *Du vrai, du beau, et du bien* would be of interest to us—
with its strong case against empiricism and its idealistic aesthetic doctrine derived from
Hegel—if we had some idea of what Jeanneret's attitude toward it was" (P. V. Turner, *The Education of Le Corbusier* (New York: Garland, 1977), pp. 81–3). Of greater importance to Le
Corbusier, as both Reyner Banham and Turner have pointed out, was his reading of Hermann
Muthesius, who certainly reflected the influence of Hegel on German aesthetic thought in valu-
ing the "spiritual" above the "material," and "form" above mere "function" (see ibid., p. 77,
and R. Banham, *Theory and Design in the First Machine Age* (Cambridge: MIT Press, 1960), p. 75).
Of special note is one of the first books on art theory Jeanneret read, Henry Provensal's *L'Art de
demain*, published in Paris in 1904, and characterized by Turner as "in the nineteenth-century
German philosophical tradition of Schelling and Hegel" (p. 11).

14 I quote from the translation by Frederick Etchells, *Towards a New Architecture* (New York: Praeger,
1960), p. 7. Another expression of Le Corbusier's idea is worth quoting: architecture "expresses
a thought. A thought which reveals itself without word or sound, but solely by means of shapes
which stand in a certain relationship to one another . . . The relationships between them have
not necessarily any reference to what is practical or descriptive" (p. 187).

The distinction Le Corbusier draws between engineering and architecture is the basis for a comparison between the two stressing the contemporary "unhappy state of retrogression" of the latter and the former's present-day achievement of "its full height." In particular, Le Corbusier contrasts the sorry state of French architecture with industrial design, especially as practiced in the United States:

> We are all acquainted with too many business men, bankers and merchants, who tell us: "Ah, but I am merely a man of affairs, I live entirely outside the art world, I am a Philistine." We protest and tell them: "All your energies are directed towards this magnificent end which is the forging of the tools of an epoch, and which is creating throughout the whole world this accumulation of very beautiful things in which economic law reigns supreme, and mathematical exactitude is joined to daring and imagination. That is what you must do; that, to be exact, is Beauty."[15]

Great architecture requires a synthesis of efficiency and beauty, in which the means of modern technology are mobilized for the ends of fundamental form.

With such words the young architect addressed himself to a ruling class whose aesthetic was still rooted in the nineteenth century.[16] Following a world war which revealed the economic and political might of the United States and led to social revolution in Russia, Le Corbusier offered principles of design evoking the system of production identified with the names of Taylor and Ford: standardization, repetition, accuracy, efficiency. Illustrations in his book took American commercial buildings as models for apartment houses assembled from modular units. Similarly, *L'Esprit nouveau*, the journal Corbusier edited with Ozenfant, celebrated modern office furniture for its clear and efficient design and praised Fernand Léger for reconfiguring such classical themes as the group of women in an interior so as to incorporate into painting the principles employed in the construction of steamships.[17]

At the same time, the limits of standardization emerge in Le Corbusier's text when he differentiates between two distinct architectural needs:

---

15 Ibid., p. 22.
16 For a discussion of the professional situation Le Corbusier confronted in the 1920s, see Reyner Banham, *Theory and Design*, Chapter 16; the book as a whole is fundamental for an understanding of modernist ideologies of design. See also *Rassegna* 2:3 (*I clienti di Le Corbusier*) (1980).
17 In the same vein, Walter Gropius, propagandizing the spirit of the Bauhaus to an English and American audience in the mid-1930s, would assert that standardization "is not an impediment to the development of civilization, but, on the contrary, one of its immediate prerequisites." It works "by the elimination of the personal content of their designers and all otherwise ungeneric or non-essential features" (Walter Gropius, *The New Architecture and the Bauhaus* (Boston: Charles T. Branford, 1935), p. 34).

> On the one hand the mass of the people look for a decent dwelling, and this question is of burning importance. On the other hand the man of initiative, of action, of thought, the LEADER, demands a shelter for his meditations in a quiet and sure spot; a problem which is indispensable to the health of specialized people.[18]

Accordingly, the apartment blocks imagined for the masses complement the villa, stocked with Purist paintings, that Le Corbusier designed in 1923 for the Swiss banker Raoul La Roche. In practice the nature of rationalization is clarified: its technical aspect serves a social content, class difference, just as the supposed superiority of the capitalist organization of labor, vaunted by theorists from Adam Smith to Taylor, with its prohibition of dawdling or "soldiering," reflects the viewpoint of the employer, not the employee. The irrational element of the social system emerges in Le Corbusier's text in the figure of the charismatic leader, with whom the architect completely identifies, dreaming as he does of the destruction of the ancient city of Paris and its reconstruction according to his "rational" design.

At the center of the urban ideal Le Corbusier presented to the public in his plans for a "Contemporary City for Three Million Inhabitants" of 1922, glass towers housed the administrative elite: "captains of business, of industry, of finance, of politics, masters of science, of pedagogy, of thought, the spokesmen of the heart, the artists, poets, musicians."[19] Luxury apartment houses for the elite surround the towers, while lower-level bureaucrats and workers live in more modest suburban areas. Le Corbusier's conception of the governing elite clearly descends from the nineteenth-century capitalist utopian Henri de Saint-Simon's doctrine of the class of creative *industriels*, and indeed Le Corbusier had good relations with French neo-Saint-Simonians, as well as with the similarly-minded Redressement français, a technocratic movement under the leadership of utilities magnate Ernest Mercier that aimed to reinvigorate the national economy by means of efficient mass production and a government headed by "experts."[20] The Redressement's monthly bulletin, distributed free of charge to 25,000 to 30,000

18 Le Corbusier, *Towards a New Architecture*, p. 24.
19 Le Corbusier, *Urbanisme* (Paris, 1925), p. 93, cit. Robert Fishman, "From the Radiant City to Vichy: Le Corbusier's plans and politics, 1921–1942," in Russell Walden (ed.), *The Open Hand: Essays on Le Corbusier* (Cambridge: MIT Press, 1977), pp. 241–83. See also the extended discussion in R. Fishman, *Urban Utopias in the Twentieth Century: Ebenezer Howard, Frank Lloyd Wright, Le Corbusier* (Cambridge: MIT Press, 1977), pp. 151–263. The "Radiant City" of 1935, designed after his disillusionment with capitalist patronage led Le Corbusier to involvements with fascism and syndicalism, featured egalitarian housing, but still concentrated decision-making vertically in a centralized command structure.
20 See Mary McLeod, "'Architecture or revolution': Taylorism, technocracy, and social change," *Art Journal* 43:2 (1983), pp. 131–47. On the St.-Simonian revival, see Sylvie Schweitzer, "Rationalization of the factory, center of industrial society: the ideas of André Citroën," *International Journal of Political Economy* 24:4 (1991–2), pp. 11–34.

members of the French elite, published two pamphlets by Le Corbusier, *Towards the Paris of the Machine Era* and *To Build: Standardize and Taylorize*, in 1928. The architect's conviction that the prosperity, joy, and social harmony promised by modern technology could be realized only in a society "centrally controlled, hier-archically organized, administered from above, with the most qualified people in the most responsible position"[21] led him subsequently to the Soviet Union, from which he expected "an example of authority, edification, and leadership,"[22] to syndicalism, and to Vichy, before he abandoned his dream that some political authority would put him in charge of national urban planning.

The rationalization of architecture and urban design meant more for Le Cor-busier, however, than the gains in efficiency made possible by such measures as the centralization of decision-making, the utilization of prefabricated elements in building, and the solution of the servant problem by means of collective services. It would end class struggle and social disorder by creating a healthy and satisfy-ing life for all productive citizens, united as beneficiaries of modern technology and rational social organization. The opening up of the city to automobile traffic was no more essential in his eyes than the provision of parks, sports grounds, and exercise rooms, for the maintenance of the human machine in good order. The close contact that Le Corbusier maintained during the 1920s with Dr. Pierre Winter, French fascist and sports enthusiast, is consistent with his aesthetic vision, which calls on artists to emulate "our engineers," who "are healthy and virile, active and useful, balanced and happy in their work."[23]

Such an image brings to mind Gustav Klutsis's 1920 Soviet poster design, *Electrification of the Entire Country*, which shows a gigantic Lenin bestriding a geo-metric-abstract representation of the globe on which tiny figures either labor at the construction of the power grid or greet the Leader with gestures of joy. Only a year before, Klutsis had been making non-objective sculptural constructions. Similarly, Aleksandr Rodchenko, who by the late 1920s was producing advertis-ing graphics and art photographs of Soviet life "directly inspired by the themes of the First Five-year Plan"[24] for periodicals like *Let's Produce!*, had spent 1911–21 exploring the purest forms of non-objectivity. Both artists, however, had made

21 R. Fishman, "From the Radiant City to Vichy," p. 247.

22 Le Corbusier, letter to A. V. Lunacharsky, March 13, 1932 (Fondation Le Corbusier), cit. Jean-Louis Cohen, "Le Corbusier and the mystique of the USSR," *Oppositions* 23 (1981), pp. 81–121, 112. For a thorough discussion of Le Corbusier's relations with the Soviet Union, see J.-L. Cohen, *Le Corbusier and the Mystique of the USSR: Theories and Projects for Moscow, 1921–1936* (Princeton: Princeton University Press, 1992).

23 Le Corbusier, *Towards a New Architecture*, p. 18. On the complex relation between Le Corbusier and French fascism, see Mark Antliff, "*La Cité française*: Georges Valois, Le Corbusier, and Fascist Theories of Urbanism," in Matthew Affron and M. Antliff (eds), *Fascist Visions: Art and Ideology in France and Italy* (Princeton: Princeton University Press, 1997), pp. 131–70.

24 Margaritza Tupitsyn, "Fragmentation versus totality: the politics of (de)framing," in *The Great Utopia: The Russian and Soviet Avant-Garde, 1911–1932* (New York: Guggenheim Museum, 1992), p. 486. For the Klutsis poster, see Figure 308.

clear reference to the spirit of machine production in their abstract work, and could claim consistency of aim across the change in artistic practice. In fact, the continuity visible in the dynamic geometry carried over from earlier painting practice to the photographs and montages of their later illustrative work was more than formal. Faithful service to the Bolshevik regime points to the intimate relation between their artistic intentions and the social reality that inspired, confined, and ultimately "liquidated" them.[25]

While many of the radical artists in Russia initially kept their distance from the Bolshevik state apparatus, they were from the first powerfully affected by the Revolution and the possibilities for social progress it opened up. The times called for fresh definitions of artistic activity.[26] Additional elements of the situation were the pressures of the new regime, not particularly sympathetic to avant-garde art, and the resentment of peasants and workers toward intellectuals and artists, perceived as useless parasites. By calling themselves "Futurists," Russian avant-gardists meant something more radical than the Italian artists whose name they borrowed: they announced a "tendency to go beyond the limits of the work of art enclosed within itself, i.e. the trend towards the liquidation of art as a separate discipline."[27] Emerging as a distinct group within the avant-garde in the early 1920s, the Constructivists, among whom Rodchenko played a leading role, defined themselves not as creators and preservers of culture, but as "professionals," specialized workers in a branch of social production. Like Le Corbusier, they modeled themselves on engineers, dedicated to the efficient solution of technical problems. According to Rodchenko, "Every trace of aestheticism will drop away. Painting tends towards engineering because its course of evolution follows that of the engineer, technology and revolution."[28] Similarly, Liubov Popova asserted in 1921 that even in painting "there can be the same construction as in the locomotive, with the difference that in painting the construction will have a pictorial purpose and in the locomotive a technical one. But in neither case should there be superfluous elements or material."[29]

The comparison poses two questions: first, what might be judged "superfluous" in painting? According to Rodchenko, this included such things as "figurative

---

25 And in more than one case the artist too: Klutsis, for instance, an early member of the Bolshevik party and fighter in the Civil War, was eventually killed in the Gulag.

26 For a brilliant account of this development, to which I am greatly indebted, see Hubertus Gasser, "The Constructivists: modernism on the way to modernization," in *The Great Utopia*, pp. 291–319.

27 Ivan Puni, "Sovremennye gruppirovki v russkom levom iskusstve," in *Iskusstvo kommuny* 19 (1919), p. 3, cit. Lodder, *Russian Constructivism*, p. 48.

28 Comments in a discussion of the concept "construction" by the Objective Analysis Group of INKhUK; cit. Selim O. Khan-Magomedov, *Rodchenko: The Complete Work* (Cambridge: MIT Press, 1987), p. 84.

29 Ibid., p. 87.

image, expression of a feeling, aesthetics."[30] A painting required no more than the application of paint to a support, sculpture nothing beyond the assembly of elements capable of maintaining a determinate three-dimensional relation to each other. The artists' watchword "construction" was typically explained in terms of a contrast with "composition," which was regulated by "taste" rather than by "scientific laws" of art. As Varvara Stepanova put it in 1921, "Only construction demands the absence of both excess materials and excess elements, in composition it is just the reverse—there everything is based precisely on the excessive."[31] Construction, objective rather than subjective, was supposed to dispense with everything ornamental, expressive, or otherwise unnecessary.

Such a doctrine, however, raises the second question: what is the "pictorial purpose" that remains when the aesthetic elements of figuration, expression, and taste are subtracted? One answer is suggested by the "Credo" written for the INKhUK (the Institute for Artistic Culture, which operated within the People's Commissariat of Enlightenment, the Soviet ministry of culture, between 1920 and 1924) in 1922 by the Constructivist architect Alexander Vesnin. Just as the "modern engineer has created works of genius: the bridge, the steam locomotive, the aircraft, the crane," so the "modern artist must produce objects equal to them in strength, tension, and potential, as organizing principles in terms of their psychophysiological impact on human consciousness."[32] In comparison to this reworking of the conception of art as an emotionally powerful means of communication, Rodchenko's explanation is radically formalist: "The purpose" of one of his own works "is to create two shapes with distinct colors on a flat surface."[33] In this way the language of rationalization was mobilized in defense of the autonomy of art. The content of a work was identified with the handling of materials to produce the work, and its "function" with its very production.

In Rodchenko's *Non-Objective Painting, Black on Black* of 1918 (Museum of Modern Art, New York), for example, the restriction of color to variants of black suggests the attempt (however unsuccessful) to eliminate both imagery and expression in the usual sense, so that what remains is simply the application of paint. The negation of customary properties of painting here signifies productive efficiency, as the use of black embodies the rejection as superfluous of the pleasures of color. Rodchenko's work of two years later was even more simplified,

---

30 Ibid.

31 Varvara Stepanova, "Protokol zasedaniya INKhUKa," January 28, 1921, MS, cit. C. Lodder, *Russian Constructivism*, p. 88. This may be compared with Karel Teige's critique of Le Corbusier, which contrasted the latter's insistence on an aesthetic, emotional content in architecture with the Constructivist elimination of "ideological-metaphysical-aesthetic intentions"; see J.-L. Cohen, *Le Corbusier and the Mystique of the USSR*, p. 32.

32 Alexander Vesnin, "Kredo," in Mikhail Barkhin and Yuri Yaralov (eds), *Mastera Sovetskoi arkhitektury ob arkhitekture* (Moscow: Iskusstvo, 1975), vol. 2, p. 14, cit. J.-L. Cohen, *Le Corbusier and the Mystique of the USSR*, p. 32.

33 Khan-Magomedov, *Rodchenko*, p. 87.

with surface texture and evidence of the brush giving way to ruler-drawn lines on flatly painted planes.[34] Finally, in his hanging constructions of 1921 Rodchenko cut into the plane to allow basic geometric shapes—exemplars of impersonality—to generate structures in space: these are works pared to a minimum, with material serving only to carry the relations defining the system, while capable of assuming an infinity of configurations. In the same year he showed three monochrome canvases, each in a primary color, applying the principle of strict economy to the colored plane.

Of course, as theorists like Tarabukin pointed out, even so radical a form of painting still ended with the production of art objects.[35] This state of affairs involved an obvious theoretical instability. It expressed the equivocal position of radical artists in a society that, whatever their wishes, like its capitalist sibling in the West generated the distinction between rationalized production, on the one hand, and fine art, on the other. The description of their art as "laboratory work" proved inadequate to realize the Constructivists' desired "rationalization of artistic labor."[36] They accordingly applied their skills to the design of useful objects, along lines similar to those explored in Germany at the Bauhaus and promoted in France by *L'Esprit nouveau*; to work in the theater and cinema; and to political and product advertising.

Already in 1919 Rodchenko had produced a design, more a visualized conception than a working drawing, for a public information kiosk combining as many means as possible of disseminating information—a clock, posters, a billboard, advertisements, a space for the sale of publications, a speaker's rostrum. The envisioned physical structure of this multimedia installation, intended to tower over the spectators in the street, had political implications, as Victor Margolin observes, primarily the

> subordinate relation of the Soviet citizen to state power. The prominent display of the clock emphasizes the social importance of precision and efficiency . . . At the core of the project is the centralization of information . . . The concentration of one-way information sources within the kiosk establishes a relation between the individual and the state in

34 See the discourse of efficiency in Rodchenko's essay *The Line* of 1921:

> The paintbrush, so essential for a painting that had to convey the illusion of an object in all its detail, has become an inadequate instrument and been replaced by others which have made it easier and more convenient to treat the surface. Press, roller, pen, rule and compass have come into use.
>
> Khan-Magomedov, *Rodchenko*, p. 293

35 See Nikolai Tarabukin, "From the easel to the machine," tr. C. Lodder, in F. Frascina and C. Harrison (eds), *Modern Art and Modernism* (London: Harper and Row, 1983).

36 Statement of the First Working Group of Constructivists, from the Catalogue of the First Discussional Exhibition of Associations of Active Revolutionary Art, 1924; in J. E. Bowlt (ed.), *Russian Art of the Avnt-Garde: Theory and Criticism 1902–1934* (New York: Viking, 1976), p. 241.

which decisions made by the state are primarily transmitted via impersonal media or an orator to citizens below.[37]

This relation between state and citizen was fully realized by Rodchenko's later photographic work for the Soviet government. The replacement of painting by photography was another path to the rationalization of art, one that employed an ideological signifier of objectivity, impersonality, and machine technology, the camera, to achieve a rapprochement with the academic Realism that had gained official favor. The move of Russian modernist artists to photography, propaganda, and advertising was, in the words of one historian, "at once a symptom and a cause of the decline of Constructivism" as an artistic program, "and of its increasing compromise with existing, as opposed to projected, reality."[38] While art historians who see the Constructivists as tragically frustrated social revolutionaries are loath to admit it, these artists were only submitting to the party dictatorship to whose triumph their earlier work had meant to contribute.[39]

Perhaps the most repulsive example of the photographic activity of Constructivism is the series of photographs Rodchenko produced of the construction of the White Sea Canal in 1931, an immense project carried out with the use of forced labor from the Gulag and at the cost of perhaps a hundred thousand deaths or more.[40] Speaking about these pictures five years later, Rodchenko set his glorification of Stalinism into the context of the productivist critique of aesthetics: "I photographed simply, giving no thought to formalism. I was staggered by the acuity and wisdom with which people were being re-educated."[41]

Even in their new guise as utilitarian producers, however, the Russian "Futurists" were not able to stand up to the political and aesthetic imperatives governing a society whose very backwardness, by the standards of capitalist modernity, had produced their devotion to technological forms. The economic planners demanded old-fashioned designs to suit the tastes of Russian peasants, workers, and bureaucrats, not modern, functionalist ones. In 1924 the Constructivist

37 V. Margolin, *The Struggle for Utopia: Rodchenko, Lissitzky, Moholy-Nagy 1911–1946* (Chicago: University of Chicago Press, 1997, pp. 17–19. Margolin relates Rodchenko's project to "poet and labor theorist" Alexei Gastev's propaganda for Taylorism, a cause dear to the heart of V. I. Lenin himself.

38 C. Lodder, *Russian Constructivism*, p. 181.

39 The perspicacity of Victor Margolin's analysis of Rodchenko's kiosk project makes all the more puzzling his "regret" that the USSR was unable "to become a viable model of economic and social organization that could have fulfilled the hopes and expectations" of the avant-garde artists; as Rodchenko's design recognized, the "utopia" for which he struggled was structured by dictatorship from the start (see *The Struggle for Utopia*, p. 213).

40 See the discussion in Margolin, *The Struggle for Utopia*, p. 186; Margolin is uncomfortable with the phrase "forced labor" because, although "accurate," it "bears the emotional overtones of a society that is under totalitarian control."

41 A. Rodchenko, "Perestroike khudozhnika," *Sovetskoe foto* 5:6 (1936), p. 20, cit. Margolin, *The Struggle for Utopia*, p. 187.

theorist Osip Brik complained that "the basic idea of productional art—that the outer appearance of an object is determined by the object's economic purpose and not by abstract, aesthetic considerations—has still not met with sufficient acceptance among our industrial executives."[42] Only a few years later the imposition of Socialist Realism made it clear that acceptance of such ideas was not on the agenda.

In the end, as we know, the Five-Year Plans did not produce the transfigured life dreamed of by the Constructivists, any more than the "new spirit" of rationalized industry in the West created generalized well-being and social order. Eighty years later, the true nature of the social realities that inspired the authoritarian fantasies of Le Corbusier and the revolutionary utopianism of Rodchenko and his comrades have become visible in the merging disasters of the two modes of progress, capitalism and Soviet communism. Rationalization in its modern form has proved to be productive of waste, destructive of life and its natural basis, and the origin of misery for millions. It is not surprising that the ideal of rationality itself has lost its earlier power.

At the end of the twentieth century, an American artist again attempted to close the circuit between art and life by subordinating art to principles of commercial reason. A different moment, however, brought a different vision. The public persona Andy Warhol adopted was not that of the virile producer but of the feminine consumer. He modeled his activity not on the engineer but on the packager and sign-maker, on the technician of publicity, comparing his products not to locomotives and steamships but to advertisements, logos, and mass media images. While Le Corbusier had declared a house to be a machine for living in, Warhol said he wanted to *be* a machine. In his work, produced as efficiently as possible (given the haze of drugs filling his Factory), pretending to impersonality and absence of expression, the grids, stripped-down surfaces, and elementary structures of early modernism returned, now to suggest not the possibility of change but the endless repetition of the ever-same.

This vision seems no more likely to be realized than the transformations imagined by the artists of the 1920s. While the rationality of modern class society succeeded in producing neither a bourgeois nor a proletarian utopia, neither has it achieved the end of history announced after the fall of the Berlin Wall in 1989. Capitalism, now the truly global power Marx's 1848 *Manifesto* predicted it would be, still drives forward the "everlasting uncertainty and agitation" of modern social life. Just as art has not been "liquidated," it is not life that is aestheticized, as some postmodernist theorists suggested, but only certain of its appearances. While rationality continues to be redefined, the fiction of art's uselessness has already lost much of its force.

42 Osip Brik, "From pictures to textile prints," in Bowlt, *Russian Art*, p. 249.

6

MECHANICAL REPRODUCTION
IN THE AGE OF ART

The enormous impact on cultural theory of Walter Benjamin's famous essay on "The work of art in the age of its mechanical reproducibility" is largely due to his claim that photography has "transformed the entire nature of art," destroying its semblance of autonomy in relation to social and political processes, and liquidating "the traditional value of the cultural heritage."[1] Photographs (and especially moving pictures) cannot, he believed, be invested with the "aura" of timelessness and sanctity which Benjamin saw as essential to the classical artwork; they give themselves not to aesthetic contemplation by a chosen few but to absorption by the masses, who in this way acquire a mode of experience adequate to the social changes called for by technological development.

While Benjamin's friend and critic, T. W. Adorno, criticized his assumption of the politically and culturally "progressive" consequences of the practice of photography, a number of recent writers have questioned the very idea that photography has had these consequences. According to W. J. T. Mitchell, for instance, photography itself has been absorbed

> by traditional notions of fine art. When Benjamin [in his "Short history of photography"] praises the production of aura in Nadar, and the destruction of aura in Atget, he is praising them as moments in the formation of a new, revolutionary conception of art that bypasses all the philistine twaddle about creative genius and beauty. And yet it is precisely these traditional notions of aesthetics, with all their attendant claims about craftsmanship, formal subtlety, and semantic complexity, that have sustained the case for the artistic status of photography.[2]

Similarly, Christopher Phillips has shown to what extent Benjamin's predictions about the transformative role of photography seem to be "considerably at odds

---

1 W. Benjamin, "The work of art in the age of mechanical reproduction," in *idem*, *Illuminations: Essays and Reflections*, ed. Hannah Arendt (New York: Schocken, 1969), pp. 227, 226, 231.

2 W. J. T. Mitchell, *Iconology* (Chicago: University of Chicago Press, 1986), pp. 181–4.

with the institutional trends that have, in recent years, borne photography tri-
umphantly into the museum, the auction house, and the corporate boardroom."[3]

Phillips begins his article with a citation of Benjamin: "From a photographic
negative, for example, one can make any number of prints; to ask for the
'authentic' print makes no sense." Since according to Benjamin the uniqueness
of the "original" artwork is a key both to its authority as an object worthy of
respect and to its place in unfolding tradition, the mechanical multiplication of
the print spells the end of these essential constituents of "aura." Multiplicity also
brings manipulability: the photograph offers itself not for worship as a singular
and rare object but for whatever uses the consumer wishes to put it to. By way of
their photographic reproduction even traditional artworks are detached from
their original loci of ritualized significance and made available for the imposition
of new meanings.

However, Phillips shows, the history of the art-institutional reception of photography runs visibly counter to this prediction. In his study of the curatorial
practices of the photography department of the Museum of Modern Art in New
York, Phillips cites as essential to this reception both the establishment of the
category of the rare, original, authentic print and the absorption even of magazine and newspaper photos into the domain of art. The systematic study of the
domain of photographs—along the lines of the history of photographic images,
and by way of their formal analysis—made possible the assimilation of photographs to more traditional art objects. The meaning of a photograph came to
be seen, following a schema of "Modernism," in the photographer's effort to
solve formal, aesthetic problems posed by the medium, and so "in its relationships to other and earlier pictures—to tradition."[4] Phillips's understanding is
borne out by other studies of photography in museums; at the Houston Museum
of Fine Arts, for instance, the criteria for acquisition decided on when the photography collection was initiated in 1976 were "first of all, the evocative power
of the work, the importance of the artist, the place of the work in the artist's
development, and its inscription in the history of photography. Without exception, the subject"—the chief interest in the dominant uses of the camera, outside
the world of art—"remains a secondary consideration."[5]

---

3 Christopher Phillips, "The judgement seat of photography," *October* 22 (1982), p. 28.
4 John Szarkowski, the first chief curator of photography at MoMA, quoted in Phillips, "Judgement seat," p. 60.
5 Anne Wilkes Tucker, "Houston, Museum of Fine Arts. Politique d'acquisition et opportunités du
   moment," in Valérie Picaudé and Philippe Arbaïzar (eds), *La Confusion des genres en photographie*
   (Paris: Bibliothèque national de France, 2001), p. 88. See also, in the same volume, Mark
   Haworth-Booth's "Repositionner la photographie" (pp. 71–85), which describes the movement of
   photographs from documentation to art works within London's Victoria and Albert Museum; by
   contrast, Philippe Albaïzar's discussion of the reception of photography in the Bibliothèque
   nationale in Paris (pp. 61–75) shows how in a non-art institution subject-matter remains the dominant principle of classification, though even here a "new attention extended to the artistic aspect of
   photography will permit the acquisition of pieces whose documentary value is secondary" (p. 74).

Almost none of his commentators and critics have paid much attention to the ambiguity of Benjamin's use of the concept of "reproduction," to cover both (1) copies of (by contrast) original works of art, and (2) works which are multiple by nature, such as (to cite Benjamin's examples) "bronzes, terra cottas, and coins" in the classical period and woodcuts, lithographs, and photographs in more modern times.[6] Benjamin's failure to distinguish clearly between these uses seems to me to have two causes. One is the aphoristic and associative, as opposed to carefully analytic, character of his writing, which makes it both usefully suggestive and often hard to pin down. The other is that his real interest lies in neither of these topics per se but rather specifically in *photography* as a means for the production of images of the world in general and of artworks in particular. (This accounts also for what Sidney Tillim has rightly described as a major oversight on Benjamin's part, his failure "to deal adequately with photomechanical processes, a type of reproduction the masses—everyone—see every day."[7])

Benjamin's neglect of the distinction to be drawn between copies and multiples, however excused by its tangential relationship to his main focus, makes his already difficult discussion harder than necessary to follow. My subsequent remarks, therefore, begin with an exploration of the difference between copies and multiples, with some discussion of its relevance to the problematic "authenticity" of photographs and other multiples. A second section will deal directly with the question of the effect of reproduction on the "aura" of artworks, and I will conclude with a *brief* discussion of Benjamin's analysis in the light of contemporary artworld developments.

6 Benjamin, "Work of art," p. 218. In contrast to Adorno, who seems not to have noticed it, the painter and photographer Otto Coenen criticized Benjamin for his disregard of the copy-multiple distinction. It is perhaps worth noting that it was not the professional philosopher but an artist who insisted that "above all, concepts should always be clarified." See Uli Bohnen (ed.), *Otto Coenen, Leben und Werk* (Cologne: Wienand, 1983), p. 28.

7 "For Benjamin," Tillim continues,

> "mechanical reproduction" is really an umbrella term for processes that have some technical similarities, such as the woodcut, the photograph, and the photomechanical print. Actually, they result in completely different objects—a fact which changes their character and function and the way they are consumed. Therefore the processes have different cultural meanings.
>
> Sidney Tillim, "Since the late 18th century," *Artforum*, 21:9 (May 1983), p. 77

For a useful discussion of Benjamin's erroneous understanding of the history of mechanical reproduction and a critique of his essay in some ways congruent with mine, see Jacquelynn Baas, "Reconsidering Walter Benjamin," in Gabriel P. Weisberg and Laurinda S. Dixon (eds), *The Documented Image: Visions in Art History* (Syracuse: Syracuse University Press, 1987), pp. 331–47.

Copies and multiples

The distinction drawn by Nelson Goodman between what he calls "autographic" and "allographic" works is relevant to the discussion of "originality" and its supposed negation by photography, for it defines a contrast between works which can and those which cannot be copied. Autographic works are those of which even the most exact duplications do not count as genuine, while "allographic" covers works, like musical symphonies, for which the distinction between copy and original is meaningless: a musical performance is either of a given work or it is not, just as any copy of a novel is as genuine an instance of that novel as any other. The chief difference between the two groups, according to Goodman, lies in the availability of notations for the identification of allographic works. A musical score, for example, specifies which sequences of sounds are performances of a work, just as a given sequence of letters determines the identity of a literary work. But works like paintings, for which there is no notation, typically can be identified only by the history of production and transmission of the object in question.[8]

The point to be stressed here is that autographic works can be either singular or multiple by nature: "the example of printmaking refutes the unwary assumption that in every autographic art a particular work exists only as a unique object."[9] One print of a lithograph or photograph is as original as any other made from the same stone or negative, with "originality" defined by Goodman in terms of the history of the work in time and space. In the case of a painting, "The only way of ascertaining that the *Lucretia* before us is genuine is thus to establish the historical fact that it is the actual object made by Rembrandt." In principle the situation is the same in the case of a multiple artform like etching: "the only way of ascertaining whether a print is genuine is by finding out whether it was taken from a certain plate."[10]

Goodman is careful not to tie his concept of "genuine" here to that of artistic "originality," taken for example as implying the work of the artist's hand: "Authenticity in an autographic art always depends upon the object's having the requisite, sometimes rather complicated, history of production, but that history does not always include ultimate execution by the original artist."[11] As Rosalind Krauss has demonstrated, in an essay taking as motto Benjamin's dictum on photography's challenge to the idea of "authenticity," the history of production on which the concept of "genuine" member of a set of multiples must rest can be complicated indeed. How should we classify prints pulled (or printed) after the artist's death, or even just past the official size of an edition? What content has the notion of "authenticity" in the case of an artist like Rodin, whose plaster

8 See Nelson Goodman, *Languages of Art* (Indianapolis: Hackett, 1976), p. 113.
9 Ibid., p. 115.
10 Ibid., pp. 116, 119.
11 Ibid., p. 119, n. 12.

models were not only cast and patinated by others but also realized in marble, in a variety of sizes, by mechanical means?[12] These are good questions, but Krauss seems wrong to conclude that the concepts of "original artwork" or "authenticity" are empty with respect to such works, and that photography typifies a mode of "reproductions without originals."

It seems more appropriate to say with Goodman that, in the case of allographic works, every example *is* an original; while in the case of autographic works we can define "originality" generally in terms of a standard process of production of the final object (photographic prints, etchings, sculptures) from the relevant original (negative, plate, plaster model), and then introduce additional categories as necessary to make whatever distinctions seem important, such as "printed by the artist," "printed under the artist's supervision," "made under license," etc. And, in fact, this is what is done in the study and trade of such objects. Reproductions of photographs by August Sander, for example, fall on one side of a divide, on the other of which lie prints made from his negatives, which in themselves are sorted into prints made by Sander, with or without signatures, prints made by his son, and prints made under the authority of the Sander estate.

Such an example itself, of course, makes it clear that Krauss is right to draw attention to an area of artificiality in the concept of "original" invoked in the art business (an area covered by Goodman's philosophical rug, with all problems swept under by the phrase, "requisite history of production"). One could argue that the artist's signature on a print confers authenticity on the image by guaranteeing the artist's approval of it as a representative of his or her work, although an unsigned copy might in fact be just as acceptable a realization of the artist's intention as a signed one. But with editions of prints limited to five, ten, or whatever low number, we are clearly dealing with attempts to raise market value by restricting supply.[13] (We will return to this below.) On the other hand, we have works like Rodin's *Gates of Hell*, assembled after his death from pieces produced by the artist, apparently in some disregard of his intentions. It seems correct to

---

12 Rosalind Krauss, "The originality of the avant-garde" and "Sincerely yours," in *idem*, *The Originality of the Avant-Garde and Other Modernist Myths* (Cambridge: MIT Press, 1985), pp. 151–94. For an interesting discussion of these problems, with a penetrating criticism of Krauss, see Alexandra Parigoris, "Truth to materials: bronze, on the reproducibility of truth," in Anthony Hughes and Erich Ranfft (eds), *Sculpture and Its Reproductions* (London: Reaktion, 1997), pp. 131–51.

13 The discussion of originality and replication by Jean Chatelain cited by Krauss in "Sincerely yours" illustrates both recognition of the role of the art market in the functional definition of "originality" and the confusions arising from identifying originality and uniqueness. Limiting editions of multiples, as Chatelain explains, produces an "originality effect"; the effectiveness of the artificially restricted "original edition" is used "to give greater value to editions which, for want of being originals, will at least have the appearance of being so, by being numbered" (p. 177). But Chatelain himself, in another passage cited by Krauss, observes that, from a technical point of view, a cast "made from the original plaster is a proof, an edition; that which is not made from the original plaster is a reproduction"—in contrast to the legal efforts made to restrict the concept of "originality" to the benefit of the art trade (p. 178).

describe multiple casts of this piece as "reproductions without an original," but only because there is an element of fraud here in the claim that the work as displayed is an "original Rodin."[14] Finally, Krauss's promotion of Sherrie Levine's photographs of photos by Edward Weston and others as "work that acted out the discourse of reproductions without originals"[15] is misleading. First of all, Levine's pictures are obviously in a straightforward sense copies of originals, namely the prints by Weston *et al.* Second, they themselves also are originals, being prints of negatives made by Sherrie Levine.

In short, the distinction between original and replica seems to be meaningful for all autographic works. A reproduction of a Rembrandt etching or a Steiglitz photograph (even of one of the early photogravures) is as much a copy, to be distinguished from an original, as is a forgery or a photograph of a painting. Despite the fact that "one can make any number of prints" from a negative, it does, *pace* Benjamin, make sense "to ask for the 'authentic' print." It is this possibility of a contrast between original and copy that gives "aura" a foothold in the world of photography.

At the same time, the practice of restricting the quantity of multiple autographic works bears witness to the role played by quantity alongside that of quality in determining the appreciation of artworks. Photographs may, as Mitchell and Phillips contend, have entered the institutional world of art, but the restricted number of galleries and private dealers specializing in such images, as opposed to painting and sculpture, testifies to the limited prices they, like prints generally, can command. We must at least ask whether it is not "aura" but monetary value that is associated with uniqueness. The counterexamples offered by the great commercial success of photographers like Cindy Sherman and Andreas Gursky prove the rule: the once unthinkable prices paid for works by these producers are associated with their marketing by dealers generally associated with painting. In the case of Gursky, whose *Untitled V* sold for over $600,000 in February 2002 at Christie's London (an auction record for a photograph), the works themselves approach the appearance of painting in their large format and rich color; while not unique, editions are very small.[16]

---

14 See Krauss, "Sincerely yours," pp. 187 ff.

15 Krauss, "Originality," p. 168.

16 Judith Benhamou-Huet draws attention to another feature of this case:

> what pushes prices up is not the idea of possessing something that no one else can own, but the thought of keeping up with the neighbors. This is the new spiral of the limited edition. Art lovers have gone beyond the stage of wanting a unique work. They don't want what nobody else has. But what the person they envy or the institution they admire already possesses.
>
> *The Worth of Art. Pricing the Priceless* (New York: Assouline, 2001), p. 112

Similarly, in the case of Jeff Koons's sculpture, one observer has noted, "Rarity pays, especially when it is multiple" (Harry Bellet, *Le Marché de l'art s'écroule demain à 18h30* (Paris: NiL, 2001), p. 41).

But we are dealing here with more than the workings of price determination by supply and demand. Photographs, as Tillim observes, "read differently from paintings because the photographic surface does not 'signify' the way paint does."[17] Paintings, except for willfully designed exceptions, proclaim themselves to be handcrafted items. In contrast, photographs—both in their most common forms, returned to us by the corner Fotomat or reproduced in magazines and advertising posters, and in the form of the exhibition print—carry the signs of their origin in mechanical processes. While photographs can have the attribute of originality without uniqueness, their mode of production differentiates them from the traditional artwork. In fact, as Susan Lambert has pointed out, when formal definitions of the "original" print were promulgated in the 1960s,

> the importance that the regulations attached to a particular kind of manual involvement with the making of the printing surface on the part of the artist makes it appear in retrospect that they were framed also as a counter-movement by the old guard against a new generation of artists who were finding a powerful and personal means of expression in the photomechanical techniques of popular visual communication.[18]

Lambert's use of "old guard" here itself suggests—in agreement with the views of Mitchell, Phillips, and others—that in reality photography has entered, as an autographic production of multiples, into the domain of art. It was Benjamin's great idea to substitute for the question commonly asked at the turn of the century, whether photography is an art, "the primary question—whether the very invention of photography [has] not transformed the entire nature of art."[19] It is thus that his essay centered on the effects of photographic reproduction on the status of works of art.

"Aura" and reproduction

In Benjamin's view, traditional art is mimetic in the sense that it reproduces an experience known to its viewers outside of art, one saturated with the mystery of the "natural," that whose meaning is seemingly given independently of history. This experience is that of "aura," "the unique appearance or semblance of a distance, no matter how close the object may be."[20] By "distance," Benjamin

---

17 Tillim, "Since," p. 69.

18 Susan Lambert, *The Image Multiplied* (London: Trefoil, 1987), p. 32. Interestingly, as she points out, this "implied that the choice of technique was more important than the originality of the image which could, if the hand of the printmaker was evident enough, be inherently reproductive."

19 Benjamin, "Work of art," p. 227.

20 W. Benjamin, "A Small History of Photography," in *idem, One Way Street* (London: Verso, 1979), p. 250; see "Work of art," p. 222, for a related formulation.

explains, he means "unapproachability."[21] Object and viewer are not connected in the spatio-temporal framework of action; instead the object appears as outside of time, a given, unalterable. In an essay on Baudelaire, Benjamin speaks of objects with "aura" as returning the gaze of the viewer; such objects have been invested with human characteristics. Put less poetically, "experience of the aura . . . rests on the transposition of a response common in human relationships to the relationship between the inanimate or natural object and man."[22]

This experience, according to Benjamin, depends on certain social circumstances, those which he associates with "tradition." While Benjamin's use of this concept derives from the Romantic contrast of the culture of a lost organic totality with that of fragmented modernity, he emphasizes the slowly developing modes of production and accordingly stable modes of perception and consciousness characteristic of "traditional" society. The heart of "tradition" is *repetition* (in mode of production, in the rhythms of daily or yearly life), and the most developed form of repetition is *ritual*. In this way Benjamin finds the origin of art in the religious life of premodern society. The dissolution of earlier society brings with it "the emancipation of the various art practices from ritual" and the transmutation of the "cult value" of their products into the "exhibition value" of what is now seen as autonomous art.[23] That this alteration should allow the transmission of the property of "aura" is, in Benjamin's view, profoundly related to the uniqueness of the art object, which he believed essential to its original ritual function. Benjamin's claim seems to be that "aura" depends on two factors: the presence of a tradition, a relatively stable framework of experience, in which an object is "embedded"; and, across tradition, the continuous existence of the object as a unique physical entity.[24]

In the modern world, tradition as such has been decisively disrupted by the advent of capitalism, with its basis in industrial mass production. Since "the mode of human sense perception changes with humanity's entire mode of existence,"[25] the breakdown of earlier patterns of activity brings with it a transformation of visual experience. In his essay on Eduard Fuchs, the pioneer historian of "popular" imagery, Benjamin quoted approvingly Fuchs's statement that "every age has its own quite special techniques of reproduction.

21 Benjamin, "Work of art," p. 243 n. 5.
22 Benjamin, "Some Motifs of Baudelaire," in *Illuminations*, p. 188.
23 Benjamin, "Work of art," p 225.
24 Ibid., p. 223:

> The uniqueness of a work of art is inseparable from its being embedded in the fabric of tradition. The tradition itself is . . . extremely changeable. An ancient statue of Venus, for example, stood in a different traditional context with the Greeks . . . than with the clerics of the Middle Ages . . . Both of them, however, were equally confronted with its uniqueness, that is, its aura.

25 Ibid., p. 222.

They represent the technological potential of the period concerned and are . . . a response to the requirements of the time."[26] The employment of machinery for picture making is only the adaptation to this purpose of the method of manufacture characteristic of capitalist commodity production. It is one element in the generalization of that new form of experience that spreads from the modern workplace to the crowds of the big cities to which this mode of production gives birth.

The effect of photography on the traditional work of art is, in Benjamin's view, a special case of its effect on our perception of reality generally. To the ceaseless revolutionizing of capitalist technology corresponds the power of photographic image making to "capture images which escape natural vision."[27] This is one effect which photography can have on our experience of artworks. More particularly, suggests Benjamin, photographing artworks (like recording musical performances) "enables the original to meet the beholder halfway,"[28] by removing the image (or performance) from its original site in church, palace, or museum. Reproduction, that is, acts against the distance basic to the experience of "aura" as it "detaches the reproduced object from the domain of tradition" and allows it "to meet the beholder or listener in his own particular situation." At the same time, finally, multiple reproduction "substitutes a plurality of copies for a unique existence"; together these processes produce "a tremendous shattering of tradition." In this way, "that which withers in the age of mechanical reproduction is the aura of the work of art."[29]

Benjamin's essay, while developing themes at work in the literature of photography since its invention in the mid-nineteenth century,[30] seems to reflect more particularly the wide-ranging debate among art professionals in Germany touched off by Alexander Dorner's 1929 exhibition at the Hanover Provincial Museum, in which he matched original works with photographic reproductions. Art historian Kurt Karl Eberlein, insisting that "the mysterious,

---

26 W. Benjamin, "Eduard Fuchs, collector and historian," in *idem, One Way Street*, p. 384.

27 Benjamin, "Work of art," p. 220; note Benjamin's reversal of the cliché about photography merely copying nature, as opposed to the "creativity" of earlier art forms. This aspect of Benjamin's thinking is well developed by Joel Snyder in his article on "Benjamin on Reproduction and Art," *Philosophical Forum* 15 (1983–4), pp. 131–45.

28 Benjamin, "Work of art," p. 220.

29 Ibid., p. 221.

30 Oliver Wendell Holmes, notably, wrote already in 1859,

> There is only one Colosseum or Pantheon; but how many millions of potential negatives have they shed—representatives of billions of pictures—since they were erected! Matter in large masses must always be fixed and dear; form is cheap and transportable. We have got the fruit of creation now, and need not trouble ourselves with the core.

> "The stereoscope and the stereograph," in Alan Trachtenberg (ed.), *Classic Essays in Photography* (New Haven: Leete's Island Books, 1980), p. 81

magical, biological 'aura' of a work of art cannot be forged," directly attacked the democratic politics of mechanical reproduction: "only a brutal utilitarianism can enslave art to its purposes, making it a means to an end, and thereby reducing it to 'art for all.' . . . *There is no universal right to the arts!*"[31] Dorner, in contrast, insisted that reproduction is only one more mode of appropriation of an object, such as an altarpiece or a family portrait, whose removal to a museum is already "a violation of [its] original purpose." He too stressed the political issue at stake:

> The enemies of facsimile think of the work only as a unique and sacred thing; the advocates consider, in addition, the artwork's uses for the present. To the former, what is important is the experience of a small number of individuals; to the latter, the further development of the people as a whole is equally important. No compromise is possible between the two.[32]

Benjamin's version of these ideas has the virtue above all of treating the category "art" as itself having a history, and one continuing to be subject to drastic transformation. And from his too simplistic acceptance of the Hegelian mythology of the origin of art in religious cult Benjamin drew a picture of art as the object of a sort of secular ritual that clearly captures something central to this social practice.[33] Benjamin's conception can, however, be questioned at several points. To begin with, the idea that uniqueness is a necessity for ritual images is not well founded. Leaving aside the evidence from contemporary non-Western peoples, not to mention cult statuettes mass produced in archaic Europe, one need only remember the rows of hardly differentiated Madonnas in the Pinacoteca at Siena to doubt Benjamin's claim (though this is not to deny that particular images may, in various traditions, acquire special reputations for efficacy).[34] We

---

31 K. K. Eberlein, "On the question: original or facsimile reproduction?" in Christopher Philips (ed.), *Photography in the Modern Era: European Documents and Critical Writings, 1911–1940* (New York: Metropolitan Museum of Art/Aperture, 1989), p. 148.

32 A. Dorner, "Original and facsimile," in Phillips, *Photography*, pp. 152, 154.

33 For a stimulating attempt to work out this idea in some detail, see Carol Duncan and Alan Wallach, "The universal survey museum," *Art History* 3:4 (1980), pp. 441–69.

34 To take an example from India:

> During the period of the Pala and Sena kings, from the eighth century till the devastating Muslim invasions at the end of the twelfth, images of the Buddhist and Hindu deities were produced in Bihar and Bengal in large numbers . . . Writing about Bengali Vishnu images found "by the dozens" from the eleventh and twelfth centuries, Susan Huntington . . . has observed that "it may be surmised that workshops were given to almost factory-like production of quantities of sculptures following the now-codified formulae of both style and iconography."
>
> Forrest McGill, "Representation and revelation: two Pala images," in *The Real, the Fake, and the Masterpiece* (New York: The Asia Society, 1988), p. 13

have already seen that uniqueness is not necessary for works to have the character of authenticity; the case of prints of (to take the most obvious examples) Rembrandt and Dürer shows that it is not a necessary condition for the possession of "aura" either. Moreover, aside from prints, Benjamin's idea is based on a projection back into the history of art of a relatively modern idea of the work of art as a unique entity, issued from the sole hand of a master.

> Yet the cachet attached to the concept of originality is a relatively recent phenomenon. What we now consider as the most characteristic works of the great masters were usually preceded by full-size cartoons and painted *modelli*, which might bear more of the master's own hand than the "finished" works. These were followed by copies or variations, sometimes by the artist himself and often, as it were, under license within his milieu. In such a sequence of collective effort the idea of a single "original" is hardly relevant.[35]

But even with respect to unique artworks to which something like Benjamin's conception of "aura" certainly applied before modern times, it does not seem to be true in general that it was diminished by reproduction. This was understood by painters such as Mantegna, Raphael, and Rubens, who, realizing "the advantage of the fame that reproduction of their images brought," played important roles in the organization of the reproductive print trade of their time.[36] In the case of the classical sculptures once felt to constitute the epitome of artistic creation, it has been observed, "the taking of plaster casts from an original was an essential step in spreading the world-wide appreciation of the most esteemed antique statues."[37] Their "classical" status was *created*, not just a given.

The "aura" of these originals could be so powerful as to pervade their copies: a palace inventory made for Philip IV of Spain "valued the casts of the Farnese *Flora* and *Hercules* as each worth more than Velazquez's 'Bacchus' and twice as much as any of his portraits."[38] This transmission of "aura" to reproductions was expressed explicitly in the eighteenth-century idea of "the importance of the traveler's report, the engraved copy, the transposition from one instrumental

35 Lambert, *Image*, p. 13.

36 Ibid., p. 147.

37 Francis Haskell and Nicholas Penny, *Taste and the Antique* (New Haven: Yale, 1981), p. 3; see also especially pp. 21, 65, 98. Another author has expressed this point, quite possibly with Benjamin's argument in mind, by the assertion that "casts and all manner of copies constitute the visible aura" of antique sculpture's "elevation to canonical status" (Walter Cahn, *Masterpieces: Chapters in the History of an Idea* (Princeton: Princeton University Press, 1979), p. 110). One must also not forget that the antique statues elevated to aesthetic sainthood in early modern times were themselves reproductions, for the most part Roman copies of and variations after Greek originals.

38 Haskell and Penny, *Taste*, p. 33.

setting into another, which bring the work to a wider public and at the same time make manifest its claim to universality."[39]

This is to say, of course, that Benjamin's idea of "tradition" as a given context for experience represents a degree of mystification of the pre- and early modern past: tradition in any society must be constructed, and continually reconstructed. And, with respect to the phenomenon under discussion here, the mechanical reproduction of artworks played a considerable role in the creation of the pre-requisites for the experience of aesthetic "aura." What we call "art" exists within the structure of a social institution, a system of practices of production (by independent producers for the luxury trade), appropriation (market-based collecting), and appreciation (based on concepts of aesthetic autonomy of the work and of the original genius of the artist). It must be remembered, as I have stressed in earlier chapters, that this institution—what Benjamin in his sketch of its historical development called "the secular cult of beauty"[40]—is itself a modern phenomenon. Like all social transformations, the creation of the modern practice of art involved the development of new modes of theory and criticism. It also made significant use of the mechanical reproduction of images, invented in Europe at about the same time as the mechanical reproduction of text.

The earliest datable (woodcut) prints of precisely identifiable objects are, according to W. M. Ivins, Jr., representations of paintings, the decorations of the church of Santa Maria sopra Minerva made at the command of Cardinal Torquemada.[41] Since the rapid expansion of the printmaking industry in the sixteenth century, "most of the printed pictures that were made and collected were reproductions of paintings and drawings."[42] These were not collateral but essential to the way in which the production of "originals" developed:

> The great influence of Italy on the north, and later that of Paris on the rest of Europe, was exerted through reproductive prints which carried the news of the new styles. If we would understand those influences and the forms they took, we must look not at the Italian and Parisian originals but at what for us are the stupid prints which the publishers produced and sold in such vast quantities.[43]

39 Cahn, *Masterpieces*, p. 123. Cahn mentions the interesting remarks of travelers that, given the sorry state of repair of Leonardo's *Last Supper* in Milan, "it could be seen to better advantage through copies elsewhere" (p. 127). For this case, see Emil Moller, *Das Abendmahl des Lionardo da Vinci* (Baden-Baden: Verlag für Kunst und Wissenschaft, 1952), pp. 78, 144, and the account in S. Lambert, *Image*, pp. 191–206.
40 Benjamin, "Work of art," p. 224.
41 These images illustrate the Cardinal's *Meditations on the Passion of Our Lord* of 1467. See William M. Ivins, Jr., *Prints and Visual Communication* (Cambridge: MIT Press, 1969), p. 31.
42 William M. Ivins, Jr., *How Prints Look* (Boston: Beacon Press), p. 146.
43 Ivins, *Prints*, p. 69.

And they provided the basic visual experience of the theorists and critics of art who played an essential role in the creation and promotion of this institution. When Winckelmann first wrote on Greek art, for example, he knew it only through engravings; Lessing had never seen the original when he wrote on the *Laocoön*. This visual experience, furthermore, was provided in a form determined by the emerging institution of art. Collections of reproductions constituted (to use Malraux's phrase) a museum without walls, "transforming paintings specifically designed for a wide variety of specific purposes—religious contemplation, moral instruction, sexual arousal—into objects whose pure aesthetic enjoyment is disturbed only by occasional doubts as to the name of their creators."[44]

On the other hand, it has been suggested that the development of mechanical methods for the reproduction of antique sculpture in the nineteenth century, especially in the form of reductions, may have created a new situation: "it is possible that the promiscuous familiarity encouraged by these techniques may have unintentionally diminished the glamour of the statues reproduced."[45] This effect must surely be explained as due not simply to the changing quantity and quality of reproductions but also—and above all—to the expansion of the audience for art and so of its social composition. Admirers of the fine arts in the 1600s and 1700s represented a severely limited sector of the Euro-American population, but late eighteenth- and early nineteenth-century purveyors of classical imagery like Josiah Wedgwood were responding to "social emulation through emulative spending, . . . the lead offered by the aristocratic few being aped by the socially aspiring many, the general clambering after the example provided by the legislators of taste."[46]

That the accuracy of a method for the production of sculptural casts developed in Paris in 1839 "led to immediate comparison with the exactly contemporary daguerreotype"[47] brings us back to Benjamin, who was certainly ready to relate art's loss of "aura" to the change in the social base of its consumption, asserting that

the simultaneous contemplation of paintings by a large public, such as developed in the nineteenth century, is an early symptom of the crisis of painting, a crisis which was by no means occasioned exclusively by

---

44 Frances Haskell, *The Painful Birth of the Art Book* (London: Thames and Hudson, 1987), p. 57. One detail casts some light on the emergence of the modern conception of art: a study of the catalogues issued by the Roman print publisher de Rossi shows an "increase [between 1677 and 1724] in the number of prints included under the names of artists rather than classified by subjects" (F. Haskell, *Painful Birth*, p. 14).

45 Haskell and Penny, *Taste*, p. 125.

46 Neil McKendrick, "Commercialization and the economy," in N. McKendrick, J. Brewer, and J. H. Plumb, *The Birth of a Consumer Society* (London: Hutchinson, 1983), pp. 140–1. See also Haskell and Penny, *Taste*, pp. 125 ff.

47 Haskell and Penny, *Taste*, p. 124.

photography but rather in a relatively independent manner by the appeal of art works to the masses.[48]

This mass audience, he held, in its modern conditions of life, actually requires new forms like illustrated papers and films, for which a way is cut through the cultural detritus of the past by the "aura"—destroying work of photographic reproduction.

It is far from obvious, however, that photographic reproduction of artworks contributed to art's loss of "aura" by depreciating "the quality of [their] presence."[49] To the contrary, as Ivins points out, "the photograph made it possible for the first time in history to get such a visual record of an object or work of art that it could be used as a means to study many of the qualities of the particular object or work of art itself."[50] Here it may be noted that Benjamin's emphasis on the element of "reproduction" in photography missed that which distinguishes this from earlier graphic techniques, which is not its inherently multiple character but its relative independence from the copyist's hand and eye as a means of depiction.[51] The rise of photography as a reproductive medium in part reflected the circumstance that by the mid-nineteenth century "the sort of awe we now feel for the status of the original made it necessary for there to be an 'authentic' or direct relation between the reproduction and its original."[52] (It should be remembered also that it was not in earlier periods deemed essential that reproductions be made after the original, copies being often substituted where more convenient.) Photography made possible not only a relative gain in accuracy of reproduction, but also a qualitative leap to the very possibility of documenting the material character of artworks, such as details of facture. In this way photographic reproduction became essential to the development of modern connoisseurship and the discipline of art history, hardly loci of the desacralization of art.[53]

---

48 Benjamin, "Work of art," p. 234.
49 Benjamin, "Work of art," p. 221.
50 Ivins, *Prints*, p. 136. That there was steady pressure on technology toward this goal is shown by the development of mezzotint and similar non-linear methods of representation. By the late eighteenth century, Crozat went to extraordinary lengths "to produce absolutely faithful records of the paintings chosen for reproduction" in the volumes he had produced (Haskell, *Painful Birth*, p. 32).
51 Ivins (in *Prints*, p. 177) was of course wrong to see photographic reproduction as pure depiction, with no interfering visual syntax of its own; see Estelle Jussim's critique in *Visual Communication and the Graphic Arts* (New York: Bowker, 1974).
52 Lambert, *Image*, p. 196.
53 Although this development eventually gave rise to worries on the part of art historians that practitioners' dependence on photographs might lead to their usurping the place of the originals as objects of study, it is worth noting that the founding of an "imaginary museum" of photographic reproductions was proposed already at the first International Congress of Art History in 1873 (see the discussion in Trevor Fawcett, "Graphic versus photographic in the nineteenth-century reproduction," *Art History* 9:2 (1986), p. 8).

It is evident from the notes Benjamin made for his projected *Passagen-Werk* that he was deeply influenced, in his appreciation of photography, by Baudelaire's critique of the new medium and his assertion that "poetry and progress are two ambitious men who hate one another with an instinctive hatred, and when they meet upon the same road, one of them has to give place."[54] When Benjamin calls the photographic reproduction of artworks "a phase in the fight between photography and painting," itself "a moment in the conflict between art and technology,"[55] he is following the poet who was no doubt the greatest art critic of the nineteenth century. But Baudelaire's opinion here reflects his historical limitations, showing his attachment to Romanticism and its stress on the transfigurative activity of the imagination as the basis of art; less than a decade later the Impressionists were to embody a radically different attitude to the data of perception in their work, and count photography an ally not an enemy.

It is obviously true that photographic reproduction decreases our distance from artworks by removing them, in image form, from the special settings (museums, palaces, etc.) in which the originals sit, and by even placing them at our disposal for use on mementoes, greeting cards, and wrapping paper. But it is hardly certain that this has spelled the withering of the "aura" of the work of art, any more than the commercial distribution of religious chromos implied a decline in faith. It has even been plausibly argued that the circulation of reproductions has enhanced the "auratic" presence of the originals, by preparing the viewer for the experience of the artwork, by embodying the limits of reproduction and so the uniqueness and unreproducible properties of the original, and—last but hardly least—by being the basis of "a new form of class distinction," the difference between "those who own originals as opposed to those who own only reproductions."[56]

More broadly, we might ask, if Benjamin's analysis is correct, how are we to explain the remarkable flourishing of the art scene, with its galleries, collectors, journals, and museums—in which photography itself, along with the cinema that Benjamin celebrated as art's greatest antagonist, has its secure niche? "Aura" seems to have more than survived the effects of reproduction and the development of mechanized image making. Here, as ever, however, we must examine the reality of this appearance.

54 C. Baudelaire, "The Salon of 1859," in *Art in Paris, 1841–1862*, ed. and tr. Jonathan Mayne (Oxford: Phaidon, 1965), p. 154. This passage was quoted twice by Benjamin in his notes, at Y10a,1 and Y11,1 (W. Benjamin, *The Arcades Project*, (tr.) Howard Eiland and Kevin McLaughlin (Cambridge: Harvard University Press, 1999), p. 691).

55 W. Benjamin, *Arcades*, Y1a,3 (p. 673) and Y2a,6 (p. 675).

56 Remy G. Saisselin, *The Bourgeois and the Bibelot* (New Brunswick: Rutgers University Press, 1984), p. 174.

Art and money

In 1796 Quatremère de Quincy protested the impending removal of Roman antiquities to Paris, insisting that

> The true museum of Rome . . . consists, it is true, of statues, colossi, temples, obelisks, triumphal columns, baths, circuses, amphitheatres, arches of triumph, tombs, stucco decoration, frescoes, bas-reliefs, inscriptions, fragments of ornaments, building materials, furniture, utensils, etc., etc.; but it is composed no less of places, sites, mountains, quarries, ancient roads, the particular placement of ruined towns, geographical relationships, the mutual relationships among all these objects, memories, local traditions, still prevailing customs, the parallels and comparisons that can be made only in this very place.[57]

Here it is removal to a museum, rather than reproduction, which "detaches the [affected] object from the domain of tradition," but the thought is at base the same as Benjamin's. Ironically, precisely such detachment from tradition was (as Dorner pointed out) necessary for the transformation of objects into *works of art*—in Benjamin's terms, by transmuting their cult value into exhibition value—and for their acquisition of the "aura" experienced by art lovers like Quatremère. The object thus became removable, alienable: in the language of aesthetics, autonomous.

Napoleon's Roman acquisitions modeled on a heroic scale the formation of the great art collections of the nineteenth century. By the purchase (or theft) of objects from premodern cultures, or of objects that claimed to be descendants of these, the art lover could claim to transcend the vulgar preoccupations of the new commercial society to join an aristocracy of the spirit. The artwork is made for its own sake, not for money, and it is collected and admired for its aesthetic value, not its commercial productivity. Expressing detachment from the claims of practical life, its autonomy earns it startling prices, and its ownership thus signifies a paradoxical combination of financial success and cultural superiority to the small-minded bourgeois.

With this contradiction at its core, it is not surprising that the modern category of "art" has been a field of contradictions from its crystallization in the late eighteenth century to the present day. The internal complexity of art as ideological construct is reflected in the obscurity of Benjamin's concept of "aura," which, though defined in the first place by reference to a psychological experience, and shadowed by a metaphysical penumbra derived from Klages and Valéry, is intended also to capture an essential element of the "aesthetic attitude." "Aura" clearly includes the association with artworks of attributes of "spirituality," an

---

57 Antoine Chrysostôme Quatremère de Quincy, *Lettres sur l'enlèvement des ouvrages de l'art antique à Athènes et à Rome* [1836] (Paris: Fayard, 1989), p. 207.

order of being higher than that of the material business of everyday life, together with those of the rarity or uniqueness of the object "without price" and so for sale at a high one. Both are expressed in the concept of "authenticity," which refers at once to the direct emanation of a superior spirit, the artist, and to the claim to a special place on the market of the Real Thing.[58]

So complex—and historically developmental—a phenomenon as "aura" is of necessity a highly unstable one. While it persists today in the form of individuals' experiences—as consumers or as producers—of enjoyment of and genuine respect for the work of artists, it is indeed in steady decline as a social structure of aesthetic value. This is visible in the frankness with which a writer for *New York* magazine could describe art collecting as "the ultimate rich man's sport."[59] As, in R. G. Saisselin's words,

> the aesthetic experience has shifted from the contemplation of the work of art to its acquisition . . . [the] old idealist ethic of beauty, the old role of art as a sign of social distinction and culture, has been laid to rest. Art remains the sign only of wealth and the aura about it is the aura of gold.[60]

While this is an exaggeration, it does seem to many that authenticity must be sought elsewhere, in the world of mass consumption—in popular music and sports, for instance—in which the frankness of corporate domination paradoxically creates the illusion of a space open for the critique of dominant values.[61]

---

58 R. Saisselin, *Bourgeois*, p. 131:

> The general bibliotization of art in the nineteenth century, with its search for the real thing, its nearly so, and its approximation, was bound to come up against the problem of authenticity. Since the object of art had been uprooted from its ancient sites and functions, stripped of its religious and social and political associations, it had become, regardless of the definitions of philosophers, an object with an exchange or trade value. Thus the moment of the expert had arrived.

59 Dinitia Smith, "Art fever: the passion and frenzy of the ultimate rich man's sport," *New York* 20:16 (April 20, 1987), pp. 31–43.

60 Saisselin, *Bourgeois*, pp. 171–2.

61 This cultural development, represented in daily life by the displacement of bourgeois formal clothing by baseball caps and blue jeans, appears in academia in the revaluation of the products formerly known as kitsch by the discipline of Cultural Studies, and in certain postmodern critics' and artists' employment of mass-cultural elements to mount critiques of "High Art" (see below, Chapter 8, p. 126f). It is thus part of the story of the art-theoretical reception of Benjamin's essay during the 1980s, when it was characteristically set in contrast to Clement Greenberg's critique of kitsch, originally published only nine years after "The work of art." While Greenberg, like Adorno, condemned all "popular" art and literature, including illustrated magazines and Hollywood movies, as kitsch, Benjamin believed that mass culture could provide a realm where "the critical and receptive attitudes of the public coincide" in the appreciation of progressive art: "the reactionary attitude toward a Picasso painting changes into the progressive reaction toward a Chaplin movie" (Benjamin, "Work of art," p. 234).

Already in 1960 Meyer Schapiro noted that, with the success of Abstract Expressionism and the rapid development of a market for American art,

> The knowledge of prices and possible gain through art enters into the common perception of art. It also makes artists keenly aware of sales price as a measure of value. Attached now to the speculative market in increasing dependence, art becomes also an object of intense publicity. The literature of art assumes a new banality and a striving for public attention.[62]

Since the 1980s, "serious" artists have begun to figure in the public eye as entertainers, featured in gossip columns and advertisements. Meanwhile "commercial" entertainers are marketed as artists. The same transformation manifests itself in the increasing openness of art historians to discussing the commercial aspects of artistic activity.

One sign of the destabilization of the social category of "art" is the growing difficulty of differentiating art objects from less high-minded commodities. Painting and statuary always mingled with fine furniture, marble columns, ancient ornaments, and Renaissance ceilings. Increasingly, however, the high arts must share exhibition space not only with photography and film but with radios and toasters—or even (as at MoMA) a helicopter. Such objects as these have generally remained segregated in "design" galleries. Yet the organizers of the exhibition "What If," mounted in 2000 at Stockholm's Moderna Museet, bluntly questioned the existence of "a distinctive line between art, architecture, and design," discovering a center of contemporary artistic interests in the meeting point of "the virtually toned-down relational art, which emphasizes social, political, and psychological situations," and art "about luxury, desire, and the subjective qualities of a fashionable world."[63] The triumph of the aesthetic principle over photography conceals but poorly the extent to which the continuing domination of society by the commodity form has, while extending it, undermined the category of "art" created in earlier phases of that same society.

While techniques of mechanized image production can no more be held responsible for this than can the widening public for art, Benjamin was right to point to what are now called the "mass media" as an important terrain on which the redefinition of "art" would take place. In the absence of the revolutionary political movements for which Benjamin wished, this redefinition did not take the form of the appropriation of cultural production by the masses. Instead, we seem to be witnessing what might be called capitalism's overcoming of its earlier bad conscience about itself, the withering of the bourgeoisie's need to justify its

---

62 M. Schapiro, "On the art market," in *idem, Worldview in Painting—Art and Society. Selected Papers* (New York: George Braziller, 1999), p. 202.

63 *What if: Art on the Verge of Architecture and Design* (Stockholm: Moderna Museet, 2000), unpaginated.

triumph as at once the inheritor of the mantle of earlier civilization and the forger of a new spiritual principle. As Carter Ratcliff explained the new meaning of "art" some years ago,

> If galleries are no more nor less commercial than auction houses or business firms in general, then art is a commodity like any other . . . Above all, we will no longer have to feel qualms about the marriage of art and money. We will no longer have to wonder if it is possible to separate the esthetic value of an art work from its commercial value . . . If we are to live in our historical moment, we have to look at [van Gogh's] *Irises* [sold at auction in 1987 for $53.9 million] (or a reproduction of it) with a full sense of the price it fetched and try to see that outrageous number as part of what the painting means now.[64]

Reproduction's role is subordinate to and defined by this ongoing transformation of the social functions of the artwork, which both reflects and includes art's absorption by the sphere of mass entertainment. The high price of *Irises*, as a critic wrote, doubtless in part reflected its prominent place in a blockbuster show at the Metropolitan Museum of Art "and its reproduction on a popular poster for the show."[65] The museum, even if still the temple of art and redeemer of commercial gain, also functions as partner of auction houses and collectors in the metamorphosis of money into art and back again, a process in which mechanical reproduction has its place. As once reproduction served the creation of aesthetic aura, so it now plays its role in the open transformation of genius and authenticity into bankables.

---

64 C. Ratcliff, "The marriage of art and money," *Art in America* 76:7 (July 1988), pp. 84, 147.
65 Carol Zemel, "What becomes a legend most," *Art in America* 76:7 (July 1988), pp. 92/151.

7

PORK AND PORCELAIN

Art

Art, as understood in Europe—and gradually, under European influence, throughout the world—for the last two centuries or so, is as we have seen not a universal, or even a normal, feature of human cultures. People in all societies that we know about have decorated surfaces, made images of various sorts, organized sound rhythmically and tunefully, engaged in dancing, constructed buildings, put words together with care, and so forth. But—to take the visual arts for example— the thirteenth-century Italian crucifixes that mark the start of the Renaissance in well-appointed museums were not produced as art as we now think of it. They may have been made to be beautiful, or moving in various ways, but they were made for religious, not aesthetic contemplation. When used to describe their making, the word "art" signified the exercise of special skills, without the sense of an autonomous realm of value that it now has.

By the fifteenth century, in Italy especially, various arts became matters for educated gentlemen and ladies to concern themselves with; painters even demanded to have their craft placed among the "liberal" arts, the arts of free men, as opposed to the "mechanical" arts practiced by those who worked with their hands. By the end of the sixteenth century the *arti di disegno* had acquired the dignity of a history, and one reaching back to classical antiquity; the end of this period saw a flowering of purely instrumental musical composition, that is to say, music that served the pleasure of composer, player, and auditor rather than a text, sacred or secular. Still, it was not until the later eighteenth century that the idea of art, as a distinct domain of activities and objects characterized by "aesthetic" functions, came into something like its modern form.

Essential to this emergence was a shift in focus from the classically sanctioned idea of the imitation of natural beauty to a new conception of artistic creativity, the expression of genius. Artistic labor came to be conceptualized, as Kant famously put it, as "free"—ruled only by the internal compulsions of its creator. It is, of course, no accident that this reconception of the arts emerged in a context that involved the replacement of work for a patron, characteristic of premodern arts, by work for an anonymous market. The premodern artist worked to order, his subject-matter and even formal means controlled to a large extent not only by guild (and, later, academic) regulations but by his customer. The modern artist produces to suit himself (I use this pronoun because this figure remains by and large defined as male) albeit with the hope of finding customers.

One can see this transformation of artistic activity in the life of Mozart. What is notable for his time is not his years of service in the household of the Archbishop of Salzburg, producing music to order for the court's needs and dining with the other servants in the kitchen, but his eventual refusal to play this part and his attempt to live as an independent entrepreneur, seeking opera commissions from rulers, to be sure, but also selling tickets to a concert-going public. It was his early death rather than commercial failure that made him a nineteenth-century emblem of the artist's condition, the contingency of renown and material success. But already in Mozart's time we can see how escape from patronage into the freedom of the market produced a paradoxical uniting of the independence of the entrepreneurial creator with his dependence on the whims of those who purchase the luxury goods called art.

From the artist's side of it, art, as self-directed activity, marks superiority to the condition of wage labor that defines the lot of the mass of humankind in bourgeois society. At the same time, engagement in a profession that yields riches, and even adequate payment, only to a small minority suggests an aristocratic disdain for trade. The other side of this coin is the rise above mere money-grubbing of the art-loving businessman (perhaps represented by his wife). As the manufacturers and financiers of Europe and America bought estates and took up fox-hunting, so they filled their houses with old furniture, Old Masters, or the art of their own moment.

Both the novelty and the nature of capitalism impeded the sanctification of social power by time, which had suggested a divine allocation of preeminence to the aristocracy. Under modern conditions, only the moral qualities of the individual could justify privilege. Religious devotion lasted longer in the New World as a marker of superiority than in the Old, but everywhere, with the rise of the religion of art, an individual's taste came to signify his or her fitness to handle society's resources. For one thing, appreciation of artworks provided a reconciliation of opposites, at once embodying strictly bourgeois virtues and transcending them, since pictures (and *objets d'art* generally) were good investments as well as evidence of a superior nature.[1] Most fundamentally, given the nature of art as a

---

1 This mixture of motives is nicely brought out in Madeleine Fidell-Beaufort's discussion of the incitement to art-buying effected by the highly successful 1876 Johnston sale in New York, which featured important price increases for a number of pictures. "It was clearly the prospect of a profitable investment that was most attractive" to the new buyers, she notes,

> but also the certitude that if the expected profit did not materialize there would at least be a gain in social prestige . . . [I]t seems clear that auction sales provided an occasion for buyers to abandon themselves to even more ferocious competition from

luxury commodity, aesthetic interests beautifully combined detachment from the claims of practical life with advertisement of financial success, requiring as they do both money and the time made possible by money.

Philanthropy

The process by which the modern practice of art was put together took a long time, and followed different paths in different places. In France, for over a hundred years the world center of art in its modern form, the state played a central role. Beginning with the transformation of the royal palace of the Louvre into a public museum in 1793, the revolutionary government carried on the responsibility for culture initiated by the ancien régime—an undertaking continued, with significant changes, by the sequence of regimes until the present time. Similarly, a program of museum building was an important element in Prussia's claim to be at the center of an emerging German nation. In the United States, by contrast, the institutionalization of art was largely left to private citizens. Hence there more than elsewhere private philanthropy played a leading part.

This was a consequence of the absence of a strong, unified American state before the Civil War, and of continuing division and conflict among the industrialists and financiers who were the masters of the nation that war produced. If it is true, as I have suggested above, that the modern practice of the fine arts serves *inter alia* to represent the claim to legitimacy of those who rule the social system that produced it, it is to be expected that the formation of artistic institutions would share the history of other institutions of class rule. As Alan Wallach has expressed the point, in the United States "the bourgeoisie's inability, during the postwar period, to create a national art institution comparable to the Louvre or the London National Gallery reveals the extent to which elite factionalism remained a persistent feature of American political and cultural life."[2] It was not until 1939 that the United States acquired a National Gallery, and even then this came to begin with as a massive gift to the nation from a wealthy individual, Andrew Mellon.

Thus the creation of an institutional structure for the arts in the United States remained for a long time the work primarily of private citizens. Leading examples are the groups of worthies who brought into existence the Boston Museum of Fine Arts and the Metropolitan Museum in New York, and—perhaps the single most spectacular case—Henry Lee Higginson's founding and long-time

---

business. A fine winning bid could facilitate entry into a club or salon frequented by leaders of finance or industry, and so perhaps to partnership with them.

"Les Ventes aux enchères d'art américain au milieu du XIXe siècle," in L. B. Dorléac (ed.), *Le Commerce de l'art de la Renaissance à nos jours* (Paris: La Manufacture, 1992)

2   Alan Wallach, *Exhibiting Contradictions: Essays on Art Museums in the United States* (University of Massachusetts Press, 1999), p. 10.

support of the Boston Symphony Orchestra.[3] It is important not to exaggerate to the point of inaccuracy: the creation and maintenance of art institutions did not proceed without the aid of public authorities. Writing about the case of museums in particular, Daniel Fox has stressed "the direct and subtle influence of the need for approval, concessions, funds, and services from municipal and state governments" on the goals and activities of private philanthropists: "Private collectors and self-appointed guardians of culture were transformed into public benefactors by the interaction of their own concern for public welfare with the need to co-operate with the elected and appointed representatives of the people."[4] Nevertheless, private philanthropy has played an undeniably crucial role in the creation of artistic institutions in the United States.

The mobilization of taste for the legitimation of social distinction had a special force for American art-lovers, who did not even have much of a native aristocracy to marry into. In Fox's words,

> Many men and women derived considerable pleasure from collecting in one lifetime what European aristocrats had acquired over many generations. Possession of great works of art, especially when the collector did not have lifelong familiarity with the fine arts, seemed to represent a "natural instinct" for the best.[5]

The gift of such a collection to the public both immortalized the collector and established his (or, less frequently, her) place as a benefactor and so as superior to his fellows. In the museum field the desire for social recognition can be seen in such phenomena as donors' strong preference for giving objects, material testaments to the collector's eye, rather than cash, more abstract and anonymous, and the many attempts made to give collections as wholes rather than allow them to be dispersed throughout an institution.

On the other hand, despite the wish to demonstrate equality with those in England and elsewhere in Europe whose ancestral portraits flowed to the New World, American philanthropy differed essentially from the patronage system after which it liked to style itself. Classical patronage emphasized the distinction of the patron, in the framework of an ideology celebrating status differentiation as the foundation of social order. Under the conditions of bourgeois democracy, cultural philanthropy had to embody in institutions the membership of outstanding individuals in a social elite *and* to suggest the notion of the potential openness of social advancement to all. Only by being offered to the public could culture—

---

3 See Paul DiMaggio, "Cultural entrepreneurship in nineteenth-century Boston, part II: the classification and framing of American Art," *Media, Culture and Society* 4:4 (1982), pp. 301–22.

4 D. M. Fox, *Engines of Culture: Philanthropy and Art Museums* (Madison: The State Historical Society of Wisconsin, 1963), pp. 1–4, see pp. 40 ff.

5 Ibid., p. 20.

in this way unlike fox-hunting—signify superiority without privilege, ideologically basic to modern class relations. Class differences disappear from view within the generality of the concept of the "public," as with that of the "citizen" who is the subject of democratic politics and the rule of law.

While tycoons like Frick and Morgan may have enjoyed thinking of themselves as modern Medici, their modus operandi could not be the same as that of past Maecenases. Mozart's archbishop had wanted new masses and symphonies for every important occasion, but the musical basis of an orchestra like the one Higginson supported in Boston was the body of "classical" works that had come into existence since the turn of the nineteenth century.[6] Likewise, a notable feature of the early stages of American museums was their stocking with casts and other copies of European antiquities, and well into the twentieth century museum philanthropy, focusing on art of the past, displaced private patronage for contemporary artists. During the period between the Renaissance and the end of the eighteenth century when the modern system of the fine arts came into existence, classical objects embodied the essence of art, giving ancient authority to a modern institution. Similarly, as the nineteenth century came to its end, art was embodied for Americans in Old Masters; for later generations, the Impressionists, both foreign and rapidly set in the past by subsequent avant-gardes, came to fill this role. Collecting such works decreased the element of risk, from the viewpoints of monetary and cultural investment alike, since collectors bought only those things already certified by the "test of time." But beyond this, and beyond the wish to acquire the luster of the European past, this orientation reflected the element of remoteness from contemporary American life important to the sacralization of art. Things from earlier times and distant places could signify interests higher than those of everyday life; they both exemplified the superiority of their buyers and held out the possibility for improvement to those less richly endowed who yet cared to accept its educational influence.

This educational aspect linked arts-giving with other forms of social altruism like the establishment of libraries and social work. By making examples of humankind's best available to the benighted masses wealthy people willing to share their artistic treasures could "belong to an exclusive group and at the same time have the satisfaction of serving the Great Public."[7] Just as fundamentally, art's sacralizing role required differentiating cultural products from other commodities, not only (as suggested above) in their manner of production but also in their distribution and consumption. It is true that the chief organizational form developed for arts philanthropy was that of the corporation, ruled by a board of trustees drawn for the most part from other more conventionally economic boards. But the nonprofit character of these corporations provided a foundation

---

6 For the early history of this development, see William Weber, *The Rise of Musical Classics in Eighteenth-Century England: A Study in Canon, Ritual, and Ideology* (Oxford: Clarendon Press, 1992).

7 Fox, *Engines*, p. 21.

for the distinction from commercial forms of culture basic to the idea of fine art. This made possible what Paul DiMaggio describes as "the erection of strong and clearly defined boundaries between art and entertainment, the definition of a high art that elites and segments of the middle class could appropriate as their own cultural property, and the acknowledgement of that classification's legitimacy by other classes and the state."[8] The nonprofit philanthropic corporation thus played a key role in providing the institutional framework for high art in the United States.

The system I have described belonged to a specific period in American history and has changed radically with the times. The most visible agent of change, perhaps, has been tax law. In former Boston museum director Perry Rathbone's view, the federal income tax imposed in 1913 "drove the great patron from the scene; the local benefactor could no longer afford the role of a Maecenas."[9] On the other hand, the development of the charitable deduction stimulated cultural philanthropy to a degree clearly appreciable in the decline in giving when Congress cut the tax break for gifts to museums between 1987 and 1990. Similarly, the coming of the corporate income tax in 1935, with its deduction for philanthropy, opened a path to large-scale corporate support for the arts. Nonetheless, such giving has a different character than the philanthropy of yesteryear.

As every arts administrator is aware, individual givers still play an essential role in arts philanthropy, as they do in hospital and educational giving. But "the entry of large institutional donors, specifically private foundations, government, and corporations," as DiMaggio has observed, has "substantially altered the arts marketplace."[10] To put the situation like this, however, is to understate the systemic nature of the change within which philanthropy has its place. To begin with, as Stephen Weil explains, the effect of the charitable tax deduction has been "to make the federal government, in essence, a cocontributor" in a system in which "a relatively small handful of affluent taxpayers" is "able to spend the public's money."[11] Private giving is therefore not as distinct as it might seem from direct governmental expenditure on the arts such as that of the National Endowment for the Arts. More important, these features of the current system are related to changes in the nature of capitalist society as a whole. The acceptance

8 Paul DiMaggio, "Cultural entrepreneurship in nineteenth-century Boston: the creation of an organizational base for high culture in America," in Richard Collins, James Curran, Nicholas Garnham, Paddy Scannell, Philip Schlesinger, and Colin Sparks (eds), *Media, Culture and Society: A Critical Reader* (London: Sage, 1986), p. 196.

9 Perry T. Rathbone, "Influences of private patrons: the art museum as example," in W. McNeil Lowry (ed.), *The Arts and Public Policy in the United States* (Englewood Cliffs: Prentice-Hall, 1984), p. 45.

10 P. DiMaggio, "The nonprofit instrument and the influence of the marketplace on policies in the arts," in Lowry, *The Arts*, p. 69.

11 Stephen E. Weil, "Tax policy and private giving," in Stephen Benedict (ed.), *Public Money and the Muse* (New York: Norton, 1991), pp. 167, 173.

of the principle of the income tax by the dominant classes of the United States signaled their recognition of the necessity for governmental regulation of social relations in a country in which the forces of economic exploitation had been allowed to run quite free. As the turn-of-the-century Progressives were the first to articulate in programmatic terms, such regulation was even in the interest of a developing corporate capitalism. The New Deal, and its extension into the war economy, further applied this principle by increasing the participation of the state in economic affairs. Tax deductions and corporate giving are aspects of a general transformation of the economic system in which the leading role once played by individual barons of industry, commerce, and finance has been taken over by corporations, foundations, and the state.

The patron state

An important element in the way in which this transformation made itself felt in the domain of culture was the movement of modernism, particularly in the visual arts, to the center of the aesthetic stage. This was due to more than the gradual disappearance of Old Masters from the market. While earlier in this century the promotion of modern art served to differentiate certain scions of wealthy families from their conservative elders, the later engagement with modernism undertaken by social agents ranging from the federal government to the mass media not only proclaimed the glory of bourgeois society but specifically celebrated the political and economic triumph of the United States after the Second World War. Art came to be seen not so much as an incarnation of higher values than those of the marketplace but as a distillation of those characteristics—daring, innovation, attunement to (often previously unarticulated) social desires—that make an individual, company, or nation successful.[12] It was in these terms that calls were issued for cultural competition with World Communism; that John Kennedy, asserting the existence of "a connection, hard to explain logically but easy to feel, between achievement in public life and progress in the arts," linked a "New Frontier in the Arts" to the "surge in economic growth" and "openness to what is new" he promised;[13] and that Lyndon Johnson established the National Endowment for the Arts, together with the National Endowment for the Humanities, as facets of the Great Society.[14]

Beyond issues of international political prestige and the aristocratic pretensions

12 For an interesting discussion, see S. J. Allen, *The Romance of Culture and Commerce* (Chicago: University of Chicago Press, 1983), *passim*.
13 "Nixon, Kennedy view music and the arts," *Musical America* 80:8 (1960), p. 11, cit. Gary O. Larson, *The Reluctant Patron: The United States Government and the Arts, 1941–1963* (Philadelphia: University of Pennsylvania Press, 1988), p. 150.
14 For a survey of American government involvement in the arts, see my "Arts and the state: the NEA debate in perspective," in Peter G. Meyer (ed.), *Brushes With History: Writings on Art from The Nation, 1861–2001* (New York: Thunder Mouth Press/Nation Books, 2001), pp. 441–61.

of the very rich, the idea was gaining ground among America's upper classes—particularly in the Northeast, but also in cities like Chicago and St. Louis—that art is a Good Thing, a glamorous thing, even a fun thing. This attitude rapidly trickled down to the middle ranks, whose self-assertiveness as leading citizens of an affluent and powerful nation was expressed in a new attachment to culture.[15] The 1950s saw galleries in department stores, rising museum and concert attendance, and the commercial distribution of classical LPs and inexpensive reproductions of famous paintings. Studio training and art history departments proliferated in colleges and universities. A handful of corporate executives, in alliance with cultural entrepreneurs like Mortimer Adler and R. M. Hutchins, discovered that culture, both classic and modern, could be both marketed and used as a marketing medium.

In part the new interest in culture reflected the changing nature of the business class: while fewer than 50 percent of top executives had some college education in 1900, 76 percent did by 1950.[16] The postwar rise of the professional manager helped break down the traditional barrier between the worlds of business and culture, affecting the self-image of American society as a whole. To this was joined—with the growth of academia, research institutions, and all levels of government—the emergence of the new professional-intellectual stratum, connected in spirit to the power elite in a way unknown to the alienated intelligentsia of yesteryear. By the 1960s art, and modern art in particular, seemed to the politically dominant forces in the United States to have a part to play in the construction of a nationally authoritative ideology.

Institutionally, the triumph of modern art led to the consolidation of a system involving dealers, collectors, museums, and even artists, in which investment and public-spiritedness could work together. The NEA was prefigured, as it was later accompanied, by private efforts, not necessarily oriented toward modernist art. The Ford Foundation, which went heavily into arts funding in the later 1950s, had an exceptionally large amount of money at its disposal, but a multitude of others have followed its example. Efforts like Ford's financing of ballet companies and symphony orchestras across the country, often described as a "democratization" of culture, can also be recognized as elements of an attempt to create a unified national culture, complementing the increasingly integrated political economy. An executive or professional could now move from New York to Santa Fe or Portland and find the opera, ballet, and contemporary art waiting for him or her. While as ever in appearance open to all, this national culture remains in

---

15 This was the group described enthusiastically and in interesting sociological detail by Alvin Toffler as the "comfort class," a term intended to suggest "something not merely about the group's economic condition, but about its psychological outlook" (*The Culture Consumers. Art and Affluence in America* (Baltimore: Penguin, 1965), p. 40; see pp. 31–51).

16 And the American college itself, as Toffler points out, changed its image radically from "a hotbed of insensibility" to a place "now spending more time, money, and energy in 'culturizing' its population than ever before in history" (ibid., p. 86).

general practice class-specific, combining a continuing focus for the business elite with an associated participation by the corps of educated professionals and managers required by the postwar development of capitalism.[17]

During the 1990s, official culture, supported by private and public funds together, embraced "cultural pluralism" and "multiculturalism." As in academia, with which this development is closely connected, multiculturalism in the arts, in responding to demands made by members of formerly excluded groups (women, minorities) for greater participation in officially sanctioned cultural production bears witness to new ideological conditions. In place of the "general interest" in which it has become increasingly difficult to believe, contemporary political art tends to define itself in terms of variously conceived "communities" (ethnic, "racial," or sexual) that, whatever their real content, obscure the class differences within them as effectively as did the old idea of the "public"—an idea which makes a contemporary appearance in the phenomenon of "public art," which represents in a concentrated form the nexus of academy, corporation, and state in the production of art.

The formal sameness of much multicultural work, from the Texas–Mexico border to New York's galleries and performance spaces, points to the unifying function operating through the medium of cultural difference.[18] Subcultural tokens work alongside the equally uniform mainstream culture (represented by such artifacts as the warhorse-oriented programs of symphony orchestras) to match identities defined for a professional class internally differentiated along "racial," gender, or other lines. The same dialectic of difference and sameness can be seen in history: the variety of stylistic modes employed in the course of the development of an American national culture, from WPA social realism through high modernist abstraction to the "political art" of the late 1990s, which itself drew on such earlier styles as Dadaism, Surrealism, and folk art, testifies both to the flexibility of the evolving art system and to the tremendous absorptive power of the capitalist mode of production and consumption.

One of the chief arguments opponents of government arts spending made from the 1940s until the creation of the NEA in 1965 was the threat of govern-

---

17 See Paul DiMaggio and Michael Useem, "Cultural property and public policy: emerging tensions in government support for the arts," *Social Research* 45:2 (1978), pp. 361–5:

> Elite dominance of [arts institution] governing boards and audiences creates an opportunity for the reaffirmation of elite social and cultural cohesion. Group solidarity requires the erection of barriers of inclusion and exclusion, and collective participation by members of the elite in ritual occasions is one means of sustaining such barriers . . . Participation in the world of high culture can be particularly important for the upper-middle class, the group whose status is most marginal to the elite. Arts consumption provides this group with an opportunity for symbolic identification with the upper class and may even yield socially useful contacts.

18 For a dispiriting survey, see Lucy Lippard, *Mixed Blessings: New Art in a Multicultural America* (New York: New Press, 2000).

ment censorship or bureaucratic control of art policy. This concern was voiced by professional organizations representing conservative artists, who saw early on that modernism would be favored by any future arts policy, as it was in the few early efforts to sponsor traveling exhibitions of American art. Their position was supported by conservative congressmen who identified modern art as communist in its basic orientation, and who could be depended on to uncover the Party affiliation (generally past) of as many government-exhibited artists as they could. The ideological foundation of this position was the idea that government deficit spending violates the private-property basis of the "free enterprise" economy; concern about censorship went hand in hand with the wish to drive a stake through the heart of the New Deal. That communism was not the central element in this ideological structure can be seen in the fact that it has remained intact after 1989, a continuity embodied in the persistence of Strom Thurmond as a leader of the anti-art policy forces. After the fall of the Berlin Wall and the collapse of the Soviet Union, homosexuality and feminism replaced communism as ideological bugaboos; in 1999 a defender of the NEA like William Ivey had to promote his organization as pro-family as well as patriotic, just as the arts advocates of the 1950s and 1960s recommended government-sponsored art as a weapon against Soviet propaganda.

Art is an easy target for politicians because its relative economic insignificance accompanies its importance as a form of cultural capital. Congressmen devoted to government aid to peanut farmers or weapons builders can thunder away against using the taxpayers' money to subsidize immoral entertainment for the wealthy. The issue is evidently not state economic involvement, but government spending that does not provide an immediate subsidy to some politically powerful business interest. Naturally enough, the populist rhetoric employed by conservatives for purposes of factional politics and self-promotion fitfully reveals the class character of the fine arts only as subordinated to appeals to patriotism and "family values." After all, the religious Right, whatever its particular interests, serves the same greater class interest as liberal culture; this explains how it can be that the same corporation, Philip Morris, pluralistically (one might say) financed both arch-reactionary tobacco-state senator Jesse Helms and the sort of art he fulminated against.[19] It also explains the survival of the NEA, in however attenuated a form, alongside the more significant efforts of Keynesian economics. The mixed economy is here to stay, though budgets may be cut and welfare in particular "reformed" to aid in the general lowering of real wages at a time of increasing global instability. While the privatization of cultural institutions, as of other, more important, economic sectors, is a definite trend, governmental support for the arts continues, since it is necessary for the maintenance of institutions now central to the mode of life of the dominant classes.

---

19 "In the arts, as in business, Philip Morris is committed to innovation and embraces diversity" (*Philip Morris and the Arts* (New York: Philip Morris Companies, 1991), p. 3).

Business culture

The developments I have sketched have naturally had an effect on the conceptualization and practice of art. A hundred years ago Joseph C. Choate, speaking for the Metropolitan Museum at the opening of that institution's new building in Central Park, urged New York's millionaires

> to convert pork into porcelain, grain and produce into priceless pottery, the rude ores of commerce into sculptured marble, and railroad shares and mining stocks—things which perish without the using, and which in the next financial panic shall surely shrivel like parched scrolls—into the glorified canvas of the world's masters . . . ours is the higher ambition to convert your useless gold into things of living beauty that shall be a joy to a whole people for a thousand years.[20]

At the present time the conception of art Choate expressed, while still in force, is seemingly on the decline. A striking manifestation of this is the tendency in the work of artists, critics, historians, and collectors to accept, with whatever irony, the coexistence of the commercial character of art with its aspiration to transcendence, or even the former's dominance over the latter.[21] On the corporate side, cultural giving, "more than a passive product of business success," is now hopefully "used to stimulate income as well," so that corporations "are moving toward a 'more market-driven strategic-management, bottom-line approach to philanthropy,' report two company observers, 'to obtain a tangible return for their contributions.'"[22] To an extent, this more openly commercial attitude to the arts perhaps reflects capitalism's overcoming of its former sense of inferiority with respect to the social order it replaced, and its forthright celebration of market-certified success. The introduction to a recent volume of essays on public funding of the arts conveys the new vision of the relation between culture and commerce when it asserts that "business and culture are two integral, interdependent systems that are part and parcel of a thriving community."[23]

The two systems are hardly equals. *Le business oblige*, but culture must beg. For most artists, philanthropy represents a welcome income supplement, an element in the career-regulating art system, and a sign of the low valuation of artistic production that accompanies the claims of its spiritual importance. In the words of painter Sidney Tillim, "it can be argued that government, corporate, and

---

20 Quoted in Calvin Tompkins, *Merchants and Masterpieces* (New York: Dutton, 1973), pp. 21–4.
21 For a survey of contemporary artists' explorations of the relationship between art and commerce, see Katy Siegel and Paul Mattick, *Money* (London: Thames and Hudson, 2003).
22 Michael Useem, "Corporate support for culture and the arts," in M. J. Wyszomirski and P. Clubb (eds), *The Costs of Culture: Patterns and Prospects of Private Arts Patronage* (New York: American Council for the Arts, 1989), pp. 48, 45.
23 A. Levitt, Jr, "Introduction" to Benedict, *Public Money*, p. 23.

private foundation support, because [it does] not involve the consequential judgment of taste that is backed up by real money, by money that circulates, tends to enforce an image of the arts as irrelevant and socially insignificant."[24] Actually it is in part the incompleteness of art's absorption into the spheres of commercial entertainment and advertising that makes possible its continuing social significance, which depends on the preservation of something of its earlier aura of transcendence. Even under today's conditions, arts philanthropy preserves a basic aspect of its original social function.

The postwar rise to near-official status of American modernism made this nation's first avant-garde the world's last. A bohemia that sues for state financing (as Karen Finley and others did in vain attempts to regain NEA grants cancelled under Congressional pressure) is a contradiction in terms.[25] As Alvin Toffler observed more than 35 years ago,

> If links between business and art proliferate, it is going to be harder for the artist to remain alienated. Despite its pluralism, our society remains a business society . . . It is easy to be opposed to the central institution of one's society when one is locked outside the system by neglect, indifference, or active hostility on the part of the men who make it run. It is much harder when one is invited within the gates and permitted to share its fruits.[26]

Contemporary art nevertheless remains flavored by the sentiment of distance from the culture of business, a distance central to the identity of art in its modern sense. The work of Gerhard Richter, for instance, combines allegiance to the painterly seriousness of high modernism with explicitly political critique of modernity; there are artists whose work directly addresses the commercial operation of galleries, museums, and art fairs, like Maurizio Cattelan, Gabriel Orozco, and Rikrit Teravanija, and others, like Mike Kelley, Liz Craft, and Rachel Harrison, who make childish, opaque, or crudely constructed work that seems to set the world of big money and expensive artworks on its ear. But anyone sufficiently recognizable to serve as an example has found his or her approach to contemporary culture an avenue to success. Inevitably, scorn for

---

24 Sidney Tillim, Remarks at NEA Symposium, Los Angeles, October 1–2, 1982.

25 Raymonde Moulin, in a penetrating analysis of the market structure of contemporary art, observes that "art oriented toward the museum" and supported by institutional funds—conceptual, minimal, performance, video, installation art—as opposed to "art objectively oriented toward the market," has "the sociological characteristics of avant-garde art": "intellectual and hermetic," it contests "at once art and the market" ("The museum and the marketplace: the constitution of value in contemporary art," *International Journal of Political Economy* 25:2 (1995), p. 50). But this is—sociologically—clearly not the avant-garde of the past, for which market success paved the road to the museum.

26 A. Toffler, *The Culture Consumers: Art and Affluence in America* (Baltimore: Penguin, 1965), p. 120.

society's dominant values has been replaced among artists by an ironic sense of the limits of the powers of art. NEA chairman Ivey's insistence in a 1998 public talk that the arts "can constitute an urban business strategy," helping to revitalize downtown areas and attracting professionals and corporate headquarters, expressed the same point of view with an administrator's distance from irony.

For this moment in the evolution of cultural finance Andy Warhol's career is instructive if not emblematic. Warhol's goal, freely advertised, was to make a place for himself in the art business on the basis of his design skills and the exploitation of his pop sensibility, deriving profit additionally from his own existence as a popular icon and celebrity. He succeeded enormously, making enough money to endow a philanthropic corporation. Since his death, which brought it into being, the Andy Warhol Foundation has given large amounts of money to art institutions of various sorts. Large sums from its resources were also consumed to pay lawyers battling over the fees to be paid to certain Foundation personnel. That an artist's fortune should provide huge fees for lawyers might have appealed to Warhol's taste for irony; it is unlikely to comfort anyone who looks to art or philanthropy to light a way out of the contemporary crisis of culture.

8

THE AESTHETICS OF
ANTI-AESTHETICS

The classic one-liner on the irrelevance of aesthetics for artists was Barnett Newman's quip: "Aesthetics for me is like ornithology must be for the birds." Speaking in 1952 at a conference co-sponsored by an artists' group and the American Society for Aesthetics, Newman declared the very idea of such a conference absurd, saying that he considered "the artist and the aesthetician to be mutually exclusive terms." He went on to attack aesthetics for what he called its irresponsibility in presuming to speak on art with the authority of philosophy or even science, while refusing to involve itself in the conflict of values fundamental to the activity of artists. Moreover, said Newman, by assuming a detached, theoretical attitude the philosophical aesthetician "leaves the field wide open for the practicing aestheticians, the museum directors and newspaper critics, who daily are making decisions and establishing and disestablishing values . . . on the authority of theoretical aesthetics."[1] The terms in which Newman described the central conflict of artistic values in his time, as "the moral struggle between notions of beauty and the desire for sublimity," were themselves—as an earlier chapter of this book makes evident—taken from aesthetic discourse.[2] But the philosophy of art, as he saw it, had failed to involve itself in, or even grasp, the struggle of American modern artists to break free from the tradition of European art, thus allowing criticism, based on traditional aesthetics, to play a destructive role in the face of the emergence of new tendencies.

If few American artists of the last fifty years have expressed themselves as strongly as Newman in opposition to the claims of aesthetics to provide a basis for the understanding of art, this is largely due to a lack of contact between the two activities as deep as Newman's remarks suggest. There have been individual artists of whom this is not strictly true, such as Robert Motherwell, who studied aesthetics at Harvard and later at Columbia with the art historian Meyer Schapiro. And the many artists who engaged with Schapiro over the decades of

1 Barnett Newman, *Selected Writings and Interviews*, ed. J. P. O'Neill (New York: Knopf, 1990), pp. 304, 242–3.
2 Ibid., p. 171.

his intimate involvement with the New York scene were certainly exposed to aesthetic ideas through conversation with that remarkable man. Nevertheless, with the exception of John Dewey's *Art as Experience* of 1934, which had a certain influence on a number of painters, including Thomas Hart Benton and his student Jackson Pollock,[3] academic aesthetics has been of little interest to modern artists in the United States.

In this regard it is possible to compare the relations between aesthetics and the actual practice of the arts to those between the philosophy of science and modern physics and mathematics. While scientific figures like Einstein and Hilbert were well versed in philosophy, the problems with which twentieth-century philosophers have struggled arose out of reflection on developments in science itself, and have been for the most part happily ignored by the vast majority of working scientists. Similarly, although artists have been uninterested in aesthetics, contemporary philosophers of art have largely found their problems—such as the place of expression in art, the nature of representation and the relation of art to nature, and, above all, the definition of art—in this century's art. Just as twentieth-century physics came to call into question not only classical mechanics but also fundamental assumptions about the relation between theory and experiment and the nature of empirical evidence, so various modern art movements seemingly collided with the understanding of art at the center of the tradition of aesthetic theory.

Stemming from Enlightenment and Romantic critical thought, this tradition located the essence of art in perceptual properties of the artistic object—its ability to evoke an "aesthetic experience" in the viewer, thanks to its "intrinsic perceptual interest," what Clive Bell called its possession of "significant form." Given this orientation, aesthetic theory could absorb the abstract art that appeared in the first decades of the twentieth century, despite its challenge to artistic convention, without much difficulty. Stiffer tests were posed by various anti-art movements, by the readymade, by the Pop appropriation of commercial imagery, by aspects of Minimalism and by the Conceptualist near-disappearance of the art object itself.

While most philosophers of art simply kept their distance from contemporary developments, thus maintaining the irrelevance of their work to artists Newman had noted, a few responded theoretically to anti-art. The so-called institutional theory of art, representing an anti-aesthetic trend within aesthetics, made its appearance in 1964 in an article written by Arthur Danto under (so Danto said) the influence of Andy Warhol's Stable Gallery show of that year, but reflecting issues raised much earlier by Marcel Duchamp.[4] George Dickie produced his

---

3 See Stewart Buettner, "John Dewey and the visual arts in America," *The Journal of Aesthetics and Art Criticism* 33 (1975), pp. 381–91. Dewey's introduction to Alexander Dorner's *The Way Beyond 'Art': The Work of Herbert Bayer* (New York: Wittenborn, Schultz, 1947), dedicated to him, provides another example of that philosopher's contact with the art world.

4 Arthur Danto, "The artworld," *Journal of Philosophy* 61:19 (1964), pp. 571–84.

own "institutional theory" ten years later, but its lesser contact with the actual world of art, in favor of an elaborated analytic-philosophical apparatus, has condemned it to a complete lack of influence outside of professional aesthetics.[5] The place that Danto has achieved in the art world, meanwhile, is due more to his writing as a critic than to his strictly philosophical work.

Among artists, the divorce of art from aesthetics took its conceptual shape for the most part not in opposition to academic philosophy but in reaction to the "formalist" criticism of Clement Greenberg and his followers.[6] Greenberg's ideas, descended, as Lawrence Alloway once pointed out, "from nineteenth-century aestheticism,"[7] had closer forerunners in German anti-aesthetic conceptions of the 1920s and 1930s, when partisans of photography drew sharp distinctions between the essences of different media, reserving for painting (in the words of Moholy-Nagy) the "elementary means" of "color and plane," as opposed to naturalistic representation.[8] In his essay "Avant-garde and kitsch," published in 1939, Greenberg presented art-for-art's opposition to "utility" as the idea of art's opposition to the commercial culture of industrial capitalism. Like Theodor Adorno, who similarly (but more convincingly) traced his thinking to the aesthetics of Kant, Greenberg located art's significance in its autonomy, its freedom from determination by nonartistic ends and its governance by its own historically evolving principles.[9] Only an emphasis on aesthetic quality could keep art alive as an alternative to the market-oriented culture of capitalism. In later writings, Greenberg identified the practice of aesthetic autonomy with the exploration by each artistic medium of its specific nature. The nature of painting, specifically, was reduced in his thinking to "the pristine flatness of the stretched canvas" on which areas of color could be laid. The modernist assertion of the

5 George Dickie, *Art and the Aesthetic: An Institutional Analysis* (Ithaca: Cornell University Press, 1974). A precursor of Danto's and Dickie's efforts to reconfigure aesthetics to take modern art into account is to be found in Wittgensteinian approaches like that of Morris Weitz; see "The role of theory in aesthetics," *Journal of Aesthetics and Art Criticism* 15 (1956), pp. 21–35. For an early and thorough critique of the "institutional theory," see Steven Goldsmith, "The ready-mades of Marcel Duchamp: the ambiguities of an aesthetic revolution," *Journal of Aesthetics and Art Criticism* 42:2 (1983), pp. 191–208.

6 It may in fact be Greenberg whom Newman had in mind in complaining about claims to aesthetic "science"; in various of his writings Greenberg both stressed that criticism must be founded in aesthetics and claimed, on this basis, a science-like or at least objective character for critical judgment.

7 Lawrence Alloway, "Systemic painting," in G. Battcock (ed.), *Minimal Art* (New York: Dutton, 1968), p. 51. For a fascinating account of the *fin-de-siècle* sources of Greenbergian theory, see Joseph Mashock, "The carpet paradigm: critical prolegomena to a theory of flatness," *Arts* 51:1 (September 1976), pp. 82–109.

8 Laszlo Moholy-Nagy, *Painting Photography Film* [1925], tr. Janet Seligman (Cambridge: MIT Press, 1973), p. 14; see also the assertion on p. 16 that "painting or any optical creation has its special laws and missions independently of all others," as well as the contrast, on p. 35, of art with kitsch.

9 As Greenberg told me in a conversation a few years before his death in 1994, Adorno was a strong influence on him in the late 1930s.

value of the artwork in its own right, and not just as a representation of some beautiful or sublime reality, became a focus on "the expressive resources of the medium, not in order to express ideas and notions, but to express with greater immediacy sensations, the irreducible elements of experience."[10]

In this way Greenberg set a domain of *aisthesis* in opposition to what he referred to as "literature," or verbalizable subject-matter, insisting on the gulf between visual art and language. He invoked Gotthold Lessing as a precursor, but while Lessing's 1766 *Laocoön* located a fundamental distinction between poetry and visual art not only in the narrative capacity of the former but also in what Lessing held to be the greater abstractness of linguistic signs, Greenberg saw language (outside of modernist poetry) as transparent in relation to subject-matter and viewed the "opacity" of its medium as basic to visual art, whose character "exhausts itself in the visual sensation it produces."[11] Concern with medium, as opposed to subject, or even expression, had made abstraction of supreme importance in modern art, in which the autonomy of the aesthetic thus became, in painting at least, the substance of art itself.

In "Nature of abstract art," published two years before "Avant-garde and kitsch" but written as a contribution to the same discussion among politically minded artists and writers that Greenberg's essay would enter, Meyer Schapiro argued that despite both appearances and the beliefs of artists and critics, "the pretended autonomy and absoluteness of the aesthetic" present in its purest form in abstraction was a myth. Here as elsewhere in art, he observed, formal construction is "shaped by experience and nonaesthetic concerns."[12] And indeed the absence of "literature" in what Greenberg called "modernist" painting really meant not the lack of reference other than to the formal conditions of the work, but just the absence of representation (or denotation). Nonetheless, Greenberg's formulation corresponded sufficiently to fundamental features of the artistic field as it evolved with the success of American abstract art in the postwar period to have influence, positive and negative, on critics and artists for several decades.

The concept of "artistic field" is borrowed from the writing of Pierre Bourdieu, who defines a field of cultural production as a system of relations among a set of agents and institutions—in the case of the art system, these include artists, dealers, critics, collectors, art magazines, and museums—constituting "the site of struggles for the monopoly of the power to consecrate" works as culturally valuable, "in which the value of works of art and belief in that value are continually generated."[13] Such fields may be characterized in terms of alternative

---

10 Clement Greenberg, "Towards a newer Laocoön" [1940], in John O'Brian (ed.), *Collected Essays and Criticism*, vol. 1, p. 36.

11 Ibid., p. 34.

12 Meyer Schapiro, "Nature of abstract art," in *idem, Modern Art: 19th and 20th Centuries* (New York: Braziller, 1978), pp. 185, 196.

13 *The Field of Cultural Production: Essays on Art and Literature* (New York: Columbia University Press, 1993), p. 78.

"positions," embodied in individual and group styles (like Pop, Minimalism, and Color Field painting) and championed by competing critics, collectors, curators, and gallerists. While the 1950s saw the artistic field, as Raymonde Moulin observes, "roughly divided between the seemingly opposite positions of abstraction and representation," succeeding decades produced, in the United States, "an artistic field with no normative aesthetic."[14] Nonetheless, the rise to global prominence of an American avant-garde style, Abstract Expressionism, kept alive earlier conceptions of modern art based on the autonomy of the artistic act and the associated high cultural value of abstraction, even while the commercial and political success of the new American art was undermining the idea of a necessary conflict between "advanced art" and the dominant culture.

Thus "literature" in Greenberg's sense remained absent from Minimalism, which tended to restore the emotionalism and sublimity of Abstract Expressionism both by emphasis on such "formal" matters as scale and the nature of materials and by a new attentiveness to physical and social context. But the work of artists like Frank Stella, Donald Judd, Carl Andre, Robert Morris, and Dan Flavin, using such devices as shaped canvases, colored three-dimensional surfaces, nearly flat assemblages, and colored light, pointedly crossed the boundary between painting and sculpture that Greenberg had both defined and insisted on as primary for quality modernist art. Critic and art historian Michael Fried, in 1967 evidently a disciple of Greenberg's, explicitly recognized in Minimalism the staking-out of a competing position—both of production (and sales) and of critical promotion—in the artistic field. This "enterprise," as he put it, "seeks to declare and occupy a position—one that can be formulated in words, and in fact has been formulated by some of its leading practitioners," a feature that "distinguishes it from modernist painting and sculpture" and "also marks an important difference between Minimal Art . . . and Pop or Op Art."[15] The struggle for cultural value could be waged as a conflict of theoretical categories.

The Greenbergian emphases on "opticality" and "quality" as central to modernism were clearly among the targets aimed at by Robert Morris's 1963 notarized "Statement of Esthetic Withdrawal":

14 Raymonde Moulin, "The museum and the marketplace: the constitution of value in modern art," *International Journal of Political Economy* 25:2 (1995), pp. 35, 34.

15 Michael Fried, "Art and Objecthood," in Gregory Battcock (ed.), *Minimal Art: A Critical Anthology* (New York: Dutton, 1968), pp. 111–17. Greenberg himself took a loftier as well as a more nuanced tone. On the one hand, he considered Minimalism, along with Pop, Op, and others, a branch of "Novelty Art," arousing interest by an anti-art flavored "far-outness" aping avant-garde daring but actually constrained by canons of conventional good design. On the other, he came to believe that the nature of sculpture allowed it both to appropriate properties of painting and to continue to refer to nature without damage to its modernist possibilities. See "Sculpture in our time" (1958) and "Recentness of sculpture" (1967) in Clement Greenberg, *The Collected Essays and Criticism*, vol. 4, ed. John O'Brian (Chicago: University of Chicago Press, 1993), pp. 51–61 and 251–6.

> The undersigned . . . being the maker of the metal construction entitled
> Litanies . . . hereby withdraws from said construction all esthetic qual-
> ity and content and declares that from the date hereof said construction
> has no such quality and content.[16]

The thought implicit in this declaration was expressed at characteristically greater length by Joseph Kosuth in his text of six years later, "Art after philosophy": "It is necessary to separate aesthetics from art." Since art once had an important decorative function, "any branch of philosophy that dealt with 'beauty' and thus, taste, was inevitably duty bound to discuss art as well. Out of this 'habit' grew the notion that there was a conceptual connection between art and aesthetics, which is not true."[17]

The basis for such ideas is the post-1900 displacement of the conceptual center of art from reference to the world to the artist's creative vision, to an emphasis on the artist's act, not properties of the object it produces, as definitive of that object's artistic status. It was, of course, Marcel Duchamp who first drew the radical consequences of this emphasis, in his work after 1912 and in explanations of it as involving an attempt to escape the rule of taste by the use of mechanical techniques and the artistic recycling of "readymade" objects.[18] Once any object chosen by an artist can be art, he claimed, art is no longer aesthetic— that is, effective through its perceptual properties—in nature. In a 1961 lecture on his invention of the readymade as an art form, Duchamp emphasized that "the choice of these 'Readymades' was never dictated by esthetic delectation. This choice was based on a reaction of visual indifference with at the same time a total absence of good or bad taste."[19]

This statement is questionable: not only is the distinction between choice and the exercise of taste far from clear, Duchamp's choices in fact exemplify a consistent (and specifically modernist) set of formal interests.[20] But the readymade undoubtedly involved a shift in the concept of taste from the expressive action of a uniquely gifted individual to—let us say—the design decisions of an informed consumer. This change Duchamp expressed as a desire "to get away from the

---

16 Museum of Modern Art; ill. in *Robert Morris: The Mind/Body Problem* (New York: Solomon R. Guggenheim Museum, 1994), p. 119.

17 Joseph Kosuth, "Art after philosophy I," [1969], in Gregory Battcock (ed.), *Idea Art* (New York: Dutton, 1973), p. 76.

18 See Michel Sanouillet and Elmer Peterson, *Salt Seller: The Writings of Marcel Duchamp* (New York: Oxford University Press, 1973), p. 134.

19 M. Duchamp, "Apropos of 'Readymades'," in ibid., p. 141.

20 For an excellent discussion of formal considerations involved in the production of the 1913 *Bicycle Wheel* and the transformation of a bottle rack into the first "unassisted readymade" in 1914, see Herbert Molderings, "The Bicycle Wheel and the Bottle Rack. Marcel Duchamp as a sculptor," in *Marcel Duchamp Respirateur* (Ostfildern: Staatliches Museum Schwerin/Hatje Cantz, 1999), pp. 141–69.

physical aspect of painting" and "to put painting once again at the service of the mind." This meant, for instance, that "the title was very important,"[21] as part of a general emphasis on the role of language in establishing the significance of an artwork, a language no longer employing the vocabulary of aesthetics.

As Thierry de Duve has put it, when

> anything visual can be called art . . . [t]he sentence "this is art" is a convention. Historical knowledge alone is required to make and judge art, some intellectual interest for the "logic" of Modernism, some strategic desire or interest to see it further extrapolated and tested on mere institutional grounds. Art fades into "art theory."[22]

This leaves unasked the questions of who is authorized to do the calling, and how an object or action arrives at the point where the convention of art can act on it. It also treats as an outcome of artistic decision-making what was in reality a more complex social development. This included changes in the marketing of art, to be discussed later, and the decisive entrance of art into the expanding embrace of academic institutions. At a time when the center of art education moved from craft skills (centered traditionally on techniques of representation) to an awareness of current artistic activities and a readiness to participate in them,[23] art theory, long inherent in the self-consciousness of modern artistic practice, crystallized out of the discourse of artists, critics, and art historians (later incorporating elements of francophone and -phile literary "theory") as an expression of the institutional autonomy of art as an academic discipline. School aesthetics was left behind, reflecting philosophy's character as (in Kosuth's words) "an academic subject with no real social life and no cultural effect."[24]

Despite the central role played by language in Conceptual artworks, in addition to the flood of words that accompanied them in the form of theory, "literature" in Greenberg's sense remained paradoxically absent here. Kosuth's account of Conceptualism is remarkably like the "formalism" he vociferously attacks, describing artworks as "analytic propositions" providing no information about the world outside art but "asserting" only that they *are* works of art. Despite Kosuth's insistence that Conceptualism had abandoned imagery for a form of philosophizing, and such critical claims as Benjamin Buchloh's scientistic celebration of "the *precision* with which these artists analyzed the place and

21 Marcel Duchamp, "The great trouble with art in this country," interview with James Johnson Sweeney, *The Bulletin of the Museum of Modern Art* 13:1–5 (1946), quoted in *Salt Seller*, p. 125.

22 Thierry de Duve, "The monochrome and the blank canvas," in Serge Guilbaut (ed.), *Reconstructing Modernism* (Cambridge: MIT Press, 1990), p. 272.

23 For a pathbreaking study of this development, see Howard Singerman, *Art Subjects: Making Artists in the American University* (Berkeley: University of California Press, 1999).

24 Interview with Jeanne Siegel on April 7, 1970, in J. Siegel, *Artwords: Discourse on the 60s and 70s* (Ann Arbor: UMI Research Press, 1985), p. 228.

function of aesthetic practice within the institutions of Modernism,"[25] ideas are typically present in Conceptual work, as in that done with traditional mediums, only as exemplified, illustrated, or suggested. Otherwise, indeed, a work like Hans Haacke's commentary on the socio-economics of the Ludwig collection of contemporary art—which assembles information about Peter Ludwig's economic holdings, the treatment of the workers in his factories, and his art collecting—would give up its "art" status for that of an unusually presented bit of art theory.[26] As Greenberg once explained, in modernism the arts had to demonstrate "that the kind of experience they provided was valuable in its own right and not to be obtained from any other kind of activity."[27] It is precisely the absence of the discursive apparatus on which possible actual conceptual development depends, and which is required for analytic precision, that, along with presentation on the walls of a gallery or museum, keeps Haacke's work in the domain of art rather than in that of the sociology of culture, whatever its power to suggest ideas or raise political questions for a suitably prepared spectator.[28]

One of the most striking features of Sol LeWitt's "Paragraphs on Conceptual Art" of 1967 is the extent to which this key statement of principles preserves elements of the understanding of art traceable to Kant's aesthetics even while emphasizing the unimportance of aesthetic features. On the one hand, LeWitt affirms that what "the work of art looks like isn't too important." What is crucial is that "it must begin with an idea."[29] But not only does the claim that "the idea or concept is the most important aspect of the work" have a lineage stretching back at least as far as Leonardo's insistence on the intellectual nature of painting, LeWitt also accepts fundamental aspects of the modern conception of art in describing Conceptualism as "intuitive," "purposeless," and "non-utilitarian."[30]

More recently, Hal Foster explained the expression "anti-aesthetic," to which he helped give currency in the early 1980s, as signaling "a practice, cross-disciplinary in nature, that is sensitive to cultural forms engaged in a politic (e.g. feminist art) or rooted in a vernacular—that is, to forms that deny the idea of a privileged aesthetic realm."[31] In reality, however, even when texts, or objects and

25 Benjamin H. D. Buchloh, "Allegorical procedures: appropriation and montage in contemporary art," *Artforum* 21 (1982), p. 48.
26 For documentation, see "Der Pralinenmeister," in Brian Wallis (ed.), *Hans Haacke: Unfinished Business* (Cambridge: MIT Press, 1986), pp. 210 ff.
27 C. Greenberg, "Modernist painting," in Gregory Battcock (ed.), *The New Art* (New York: Dutton, 1966), p. 162.
28 Speaking of Haacke's installation *MetroMobiltan*, Leo Steinberg identifies the art-experiential correlate of this form and location: "nothing practical can or will come of it, because [it] is wholly addressed to the mind and eye, to imagination and feeling" ("Some of Hans Haacke's works considered as works of art," in Wallis, *Hans Haacke: Unfinished Business*, p. 18).
29 Kristine Stiles and Peter Selz (eds), *Theories and Documents of Contemporary Art: A Sourcebook of Artists' Writings* (Berkeley: University of California Press, 1996), p. 824.
30 Ibid., pp. 822, 825.
31 Hal Foster, "Postmodernism: a preface," in *idem*, (ed.), *The Anti-Aesthetic* (Seattle: Bay Press, 1983), p. xv.

processes taken from hitherto non-art contexts, are substituted for the imagery and media central to earlier art, the result tends to function institutionally like the properly "aesthetic" art to which it offers itself as an alternative possibility. This is visible in the very terms with which Foster makes his claim, which locate a border-crossing from art to politics in the domain of form: the use of visual elements with political significance or "import," like the readymade, "in a vernacular." Foster claimed, in effect, that the political significance of an artistic act is under the control of the artist, embodied in decisions about visual sources and media.[32] (Haacke's wish to keep his Ludwig piece out of the hands of its eponymous collector represents a similar idea of politics by artistic will; in the event, it did not take long for Ludwig to acquire the work for his collection.)

Foster intended to define a "postmodernist" position able to come to terms with modernism's failure to deploy "the aesthetic as subversive." Modernism—here Foster refers to Adorno's formulation—was to accomplish this by insisting on art's autonomy in relation to capitalist instrumental rationality. But capitalist culture proved the stronger. "Originally oppositional, modernism defied the cultural order of the bourgeoisie . . .; today, however, it is the official culture."[33] It seems to Foster that art must respond by moving to the opposite tack: an oppositional position can be maintained only by abandoning autonomy for a direct engagement with politics and "vernacular" culture—that is, by an abandonment of the aesthetic. What remains constant in this conceptual turn, however, is the idea of art and its purported oppositionality. While an early ideal of transcendence is abandoned, art is now given the task of transcending its own institutional context. The immediate absorption of postmodernism by official culture, however, might have alerted its promoters to the presence of a flaw in their reasoning.[34] (We will return to the idea of artworks as "resistant" to the social order in Chapter 10.)

32 Art historian Thomas Crow makes a similar argument, tying political efficacy to formal choices, in his book *Modern Art in the Common Culture* (New Haven: Yale University Press, 1996). According to Crow, Conceptualism is "potentially available to a much wider audience" than modernist painting, thus enabling a meaningful confrontation with political issues, because in its use of vernacular images and media it possesses "the keys to new modes of figuration, to a truth-telling warrant pressed in opposition to the incorrigible abstraction that had overtaken painting and sculpture in traditional materials" (p. 217). In this he echoed John Baldassari's 1987 explanation that he "began using photographic imagery and words" because "it seemed to be a common parlance more so than the language of painting, which seemed to be kind of an elitist language" (Jeanne Siegel (ed.), *Art Talk: Discourse on the Early 80s* (Ann Arbor: UMI Research Press, 1988), p. 39). Actually, the closer the materials used in art are to raw elements of "vernacular" culture, the greater the amount of sophistication and inside knowledge required to understand even the claim made to the status of art, let alone decipher its meaning or judge its quality (see my review of Crow in *The Nation*, October 14, 1996, pp. 31–5).

33 H. Foster, "Postmodernism," pp. xv, ix.

34 Fredric Jameson ends his contribution to Foster's anthology by observing that "there is a way in which postmodernism replicates or reproduces—reinforces—the logic of consumer capitalism; the more significant question is whether there is also a way in which it resists that logic." To which he offers only the feeble response, "that is a question we must leave open" ("Postmodernism and consumer society," in Foster, *The Anti-Aesthetic*, p. 125).

According to Margaret Iversen, the text- and photo-based feminist work of artists like Mary Kelly and Cindy Sherman reflects the anti-aesthetic lesson learned from Minimalism that art can be "deflated" by being reduced "to a thing in the world, undifferentiated from other objects."[35] In reality, such reduction makes this kind of work, while visibly quite different from other objects, unreadable as art by any public other than that educated in advanced aesthetic theory. A good example is Kelly's *Post-Partum Document* of 1971–8, intended to speak of fundamental matters of life outside the world of art, specifically of women's experience of childrearing.[36] In this as in her later work, Kelly "describes her practice as like that of an indigenous ethnographer of a community or, better, communities of women—observing, recording, and analyzing her data, yet without assuming a privileged position."[37] Yet, as two sympathetic critics wrote of the *Document*, the objects composing it—soiled diapers and texts such as diary entries, transcribed mother–infant conversations, and psychoanalytical commentaries—"come across as disconnected visual clues to some academic discourse which do little more than expose the ignorance of the viewer."[38] Even in championing this work Iversen has perceptively compared it, for the difficulty of imagery and "explanatory" documentation alike, to Duchamp's classically inscrutable *The Bride Stripped Bare by Her Bachelors, Even.*[39] While the anti-aesthetic has meant a repudiation of Greenberg's identification of modernism with non-linguistic visuality, language here still hovers outside the artwork (even when that work consists of a text) as the explanation, external to it, necessary for its full functioning as art.

The relative inaccessibility of much Conceptualist art, and its accompanying theory, to nonspecialist viewers is, as suggested above, an index of the extent to which art training, production, and reception have been absorbed by academic institutions. Beyond this, it only presents in an exaggerated way, and so makes visible a feature of every work of art, that its readability depends on mastery of the cultural code utilized in its production.[40] This is normally unrecognized by the educated viewer, for whom the learned codes have become a second nature.

---

35 Margaret Iversen, "The deflationary impulse," in Andrew Benjamin and Peter Osborne (eds), *Thinking Art: Beyond Traditional Aesthetics* (London: Institute of Contemporary Art, 1991), p. 85.
36 For a presentation of this work in book form, see Mary Kelly, *Post-Partum Document* (London: Routledge and Kegan Paul, 1983).
37 Iversen, "Deflationary impulse," p. 92.
38 Margot Waddell and Michelene Wandor, "Mystifying theory," in Hilary Robinson (ed.), *Visibly Female* (New York: Universe, 1988), p. 103.
39 Margaret Iversen, "The bride stripped bare by her own desire: reading Mary Kelly's *Post-Partum Document*", in M. Kelly, *Post-Partum Document*, p. 206. For a refreshingly straightforward critique, see Cassandra Langer's report on a symposium on Kelly's work, reprinted as "Language of power" in Judy Siegel (ed.), *Mutiny and the Mainstream: Talk That Changed Art, 1971–1990* (New York: Midmarch Arts Press, 1992), pp. 311–12.
40 For a concise presentation of this point, see Pierre Bourdieu, "Outline of a sociological theory of art perception," in *idem, The Field of Cultural Production*, pp. 215 ff.

Older naturalistic art—at the present time, Impressionism is the central case—may seem immediately accessible even to the aesthetically uneducated, since it makes use of conventions shared with culturally dominant modes of representation, particularly in photography. But even here a fuller comprehension is available only to those aware of more esoteric (for example, historically outmoded) modes of signification employed in such art. A contemporary case is Barbara Kruger's work, which—thanks to its use of imagery and verbal forms borrowed from mass communications—is fairly accessible to a general public, while revealing what further complexities it has only to those able to set it conceptually within its art-world context.

To a great extent, it is worth noting, the art celebrated under the rubric of the anti-aesthetic shares formal features with art of the earlier avant-garde, in particular with Dada and Surrealism in its use of performance, text, photography, and stylishly ordered juxtapositions of images and objects. As Harold Rosenberg observed in relation to the "*arte povera*" of the 1960s, "Denying all aesthetic aims in a work permits the artist to draw freely on the entire aesthetic vocabulary of modern art." The earthworks, material arts, and conceptual pieces he was discussing "are strung on a line that meanders from Duchamp and Futurism through Dada, Surrealism, Action Painting, Pop, Minimalism, and Mathematical Abstraction."[41] Again, despite the lip service paid in recent times to "mass culture," video art typically has little of the "vernacular" character of television, and indeed (to use Max Kozloff's expression) for the most part functions in galleries and museum shows as "crypto-painting (and sculpture)."[42]

More important to the present discussion is the preservation by "anti-aesthetic" work of the fundamental feature of the aesthetic experience of art, which has to do not with perceptual experience directly but with the social distinctiveness conferred on perception by the art context. The illusion that aesthetic experience is an unmediated apprehension of a work depends precisely on the unconsciousness with which the codes necessary for that apprehension are activated. Actually, as Bourdieu has well said,

> The perception of the work of art in a truly aesthetic manner, that is to say as a signifier which signifies nothing other than itself, does not consist, as is sometimes said, of considering it "without connecting it with anything other than itself, either emotionally or intellectually," in short of giving oneself up to the work apprehended in its irreducible singularity, but of noting its *distinctive stylistic features* by relating it to the whole of the works forming the class to which it belongs, and to these works only.[43]

41 H. Rosenberg, *The De-Definition of Art: Action Art to Pop to Earthworks* (New York: Horizon, 1972), p. 36.
42 Max Kozloff, "Painting and anti-painting: a family quarrel," *Artforum* (September 1975), p. 42.
43 Pierre Bourdieu, "Outline," p. 222.

To do this is to classify it as a work of *art*. It is by being set into relation to the field of art that "anti-aesthetic" art, like earlier art, has its social significance. Although by different means, it seeks like the art of the past to provide an experience serving the exercise of a sensibility momentarily freed from engagement in the daily business of life, and thus emblematic at once of the privilege signified by such freedom and of the art lover's worthiness to enjoy it. (It is, of course, just the distance from the demands of life experienced even in the representation of those demands, say by documentary photography or explicitly political art, that is signified, in Kant's conception, by the concept of the aesthetic.)

This explains the paradox of anti-art noted by Bourdieu, that

> Nothing more clearly reveals the logic of the functioning of the artistic field than the fate of these apparently radical attempts at subversion. Because they expose the act of artistic creation to a mockery already annexed to the artistic tradition by Duchamp, they are immediately converted into artistic "acts," recorded as such and thus consecrated and celebrated by the makers of taste. Art cannot reveal the truth about art without snatching it away again by turning the revelation into an artistic event.[44]

Perhaps among artists Andy Warhol understood this best; at any rate he made use of it as the basis for his artistic career. Once art was separated from aesthetics as traditionally understood, he saw, it could be treated as a marketing category— one that maintained its original luxury character. Thus Warhol could appreciate the aesthetics of commercial design and describe art as "just another job" while preserving the definition of art in terms of autonomy: "An artist is somebody who produces things that people don't need to have but that he—for *some reason*— thinks it would be a good idea to give [*sic!*] them."[45] The philosophical treatment of Warhol's work as revealing the theoretical (or "institutional," analyzed in an abstract and ahistorical way) nature of art is an analogue in aesthetic theory to the self-cancellation of anti-art noted by Bourdieu.[46] It represents on the analytic level the same procedure as that by which the gallery and museum in folding the

---

44 P. Bourdieu, "The production of belief," in *The Field of Cultural Production*, p. 136. Inconsistently, Bourdieu asserted in a dialogue with Haacke that the latter proves "that a person, almost alone, can produce immense effects by disrupting the game and destroying the rules, often through scandal, the instrument par excellence of symbolic action" (Pierre Bourdieu and Hans Haacke, *Free Exchange* (Stanford: Stanford University Press, 1995), p. 84). The "immense effect" under discussion was an artists' boycott of art events sponsored by the Philip Morris Corporation, stimulated by a Haacke work, which eventually led the corporation to give some money for the fight against AIDS. This is, of course, a nice thing for an artist to stimulate but the rules of art have hardly been destroyed, nor the game disrupted.

45 Andy Warhol, *The Philosophy of Andy Warhol* (New York: Harvest/HBJ, 1977), pp. 178, 144.

46 Notably by Arthur Danto in "The artworld." See Chapter 9 below.

readymade within their embrace removed the sting of its challenge to earlier conceptions of art. That is, it obscures the turning point in the history of the modern practice of the fine arts signaled by the attempt to produce a radical disjuncture of art and aesthetics.

This is why it would also be wrong to dismiss Warhol's analysis too quickly as an ironisation of the complex relationship a poor boy from Pittsburgh had to the world of glamour and financial success into which his very social and psychological distance from art opened a path. Kant's analysis of the judgment of taste assumed a fundamental universality among human beings, here localized in the "sensus communis," which alone made comprehensible the demand for uniformity of judgment that he took to be implied by claims of aesthetic quality.[47] Philosophers argued that the actual lack of unanimity revealed, for example, in the German "reading debate" of the eighteenth century,[48] and in the vast outpouring of literature in all European languages concerned with the nature and standard of taste, would be overcome in the course of time through the aesthetic education of the vulgar; their assurance seemed justified for a hundred-odd years by the general acceptance of the taste of the educated classes as better, whatever the actual preferences of people in any class. Yet the chasm between "high" and "low" taste was never bridged; it seemed to Clement Greenberg in 1939 that the domain of the low ("kitsch") had so expanded that the high remained only on the threatened margin.

His dire prediction of the fate of art under capitalism seemed to be proven correct in the 1960s, when the authority of taste in the world of high art itself was badly shaken by the market success of Pop art, which forced critics who had initially condemned or even dismissed it to take it seriously and eventually to appreciate it with all the resources of learned discrimination. This development was not an anomaly; the critics whose power had earlier made them threatening figures to Barnett Newman never recovered their authority. By the end of the 1970s, their place as arbiters of artistic value was taken by a de facto alliance of museum curators and the auction market.[49] In retrospect, the structural fit

---

47 See David Summers, "Why did Kant call taste a 'common sense'?" in Paul Mattick (ed.), *Eighteenth-Century Aesthetics and the Reconstruction of Art* (Cambridge: Cambridge University Press, 1993), pp. 121–51.

48 See above, Chapter 3, p. 39f.

49 For the role of museum curators in the creation of artistic value, see R. Moulin, "The museum and the marketplace," pp. 31–62. For the rise in importance of the auction market after 1970, see Diana Crane, *The Transformation of the Avant-Garde: The New York Art World, 1941–1985* (Chicago: University of Chicago Press, 1987), pp. 114 ff; Nancy Sullivan's penetrating article, "Inside trading: postmodernism and the social drama of *Sunflowers* in the 1980s art world," argues that the art community is defined sociologically "by its proximity to the auction market, which is itself based in New York auction houses" (in George E. Marcus and Fred R. Myers (ed.), *The Traffic in Culture: Refiguring Art and Anthropology* (Berkeley: University of California Press, 1995), p. 257). The crowning artistic monument to this development is perhaps Sol LeWitt's *Wall Drawing #896*—exemplifying a type of object art-historically celebrated as "dramatically

between the incessant innovation of avant-gardism and the repetition of novelty required for a lively speculative market was bound over time to undermine the claim to disinterest that Kant had made definitional of the aesthetic.[50]

As Paul Ardenne observes, the institutional basis for this was laid by the nineteenth-century achievement of "the real or supposed autonomy of art relative to society," which "created an aesthetic sphere unto itself, an absolute and solipsistic universe of value." The Renaissance system that priced work in relation to its material constituents as well as the design agreed upon by patron and maker had a residue in the Parisian system of pricing by picture sizes ("points") still in place in the earlier twentieth century. But the autonomy of the aesthetic, as the conceptualization of the modern emergence of "art" as a distinct field of social practice, made the anti-aesthetic possible, by underwriting the twentieth-century tendency for the artwork to evolve from an object with particular perceptual and referential properties toward an object whose social and economic value was increasingly determined by its character as art.[51] Thus (in Ardenne's words) the readymade, "of little inherent material value, acquired value only by virtue of the credit bestowed upon it (or not) by the source of legitimation," the artistic field. Anti-aesthetics is the theoretical counterpart to a contemporary art system in which high prices "are the best indication" that the works that bear them "do indeed belong to the sphere of art."[52]

The present-day conservatism of philosophical aesthetics (the articles in a publication like the American Society for Aesthetics's *Journal of Aesthetics and Art*

challenging traditional thinking about the art object and its place in the world," in particular making "art available to a broader public"—made for the lobby of Christie's auction house in the Rockefeller Center, New York in 1999 (John S. Weber, "Sol LeWitt: the idea, the wall drawing, and public space," in Gary Garrels (ed.), *Sol LeWitt: A Retrospective* (New Haven: Yale University Press, 2000), p. 89).

50 In her 1967 survey of the French art market, Raymonde Moulin had already suggested that "characterized, in its most advanced tendencies, by a continual questioning of accepted values and by an accelerated series of changes, art by its very nature offers an incitation to the speculative behavior that is one of the dominant traits of the post-war market" (*Le Marché de la peinture en France* (Paris: Editions de Minuit, 1967), p. 69).

51 In *Dialectic of Enlightenment* (1944), Max Horkheimer and Theodor Adorno argued that "the purposelessness of the great modern work of art depends on the anonymity of the market. Its demands pass through so many intermediaries that the artist is exempt from any definite requirements—though admittedly only to a certain degree." Even so, they asserted prophetically,

> a change in the character of the art commodity is coming about. What is new is not that it is a commodity, but that today it deliberately admits that it is one; that art renounces its own autonomy and proudly takes its place among consumption goods constitutes the charm of novelty.
>
> Tr. John Cumming (New York: Continuum, 1987), p. 157

52 Paul Ardenne, "The art market in the 1980s," *International Journal of Political Economy* 25:2 (Summer 1995), pp. 111–3.

Criticism are as irrelevant to contemporary art today as when Newman complained about philosophical detachment from the art world struggle over aesthetic legitimacy and significance) is itself a symptom of the ongoing transformation of the practice of art signaled by the rise of the anti-aesthetic. Art, once securely positioned as the highest secular religion of modern society—higher than science, for all practical purposes, because it is both more accessible to the nonspecialist and freer of the taint of commercial (not to mention military) utility—has now become an area of confusion and contestation. The taking up of this field of production and consumption, and in particular of the avant-garde area within it, by institutions of state and academy, together with the enormous and rapid expansion of the market for art, have done much to erode the earlier conception of art as founded on the transcendence of social particularity achieved by the heroic, creative individual.

At the same time, the importance of the role of the practice of art in the development of modern society, visible in the use of the museum and concert hall as reliquaries for the material embodiments of its "higher self," means that it remains with us despite the ever more apparent incoherence of its conceptual structure. As a result of this practice's continuing life, even attempts to question basic elements of aesthetic ideology can function in the struggle for art world legitimacy and commercial success. For example, the success of "postmodern" critics and artists in defining "feminist art" in terms of the use of non-traditional media has made possible the creation of an artistic (and marketing) niche for critical women's work, while also largely accepting as a given the centuries-old definition of painting—still the core (and highest priced) commodity of the art business—as masculine, despite the activity of women and feminist painters.[53] Here too we see that the refusal of aesthetics is no more a guarantee of actual transformation of the social significance of art than the autonomy of form once seemed to some to be.

---

53 One can get a sense of the breadth of women's artistic activity in the 1970s and 1980s, and the constrictive force of the play of positions exercised within the artistic field, from the accounts of artists' panels, and reactions to them, in Judy Seigel (ed.), *Mutiny and the Mainstream*.

9

THE ANDY WARHOL OF PHILOSOPHY AND THE PHILOSOPHY OF ANDY WARHOL

It is only shallow people who do not judge by appearances.

Oscar Wilde, *The Picture of Dorian Gray*

Andy Warhol himself once explained, in words close to Wilde's, "If you want to know all about Andy Warhol, just look at the surface: of my paintings and films and me, and there I am. There's nothing behind it."[1] This remark, whether taken as all too true or as coyly misleading, is itself generally judged in a superficial way. Wilde's aphorism may help us remember that it is a mode of shallowness to be unable or unwilling to explore the structure and content of appearances. From this point of view, much of the consideration critics, art theorists, and philosophers have given Warhol's work is superficial. Finding that work's surfaces insufficient, such thinkers either condemn it as evidence of cultural decline or seek to give it significance by setting it within a framework of theory that possesses depths invisible in the work itself.

This essay examines accounts of Warhol's work, by a philosopher and three art historians, that seek significance for it in this way. I will argue that despite their differences and their many interesting features, they are all flawed in being critically shallow—I mean, shallow as criticism. I will suggest that we can do better, in some respects at least, by paying close attention to Warhol's surfaces.

To begin with an eminent example, the issue of the relation between surface and deep meaning lies at the heart of the lesson the critic-philosopher Arthur Danto drew from *Brillo Boxes*, which Warhol exhibited at the Stable Gallery in New York in 1964. Twenty-five years later, reviewing Warhol's postmortem retrospective at the Museum of Modern Art, Danto called him "the nearest thing to a philosophical genius the history of art has produced." This is because

---

1 Gretchen Berg, "Andy: my true story," *Los Angeles Free Press* (March 17, 1967), p. 3.

Warhol "revealed as merely accidental most of the things his predecessors supposed essential to art."[2] More particularly, Danto takes Warhol to have demonstrated that art is not to be defined aesthetically—that is, in the case of visual art, by visual features (such as those which, in traditional philosophical aesthetics, were supposed to give rise to aesthetic experiences in sensitive observers). *Brillo Boxes* demonstrated this by being "indiscernible" from the boxes on which it was modeled; they showed that "no sensory examination of an object will tell [the observer] that it is an artwork, since quality for quality it may be matched by an object that is not one, so far at least [as] the qualities to which the normal senses are responsive are concerned."[3]

Danto's argument rests on the idea of a contrast between art and "commonplace" things that he shares with the traditional aesthetic theory his views are intended to supplant. This contrast is indeed fundamental to the modern conception of fine art, which sets art in opposition to practices and objects associated with what is typically called, in this discourse, real or ordinary or everyday life. Warhol's boxes seem to Danto to have shown that this opposition cannot be perceptual in nature by enacting a comparison of works of art to extremely mundane objects indeed. Thus what struck Danto most about the *Brillo Boxes* "was that they looked sufficiently like their counterparts in supermarket stockrooms that the differences between them could hardly be of a kind to explain why they were art and their counterparts merely cheap containers for scouring pads."[4]

Since 1964, when Danto first presented this notion in his essay "The artworld," many people have pointed out that Warhol's boxes and the real thing are not actually indiscernible. In a recent essay on these works Danto states the problem that *Brillo Boxes* posed for the philosophy of art as the question, "How is it possible for something to be a work of art when something else, which resembles it to whatever degree of exactitude, is merely a thing, or an artifact, but not an artwork?"[5] But this term of comparison is rather far from indiscernibility, and it makes hash of Danto's analysis. Everything resembles everything else to some degree of exactitude. Of course, Warhol's boxes do look a good deal like the real thing. But you do not have to peer too closely to see the differences: they are made of wood, not cardboard; they are silk-screened, not printed; they are somewhat larger than the cartons in stores. Furthermore, as Danto himself pointed out in 1964, imagining someone displaying real soap pad cartons in an art gallery, "we cannot readily separate the Brillo cartons from the gallery they are in."[6]

---

2 Arthur C. Danto, "Andy Warhol," *The Nation*, April 3, 1989, p. 459.

3 Arthur C. Danto, *The Transfiguration of the Commonplace: A Philosophy of Art* (Cambridge: Harvard University Press, 1981), p. 99.

4 Danto, "Andy Warhol," p. 459.

5 Arthur C. Danto, "Andy Warhol *Brillo Box*," *Artforum* 32 (1993), p. 129.

6 Arthur C. Danto, "The artworld," in Joseph Margolis (ed.), *Philosophy Looks at the Arts: Contemporary Readings in Aesthetics*, revised edition (Philadelphia: Temple University Press, 1978), p. 141.

While acknowledging that this is an aspect of what would make even real boxes, under those circumstances, works of art, Danto does not, for some reason, seem to regard being stacked in a gallery a visual (as well as a spatial-locational) property of an object. Similarly, he makes it clear that what he means by an "artworld"—the context that turns a "real object" into an artwork—is not the actual world of institutions, people, and practices that we normally refer to by this phrase but "an atmosphere of artistic theory, a knowledge of the history of art": "What in the end makes the difference between a Brillo box and a work of art consisting of a Brillo box is a certain theory of art. It is the theory that takes it up into the world of art."[7] This theory is what Danto takes Warhol to have expressed in the form of his artwork, inspiring Danto to express it in words; the idea involved in *Brillo Boxes* is the idea that art is constituted in (implicit or explicit) reference to philosophical theory.

As Danto's thought-experiment of a carton-displaying artist suggests, this idea might have been provoked decades earlier by Marcel Duchamp's readymades, although it was apparently Warhol's work that happened to suggest it to him.[8] On the other hand, the visually apparent differences between Warhol's boxes and their originals suggest that the thought the philosopher took from them was no more Warhol's than it was Duchamp's. Claes Oldenburg seems to me to have had a more plausible understanding of Warhol's boxes in 1964. In the midst of a discussion of the impersonality of the Pop art style he pointed out that "there is a degree of removal from actual boxes and they become an object that is not really a box. In a sense they are an illusion of a box and that places them in the realm of art."[9] This at least reflects close looking at the objects. Danto, in contrast, offers no explanation of why, if Warhol was offering up a Dantoesque reflection on the nature of art, he should not have exhibited either an actual carton or a truly indiscernible replica.

Not only does the way the Brillo boxes look not actually support Danto's

7 Danto, "The artworld," pp. 136, 140, 141.
8 Danto's attempt to dissociate his thought from Duchamp's example (in "Andy Warhol," pp. 451–60) is not convincing; it relies, for instance, on the dubious judgments that Duchamp's chosen objects were both "arcane" and aesthetically bland ("Andy Warhol," p. 459).
9 Claes Oldenburg, quoted in Bruce Glaser, "Oldenburg, Lichtenstein, Warhol: a discussion," in Carol Anne Mahsun (ed.), *Pop Art: The Critical Dialogue* (Ann Arbor, Michigan, 1989), p. 143. This is a particularly striking remark given Danto's insistence that Warhol's work cannot be understood in terms of the traditional understanding of art as imitative. He believes that it is the modern replacement of this understanding with an emphasis on the independent reality of art-works that creates the problem—how are artworks to be distinguished from other objects?—to which Warhol's Brillo boxes suggest a solution; see "The artworld," pp. 131–6. This argument leads him to claim that Lichtenstein's paintings after comic strip panels are not imitations of them, on the peculiar ground that difference in scale rules out mimesis. Committing the same error as in the Brillo box case, Danto asserts that "a *photograph* of a Lichtenstein is indiscernible from a photograph of a counterpart panel from *Steve Canyon*," which is not true ("The artworld," p. 135).

reading of them, but there is no reason I know of to think that Warhol was particularly interested in the question "What is art?" to which Danto believes his work provides an answer. Some artists of the mid-1960s were interested in such theoretical issues—Robert Morris and Joseph Kosuth come to mind—but Warhol was not among them. Or, rather, what remarks he made on the matter lead in the other direction, toward a questioning of the difference between art and "real things" so important to the philosopher.

What actually were the appearances Warhol offered the visitor to the Stable Gallery? There were stacks of plywood boxes, with designs taken from supermarket packing cartons indicating various household items. These things drew, first of all, on the basic Pop art iconography of consumer items. They had ancestors in Oldenburg's 1961 exhibition, *The Store*, which displayed plaster versions of various goods, mostly edible ones, in a mock bodega and, more directly, in Jasper Johns's bronze *Ale Cans* of 1960. They clearly followed in Warhol's oeuvre from his Campbell's soup can paintings and other pictures of packagings, like Coke bottles. In fact, this was the origin of *Brillo Boxes*, as Warhol once explained:

> I did all the [Campbell's soup] cans on a row on a canvas, and then I got a box made to do them on a box, and then it looked funny because it didn't look real . . . I did the cans on the box, but it came out looking funny. I had the boxes already made up. They were brown and looked just like boxes, so I thought it would be so great just to do an ordinary box.[10]

Why did the cans look "funny" and not "real" on a box, while they (apparently) looked "real" enough silk-screened singly or in grids on canvas? It is certainly not trompe l'oeil similitude that is at issue here. A key lies in the fact that the subject in all the examples of Warhol's art I have mentioned—and many more besides—is not an actual product or substance but its packaging or, specifically, its label. As Lawrence Alloway observed about Pop art more generally, "it is, essentially, an art about signs and sign-systems."[11] In the case of the Campbell's soup can box, Warhol's original idea produced a discord between the box shape and the image of a cylindrical can, a funniness that does not arise with the application of designs from actual cartons to boxlike structures.[12] We can now see also why the visible difference from storeroom reality is important: both the difference in material and the inferred emptiness of Warhol's boxes play roles in emphasizing their character as 3-D signs.

10 Glenn O'Brien, interview with Andy Warhol, *High Times* 24 (1977), p. 34.

11 Lawrence Alloway, *American Pop Art* (New York, 1974), p. 7.

12 See the photograph in Kynaston McShine (ed.), *Andy Warhol: A Retrospective* (New York: Museum of Modern Art, 1989), p. 197, pl. 181.

The sign, that is, has been materialized in—or on—a new object. It is the recognizability of the sign, especially when displayed on an object more similar to the original carrier of the sign than, say, the soup can paintings are to actual cans, that allowed Danto to think of the artwork and the original as indiscernible and the difference between them as therefore problematic. But the point of the Brillo boxes, it seems to me, is not so much the difference as the more than visual similarity between the two, which the differences set off.

Warhol's boxes, knocked off in large numbers, unlike traditional trompe l'oeil representations of common objects make no claim to the transfiguration of the commonplace by artistic skill or vision. This is in part because Warhol does not scorn the so-called commonplace. After all, he had been himself a successful commercial designer. His reaction when his friend Emile de Antonio explained to him that his career as a prominent, prizewinning commercial artist was one reason Johns and Robert Rauschenberg withheld the approval and friendship Warhol dearly desired is interesting in this regard: "If you wanted to be considered a 'serious' artist," Warhol said, "you weren't supposed to have anything to do with commercial art. De [Antonio] was the only person I knew then who could see past those old social distinctions to the art itself."[13] Those social distinctions continued to have the power for Warhol himself that they had for others. This is, after all, part of why he was so set on becoming a fine artist, and why he abandoned commercial art—at least officially—as soon as he succeeded in making this transition. But at the same time his work emphasizes the similarities that coexist with the social differences.

For one thing, the sameness of the sign shared by soap pad carton and artwork draws attention to the fact that the original was already a product of the designer's craft (in fact, that of a designer who was himself a "fine" artist). In a 1963 interview Warhol observed, "It's so funny" that "the shoe I would draw for an advertisement was called a 'creation' but the drawing of it was not. But I guess I believe in both ways."[14] Further comparing his commercial work to his fine-art activity, he said, "I'd have to invent and now I don't . . . those commercial drawings would have feelings, they would have a style."[15]

Of course, Warhol's fine-art use of commercial design had style, too (something in only apparent contradiction to his desire, expressed in the same interview, to be a machine). Here a comment of Roy Lichtenstein's on comic strips is of great interest:

> This technique is a perfect example of an industrial process that
> developed as a direct result of the need for inexpensive and quick color-

13 Andy Warhol and Pat Hackett, *POPism: The Warhol '60s* (New York, 1980), p. 12.
14 Gene Swenson, "What Is Pop Art?" in Mahsun, *Pop Art* , p. 119.
15 Ibid., p. 120.

printing. These printed symbols attain perfection in the hands of commercial artists through the continuing idealization of the image made compatible with commercial considerations. Each generation of illustrators makes modifications and reinforcements of these symbols, which then become part of the vocabulary of all. The result is an impersonal form.[16]

The impersonality of the form, however, does not make its use by the individual artist less characteristic, or even less expressive, as was shown also, at around the same time, by the systematized constructions of Minimalism. Warhol's work is not only immediately recognizable but has proved surprisingly hard to forge. Graphic sensibility, direction of thought, and mode of production combine to make most of Warhol's work as distinctive as a Cassandre poster or a grid of boxes by Donald Judd.

Like the contents of the original cartons, Warhol's boxes are items for sale in a store. They can be sold as art simply because, assembled by hand in the Warhol "Factory" for gallery sale, they bear the Warhol brand name, which makes possible the detachment of the Brillo (or other) logo from its original connection with a different product to demonstrate the centrality of such signs to our visual lives, and indeed to life as a whole. Both uses of the sign function as packaging; if the one advertises scouring pads, the other advertises the Warhol persona.

In short, Warhol's boxes look like scouring pad cartons because he wishes to emphasize the similarity, not the difference, between them. The differences are obvious enough: as I mentioned earlier, the whole history of the fine arts since they came into existence as a social practice in the later eighteenth century has included as a central element their distinction from what in contrast became ordinary things. Warhol's work marks a moment of the disintegration of this venerable practice, a disintegration that art shares with other ideological constructs of modern society such as science, politics, and the self. Danto's resistance to the message of Warhol's surfaces exemplifies the investment of philosophy, as an academic discipline, in the preservation of such constructs. Perhaps he is right, after all, to think Warhol a greater philosopher than the aestheticians among whom he occupies such a prominent place.

While Danto has attempted to enroll Warhol in a philosophical cause, art historians have, equally naturally, set his work in contexts defined by their discipline. But philosophical theory plays a role here also. This is hardly surprising, given the centrality of philosophy—in particular, Hegel's and Kant's—to the art historical tradition. That this discipline as presently constituted may have a difficult

16   Roy Lichtenstein, quoted in John Rublowsky, *Pop Art* (New York, 1965), p. 43.

time assimilating Warhol's art is at least suggested by the remarkable fact that there exists no full-scale, serious historical treatment of his work.[17] The texts I will discuss are short and far from thorough, and perhaps not too much should be made of them. Rainer Crone's book-length studies were published at the start of the 1970s. Thomas Crow's often-cited short article, published in three slightly differing versions, focuses on a few of the silkscreen paintings of the 1960s. And Benjamin Buchloh's catalogue essay for the 1989 retrospective, surprisingly, deals only with the same material, which was also the focus of his lecture at the DIA Warhol symposium the previous year.[18]

In addition to their neglect of Warhol's production from the 1970s on—true even of Crone's contribution to the 1988 symposium—the texts by Crone, Buchloh, and Crow share a number of other features. Writing as leftists of one sort or another, the authors in each case are preoccupied with the question of what Buchloh calls the "affirmative" or "critical" character of their subject's response to mass culture.[19] (This is the aspect of their analyses where more explicitly philosophical ideas tend to come into play.) And they all operate with the core idea of art history, the autonomy of the art object as a signifier. This is to be seen in their shared insistence on segregating discussion of the work from consideration of Andy the public persona. More generally, they agree in removing the work from its original social contexts—the intersecting social worlds of artistic producers and consumers—to position it, as an object of study, in the art historical context materialized in the slide library. Crone constructs an artistic lineage for Warhol that starts from Jacques-Louis David and passes through Gustave Courbet and, *inter alia*, Alfred Stieglitz and John Sloan; Crow, more plausibly, launches into his treatment of Warhol's *Gold Marilyn Monroe* from an extended discussion of Willem de Kooning's *Woman I*; and Buchloh aligns Warhol with the tradition of the dandy that stretches from Charles Baudelaire

---

17   The closest thing to it is Stephen Koch's *Stargazer: Andy Warhol's World and His Films* (New York, 1985); it is perhaps the one indispensable book on the artist, but it is concerned nearly exclusively with his films. Apart from this there are exhibition catalogues, a number of what amount to coffee table books, and Patrick S. Smith's *Andy Warhol's Art and Films* (Ann Arbor: UMI Press, 1986), extremely useful for its collection of interviews, but offering little historical analysis.

18   See Rainer Crone, *Andy Warhol* (New York, 1970); Crone, "Form and Ideology: Warhol's Techniques from Blotted Line to Film," in Gary Garrels (ed.), *The Work of Andy Warhol* (Seattle, 1989), pp. 71–92; and Crone and Wilfried Wiegand, *Die revolutionäre Ästhetik Andy Warhol's* (Darmstadt, 1972). See also Thomas Crow, "Saturday disasters: trace and reference in early Warhol," *Art in America* 75 (May 1987), pp. 121–36, rpt. with alternations (and a discussion) in Serge Guilbaut (ed.), *Reconstructing Modernism: Art in New York, Paris, and Montreal, 1941–1964* (Cambridge: Harvard University Press, 1990), pp. 311–31 (the version cited below), and in Crow, *Modern Art in the Common Culture* (New Haven: Yale University Press, 1996), pp. 41–65; and Benjamin H. D. Buchloh, "Andy Warhol's One-Dimensional Art: 1951–1966," in McShine, *Andy Warhol*, pp. 31–61, and "The Andy Warhol line," in Garrels, *The Work of Andy Warhol*.

19   Buchloh, "Andy Warhol line," pp. 55, 59.

and Edouard Manet to Francis Picabia and Duchamp, while also setting his work in relation to American painting of the 1950s.[20]

In contrast, these writers exhibit almost no interest in the non-art sources of Warhol's imagery. While Crone insists, in an exhibition catalogue published in 1987, on the importance of more than art historical context, that turns out to be restricted to the worlds of literature and the theater, along with general social and economic developments.[21] And, to take a striking example, when Buchloh discusses an early Warhol drawing of Ginger Rogers in terms of the types of line employed, of which some are said to synthesize "the boredom and routine of the commercial artist" while others "assume the function of a 'free' gestural linear movement," he has nothing to say about the source of the image, a movie maga-zine, or about Ginger Rogers herself.[22] The contents of the image bank from which Warhol drew are, in fact, consistently treated as acquiring value and even interest only thanks to the artist's use of them; that is, of course, related to Buchloh's focus on the question of whether that use involved critique or shame-ful acquiescence in what he refers to as "vulgarity."[23]

Crone's writing constructs an image of Warhol placeable, as already men-tioned, in the modernist lineage conventionally spoken of as initiated by David and, more specifically, in an artistic tradition located in "Eastern and Central Europe in the 1920s."[24] Central to this construction is reference to Bertolt Brecht, whom Crone continued in 1989 to claim as an important influence on Warhol despite Patrick Smith's decisive undermining of the supposed biographi-cal basis for this hypothesis.[25] But the major theoretical presence in Crone's analysis of Warhol is Walter Benjamin. In Crone's view, the silkscreen paintings "represent an aesthetic theory put into aesthetic practice," namely that of Ben-jamin's 1936 essay, "The work of art in the age of mechanical reproduction."[26] Crone draws on Benjamin's argument that the advent of photography has "transformed the entire nature of art," destroying its semblance of autonomy in relation to social and political processes, and liquidating "the traditional value of the cultural heritage." Photographs (and especially motion pictures) cannot, Ben-jamin believed, be invested with the "aura" of timelessness and sanctity that he believed essential to the classical artwork; correlatively they give themselves not

---

20 An amusing interview Buchloh conducted with Warhol in 1985 shows the artist resisting the his-torian's attempt to fit him into the latter's preferred context. Thus he claims ignorance of Picabia's work at the relevant time, explains his formal procedures as "just something to do" rather than responses to the art-historical *Zeitgeist*; and, above all, refuses any idea of the histori-cal obsolescence of painting, even figurative painting ("Conversation with Andy Warhol," *October* 70 (1994), p. 41).

21 Rainer Crone, *Andy Warhol, A Picture Show by the Artist* (New York, 1987).

22 Buchloh, "Andy Warhol line," pp. 51–4.

23 B. Buchloh, "One-dimensional," p. 48.

24 R. Crone, "Form and ideology," p. 70; see Crone and Wiegand, *Die revolutionäre Ästhetik*, p. 27.

25 See Smith, *Andy Warhol's Art and Films*, pp. 71–9.

26 R. Crone, *Andy Warhol*, p. 10.

to aesthetic contemplation by a chosen few but to absorption by the masses.[27] Crone emphasizes the "mechanical" and reproductive character of Warhol's methods of image production, from the blotted-line technique of his advertising work of the 1940s and 1950s—which was both a sort of homemade offset printing and produced an image easily reproduced by mechanical offset—through the use of applied gold leaf, stamps, and stencils, and the imitation of printed pictures, to the silkscreen printing of photographs.[28] From this point the obvious move was to film itself, where again the methods used serve to foreground "the conditions of production, which determine the character of the product."[29]

According to Crone, the orientation to reproduction, exactly as Benjamin had argued, "robs the artwork of its uniqueness and authority, imparting significance instead to the image reproduced."[30] By making visible the structure of the medium used (the Brechtian alienation effect) and by depersonalizing the actual production of art (the Benjaminian principle of mechanical reproduction) Warhol counters the fetishization of art in bourgeois society and makes it available for use as a medium for political education. His work functions then as what Crone calls "documentary realism," an impersonal technique allowing attention to be focused both on the system of visual communication developed by modern society, from which the images are drawn, and the reality it depicts. That reality is a social system based on "manipulating people to consume," which leads to "the destruction of personality, of the individual."[31] While Warhol's aim was "to fight the system of consumer society, he took a different strategy than some idealistically oriented European artists."[32] His strategy of depersonalization dictated that the picture should not express his critical attitude; rather, its political character lies in the content itself, which the elimination of traditional aesthetics makes fully visible. Thus, as Crone explains, referring in particular to the car crash paintings of 1961–3, these pictures "*become* criticism as soon as they are received into the machinery of the art market and thus accepted by society as viable artworks. Only a mirror held up without comment reflects society's ills—therein lies the criticism."[33]

Central to Crone's construction is the unification of Warhol's oeuvre around the concept of depersonalization, seen as active in both form and content. The emphasis on mechanical reproduction leads him to ignore the obvious differences, in medium, style, content, and social position, between Warhol's commercial and fine-art work. On the other hand, paradoxically, even in his

---

27 Walter Benjamin, "The work of art in the age of mechanical reproduction," in *idem*, *Illuminations*, tr. Harry Zohn (New York: Schocken, 1969), pp. 227, 221.
28 Crone, "Form and ideology," p. 74.
29 Crone, *Andy Warhol*, p. 31.
30 Ibid., p. 10.
31 Ibid., pp. 10, 23.
32 Crone, "Form and ideology," p. 134.
33 Crone, *Andy Warhol*, p. 29.

1989 text Crone completely ignores Warhol's return to painting in the 1970s. To deal with it would either contradict the Benjaminian logic which is supposed to explain the move to film, or require the bifurcation of the artist into the Critical (Good) Warhol of the 1960s and the Corrupt (Bad) Warhol of the 1970s and 1980s—a move made in Crow's account of the artist.

In fact, Warhol's adventures as a filmmaker can be understood without refer ence to the supposed historical movement from painting to mechanical reproduction. The underground cinema of the 1960s was part of a wider field of art activities including experimental dance, music, poetry, and performance. Typically, Warhol combined *his* filmmaking with adventures in the less arty realm of rock-and-roll spectacle, alongside quasi-automatic writing (as in the tape-recorded *a* (*a novel*)). Crone's theoretical fixation prevents him from noting the surface similarities between Warhol's films and paintings (a point Warhol made himself when he screen-printed enlarged frame sequences of his films). While the out-of-focus picture, meaningless camera movement, and non-narrative action of a film like *Poor Little Rich Girl* make it almost more like a painting than a film, *Empire*'s unchanging view is so like a Warhol multi-image silkscreen work that the differences in medium—"the conditions of produc-tion"—can be taken as relatively unimportant. Such considerations also make Warhol's eventual "return to painting" less mysterious. And anyway, despite the 1965 announcement of his retirement from painting to consider a (probably fic-tional) offer from Hollywood, the production of paintings—in addition to the printed *Cow Wallpaper* of 1966—never actually stopped.

A basic problem with Crone's analysis, as with Danto's, is that Warhol's career is being used to illustrate a theory that it fits only very imperfectly. While Brecht's alienation effect operated against the conventions of theatrical natural-ism, Warhol's explicitness about matters of form and medium is—despite the dismay his work aroused among modernist critics—quite at home in the context of American modernism. And with respect to the employment of reproductive techniques, the effect is, as I observed earlier, not one of anonymity (as in Laszlo Moholy-Nagy's paint-by-telephone experiments, to which Crone compares it). Warhol's enormous success as a commercial artist depended, after all, on a sig-nature style; and the artistic (as well as commercial) achievement of the silkscreen paintings has much to do with the nonmechanical, handmade charac-ter of the marks by which they are realized: the varying heaviness of the paint, the off-register effects, the smears and other imperfections that are traces of the handling of the silkscreen (just as the wilfully crude cinematic technique both emphasizes the mechanics of the medium and marks each film, no matter who actually made it, as a Warhol).

At the same time, it is clear that Warhol's use of photography and silkscreen for his paintings, along with his choice of subject-matter, brought the imagery of commercial culture into art culture in a particularly powerful manner, and that this is at the heart of both the aesthetic effect and the historical significance of Warhol's work. It is not unthinkable that Benjamin's theory might cast some light on this effect and significance but it would take closer attention to the work than Crone gives it to let it do so. For instance, a comparison between versions of the race riot pictures of 1964 silkscreened onto paper and onto canvas suggests the insufficiency of identification of the mark-making mechanism for understanding the effect of the imagery. On paper, Warhol's screen print looks like a crudely printed high-contrast photograph; placing it on canvas inserts the same image into the high art tradition of oil painting, thus generating a complex interaction between the handmade and the mechanical, elite and mass media, art and politics, form and content. The flawed printing now reads as "painting"; the aura of art, to use Benjamin's expression, struggles with the familiarity of news photography.

In direct opposition to Crone's insistence on the "impersonality" of Warhol's imagery, Crow finds in it what it seems appropriate to call a humanistic content, at once an expression of feeling and a critique of the emotional poverty of consumer culture. As a sort of material foundation for this interpretation of Warhol, Crow, like Crone, emphasizes the artist's working-class background, discovering in the work of the 1960s "a kind of loyalty to his origins" that mysteriously disappeared after that period, producing the meretricious work of the later decades.[34] He sees the making of the Marilyn Monroe pictures immediately following the actress's death as an "act of mourning," and the *Jackies*, read as "Kennedy assassination pictures," as "a sustained act of remembrance." Finding these works "a kind of history painting," in a tack reminiscent of Crone's invocation of David, Crow finds no alienation effect here, no attempt to "direct our attention to some peculiarly twentieth century estrangement between an event and its representation," and no mockery "of our potential feelings of empathy." Rather, they exhibit "instances in which the mass-produced image as the bearer of desires was exposed in its inadequacy by the reality of suffering and death."[35] The very imagery in which consumer society made its promises to the American people is used to expose its failure to keep them. For instance, Crow sees the car crash pictures as exposing, behind "the supreme symbol of consumer affluence," the reality of "sudden and irreparable injury." Beyond this, he views the race riot and electric chair pieces as bringing explicitly political issues into this "stark, disabused, pessimistic vision of American life."[36]

This interpretation of the celebrity and disaster pictures is framed in terms of Warhol's (supposed) intentions. The question of the nature of Warhol's attitude to the phenomena that served him as subject-matter was a live one already in the 1960s; now Crow (like Crone) finds social criticism where others find a cynical celebration of consumer culture and John Coplans, in his 1971 catalogue,

34 T. Crone, "Saturday disasters," p. 327.
35 Ibid., pp. 313, 317, 320, 313.
36 Ibid. pp. 322, 324.

found a "strictly neutral" attitude, "neither for the material nor against it."[37] Coplans's view at least had the virtue of conforming to Warhol's own description of his work as expressing not a political position but indifference.[38] But Warhol is well known for the falsity of his information about himself, which lends force to Crow's insistence that any critical account of the work "will necessarily stand or fall on the visual evidence."[39]

But how is that evidence to be understood? Crow's readings of individual images, basically associationist in method, are imaginative. The silkscreened face of the star in *Gold Marilyn Monroe* (Figure 9.1, overleaf), for example, seems to him to resemble memory in being selective, elusive, vivid in parts, and "always open to embellishment as well as loss." The sentiment in the Jackie portraits strikes him as "direct and uncomplicated"; these pictures recognize by their use of the "impoverished vocabulary" of news photographs "the distance between public mourning and that of the principals in the drama." In the *Tunafish Disaster* pictures "the repetition of the crude images" forces "attention to the awful banality of the accident and the tawdry exploitation by which we come to know the misfortunes of strangers."[40]

None of this, I have to say, seems to me to follow upon "the visual evidence." Basic to these interpretations is the idea that Warhol's treatment of his sources effects a distancing from them—a distancing which, given the nature of the material and his own attitudes to it, Crow cannot help but see as critical. It was this idea that led him, against the visual evidence, to seek the source of *Gold Marilyn Monroe* in a combination of two studio stills.[41] In the revised version of his article, Crow views Warhol's cropping and enlargement of a black-and-white still as draining away "much of the imaginary living presence of the star." In this way Warhol's treatment is said to avoid, at least to a significant extent, Hollywood's "reduction of a woman's identity to a mass-commodity fetish" and to exhibit "a degree of tact, even reverence, that withholds outright complicity" with that reduction.[42] It is, of course, true that Warhol's picture looks different from and functions differently from a publicity still. As a picture *of a photograph* it comments directly on what Crow calls the fetishization of the person pictured. And it is a response to a death. But to reduce it to an expression of the sentiment of mourning is to leave unexplained much of its interest and power.

First of all, as Crow seems to have forgotten, while the actual woman was dead, the image remained (and remains) very much alive. The Marilyn pictures unite two of Warhol's lifelong preoccupations, death and celebrity. As an image

37 John Coplans, *Andy Warhol* (Greenwich: American Graphic Society, 1970), p. 49.
38 See the discussion with Glaser and others in Mahsun, *Pop Art*, p. 153.
39 Crow, "Saturday disasters," p. 312.
40 Ibid., pp. 316, 317, 320.
41 Compare the version of "Saturday disasters" in *Art in America*, p. 133, with that in the Guilbaut volume, p. 326 n. 8.
42 Crow, "Saturday disasters," p. 315.

Figure 9.1 Andy Warhol, *Gold Marilyn Monroe*, 1962, © The Andy Warhol Foundation for the Visual Arts, Inc./ARS, NY and DACS, London 2003. Courtesy of The Museum of Modern Art/Licensed by SCALA/Art Resource, NY.

of fame, Monroe's face is like the Campbell's label or the portraits of Mao Warhol later copied; as a memento mori it sits alongside the *Tunafish Disaster* victims, the electric chair, and the skull paintings of 1976. (Crow seems to me wrong to declare that the *Flowers* series and silver pillows of 1961–6 "have little to do with the imagery under discussion here";[43] as Coplans observed, these too can usefully be considered part of his wide-ranging iconography of death.)[44]

These themes do not just cohabit here; death and glamour are closely related in Warhol's world.[45] Crow has missed this because his *kulturkritisch* framework allows him to see in the studio still nothing but "the reduction of a woman's

43 Ibid., p. 324.
44 Coplans, *Andy Warhol*, p. 52.
45 Smith explores this, obscurely, in *Andy Warhol's Art and Films*, pp. 121–5.

identity to a mass-commodity fetish," a commercial pandering to "the erotic fascination" felt for Monroe by "male intellectuals of the fifties generation" like Norman Mailer and de Kooning.[46] In the only reference to Warhol's sexuality in Crow's essay, he is said to have "obviously had little stake" in the erotics of MM. This is to misunderstand profoundly the stake of the gay male subculture within which Warhol moved—as it misunderstands the stake of many others in female movie stars, as representatives of desire and desirability, of the artificiality of gender roles, and of the conflict between appearance and reality. Monroe dead, for some purposes, can be superior to Monroe alive; the image of pleasure stands then in counterpoint to a secret reality of pain, and the eternal life of the visible acquires a kick from the sad destruction of the bodily unseen.

Warhol's *Marilyns* should be put not in the context of the artist's imagined sentiments at her death but in that of his lifelong interest in female sexual glamour precisely as separable from the "woman's identity,"[47] which in any case has no existence, as a reality distinct from the complex of discourses constructing the star, for the movie fan. Similarly, given that there is no reason in the biographical record to imagine any deep attachment to John F. Kennedy on Warhol's part, it sees to me more plausible to see the various *Jackies* as a response to her TV stardom at the time of her husband's assassination, which only added to the complexity of her already glamorous image.[48] She lines up not only with Marilyn and Liz but with all the self-destructive "superstars" of Warhol's filming days, Edie Sedgwick in the forefront; with his collection of designer dresses of years gone by; and with the drag queens by whom the artist was always deeply fascinated, above all the beautiful, Marilyn-imitating Candy Darling (and let us not forget Christopher Makos's portrait photograph of Warhol in blond-wig drag). "Drags are ambulatory archives of ideal moviestar womanhood," Warhol wrote in *The Philosophy of Andy Warhol*. "They perform a documentary service, usually consecrating their lives to keeping the glittering alternative alive and available

---

46 Crow, "Saturday disasters," p. 315.

47 Which, if represented anywhere in Warhol's oeuvre, might be identified, unpleasantly, in the *Cow Wallpaper*—or even in *Tunafish*.

48 The closest I have encountered is John Giorno's memory:

> We heard Walter Cronkite say "President Kennedy died at 2 p.m.," we started hugging each other, pressing our bodies together and trembling. I started crying and Andy started crying. We wept big fat tears. It was a symbol of the catastrophe of our own lives. We kissed and Andy sucked by tongue. It was the first time we kissed. It had the sweet taste of kissing death. It was all exhilarating, like when you get kicked in the head and see stars.
>
> Quoted in Andrew O'Hagan, "Many Andies," review of *Shoes, Shoes, Shoes*, by Warhol; *Style, Style, Style* by Warhol; *Who Is Andy Warhol?*, ed. Colin MacCabe, Mark Francis, and Peter Wollen; *All Tomorrow's Parties: Billy Name's Photographs of Andy Warhol's Factory*, by Billy Name; and *The Last Party: Studio 54, Disco, and the Culture of the Night*, by Anthony Haden-Guest, *London Review of Books* (October 16, 1977), p. 12

for (not-too-close) inspection."[49] I do no more than touch on the implications of this statement with regard to Warhol's "documentary" pictures when I note that the "alternative" cherished is relative to straight, "middle-class" existence (the very one that meets its comeuppance in the *Tunafish Disaster*, which also features dead women). It is the life of fame, wealth, and glamour Warhol always wanted, even while he saw its limitations and costs, the gap that would always exist between the appearance and reality of wealth and power, and the fact that in the end you die.

And this is the source, I believe, of the effectiveness of his *Marilyn* pictures. Crow's contrast with James Rosenquist's *Marilyn II* (Figure 9.2)—that the latter preserves the star's "false [*sic*] seductiveness" while Warhol's portrait strives for "some seriousness"—seems to me to get it just backwards.[50] Rosenquist subordinates Monroe to his signature style, actually cutting up her image in the process, while Warhol keeps that face, with its signature smile, intact. Warhol's use of the image is so close to the image itself—thanks to the photo-based silkscreen technique, which interposes only the thinnest Warholian layer between the original still and the artwork we see—that it partakes of the mass of dissonant meanings carried by Monroe's face. To understand this requires response to Monroe not just as an exemplar of women's oppression but as a star, just as appreciation of the electric chair images must acknowledge a psychologically complex fascination with the instrument pictured. And this in turn means taking as seriously as Warhol did what Crow has elsewhere called "the degraded materials of capitalist manufacture"[51] and which he is here too quick to dismiss as mere "pulp materials."[52]

Less inclined to sentimentalize about Warhol's emotional response, Benjamin Buchloh shares with Crow (and Crone) a preoccupation with art and mass culture as twin products of bourgeois society and a characterization of avant-garde art as a matter of "strategies of negation and critical resistance" in the face of that society.[53] As he sees it, Warhol "'embodied' the paradox of modernist art: to be suspended between high art's . . . critical negativity and the pervasive debris of corporate-dominated mass culture."[54] In Warhol's case this "paradox" took the form of a contradiction between his own "opportunistic, conformist, and conservative" politics and his work's "interventions in traditional ideologies of artistic production and reception." Where Crone and Crow, in different ways, deal with this problem by constructing a personality capable of "critical negativity,"

49 Warhol, *The Philosophy of Andy Warhol (From A to B and Back Again)* (New York, 1975), p. 54.
50 Crow, "Saturday disasters," p. 133.
51 Thomas Crow, "Modernism and mass culture in the visual arts," in B. Buchloh, S. Guilbaut, and D. Solkin (ed.), *Modernism and Modernity* (Halifax, 1983), p. 215.
52 Crow, "Saturday disasters," p. 324.
53 Buchloh, "Andy Warhol line," p. 55.
54 Buchloh, "One-dimensional," p. 39.

Figure 9.2 James Rosenquist, *Marilyn II*, 1962, © James Rosenquist/VAGA, New
York/DACS, London 2003. Image courtesy of The Museum of Modern
Art/Licensed by SCALA/Art Resource, NY.

Buchloh sees the political limitations of Warhol's personality as ultimately setting
limits to the "aesthetic and subversive 'intensity'" of his art.[55]

What Buchloh says about Warhol's earliest work with art-cultural pretensions
sets the pattern for his analysis of the production of the 1960s as a whole: that
the "task" Warhol set for himself was the destruction of the "metaphysical residue" that, clinging to painting, limited its utility as a "device" of negation. This

55 Buchloh, "Andy Warhol line," p. 64.

he accomplished by the "contamination" of the modernist artwork "with the vulgarity of the most trivial of commonplaces" (Buchloh here has in mind the matchbook-cover paintings of 1962). The adoption of the silkscreen technique emphasized the photographic image and substituted a mechanical mark for Abstract Expressionist gesture.[56] In this Buchloh follows in Crone's footsteps; all that is missing is a quotation from Benjamin (the other major source of the analytic framework employed here is, of course, Benjamin's fellow Frankfurter, Theodor Adorno).

Corresponding on the iconographic plane to the use of mechanical reproduction, according to Buchloh, is "the abolition of the hierarchy of subjects worthwhile representing." As Buchloh sees it, the lasting fascination of the paintings of Marilyn, Liz, and Elvis "does not originate in the myth of these figures, but in the fact that Warhol constructed their images from the perspective of the tragic condition of those who consume the stars' images."[57] Because he made the point of view of these consumers that of his art Warhol was unable to pass beyond the demolition of art's pretensions to an active resistance to the "state of general semiotic *anomie*" represented by "the advanced forms of the culture industry."[58]

Just as the conventional emphasis on the mechanical aspect of serigraphy misses, I have argued, the actual effect of paint handling produced in the printing process, so Buchloh's idea that Warhol's images reveal glamour to be only the reflex of "collective scopic fixation" reduces the consumers of mass culture to manipulated victims, erasing them as subjects.[59] This is—to repeat an argument I have already made, in a different form, with respect to Crow—to ignore the ways in which mass culture, like art culture, serves as a means for the active construction of subjectivity. Buchloh speaks of "semiotic *anomie*" because he does not care about the semiotics of the movies, advertising, fashion, and the news. But Warhol did care about such things. For him, as for most people, the myths mattered. It was this actual involvement in "vulgarity" that led Warhol to the insight that Marilyn, Jackie, and Mao share an identity as media constructions, along with the victims of car accidents and civil rights marchers attacked by police dogs. This identity is artificial, but it provides materials that people work with, just as leftish art writers can find in Warhol's paintings a critique of consumer culture.

In criticizing the writings on Warhol by Danto, Crone, Crow, and Buchloh, I have not meant to assert an incompatibility between close observation of works of art and the employment of theory, philosophical or otherwise, in their interpretation. What I have meant to challenge is the insistence on certain theoretical constructs in the face of artistic phenomena—meaning both artworks and their

---

56 Buchloh, "One-dimensional," p. 48; see p. 50.
57 Ibid., p. 53.
58 Buchloh, "One dimensional," pp. 65, 66; see also p. 68.
59 Buchloh, "One-dimensional," p. 57.

contexts of production and consumption—which they are not suited to describe. In all the cases I have considered, despite the important differences between the writers' perspectives, analysis rests on a certain conception of art as the carrier of high spiritual value, in contrast to the artifacts of everyday life. For Danto, to quote the title of his first book on aesthetics, art involves "transfiguration of the commonplace," indeed, the expression in visual form of philosophical insights. For Crone, Crow, and Buchloh, in variants of what one might call a left-modernist version of this idea, art embodies, or ought to embody, a critique of the alienation and oppressiveness of capitalist society by constituting a concretely existing alternative to the meretricious products of consumer culture. But it was exactly this conception of art in opposition to the everyday that Warhol's work challenged.

Warhol is certainly part of the history of art, but his story marks an acceleration of the decline of the classical form of that institution. This decline is evident in a range of phenomena, from the expansion of the category of art (as embodied, for instance, in museum practice) to contain not just photographs and films but mass consumption goods themselves, to the growing willingness of even those concerned professionally with art to acknowledge its commodity character.

Far from seeking to justify the specialness of art, mounting a critique of its degradation under modern conditions or of the emptiness of consumer culture, Warhol embraced the commercial aspect of high art and celebrated the sign system of "popular" culture. This is one reason it is a mistake to sever Warhol's work of the 1960s from his later production, for the earlier work foreshadowed what one writer has called the "unexpected marriage" consecrated in the 1980s: "The slow, inexorable decline of ideology typical of this entire period was matched by a euphoric celebration of art and the market—business joined hands with creativity."[60] Warhol did not need to take on the Benjaminian or Adornian "task" of demystifying art; rather, the development of bourgeois society in accomplishing this created a space into which he could move to make a place for himself in the art business. The fit between his sensibility and that space is at least one important reason why his work has the power it does, a power as great, at times, as that of the movies or newspaper photos themselves. The key to its power lies on the surface, not in philosophic depths—on surfaces like Marilyn's face, a newspaper headline, or a cereal box, with depths enough of their own for millions to swim in.

---

60 Paul Ardenne, "The art market in the 1980s," *International Journal of Political Economy* 25:2 (1995), p. 100.

10

THE AVANT-GARDE
IN FASHION

The March 1, 1951 issue of *Vogue* contained four pages reproducing photographs made by Cecil Beaton in the Betty Parsons Gallery in New York, which have become well-known images among art historians and theorists dealing with Abstract Expressionism (Figure 10.1).[1] They are part of a story called "American Fashion: The New Soft Look," which follows a "Quick Tour of the Paris Collections." The backdrops are paintings by Jackson Pollock, described in the accompanying copy as "spirited and brilliant," "dazzling and curious" pictures that "almost always cause an intensity of feelings." This aesthetic description is doubled by a social one: they are said to be admired by "some of the most astute private collectors and museum directors in the country."

It is easy to see why these images have come to haunt contemporary studies of Pollock's work: their elegant composition brings into juxtaposition a set of polar categories that have been used to talk about art throughout the modern period: avant-garde and fashion, abstraction and representation, autonomy and decoration, painting and photography, production and consumption, masculinity and femininity, art and commerce. As we have seen in earlier chapters of this book, these pairs are not independent of each other; as a group they structure the field of discourse concerning the making and receiving of modern art. Beaton's pictures take us to particular versions of these issues activated in New York in 1951, but which are still alive today, half a century later.

Thus T. J. Clark begins and ends his much-discussed essay on Jackson Pollock's abstract painting, reworked for his book *Farewell to an Idea*, with Beaton's pictures. The "idea" of Clark's title is modernism, which he defines in the tradition of Theodor Adorno and the early Clement Greenberg as an aesthetic analogue to socialist politics. In Clark's words:

---

1 So far as I know, the first art-historical mention of Beaton's pictures is in Phyllis Rosenzweig, *The Fifties: Aspects of Painting in New York* (Washington: Hirshhorn Museum and Sculpture Garden, 1980), p. 13. The historically best-informed treatment remains Richard Martin, "'The New Soft Look': Jackson Pollock, Cecil Beaton, and American fashion in 1951," *Dress* 7 (1981), pp. 1–8.

Figure 10.1 Cecil Beaton, "Jackson Pollock's Abstractions," *Vogue*, March 1, 1951,
p. 159, © *Vogue*, The Condé Nast Publications Inc.

There is a line of art stretching back to David and Shelley which makes
no sense—which would not have existed—without its practitioners
believing that what they did was resist or exceed the normal understandings of [bourgeois] culture, and that these understandings were
their enemy. This is the line of art we call modernist.[2]

2 T. J. Clark, *Farewell to an Idea* (New Haven: Yale University Press, 1999), p. 364; subsequent page
  references to this volume will be placed within parentheses in the text.

Just as—to take another matter discussed in Clark's book—the Russian Revolution embodied aspirations for a better world, modernism attempted to break with artistic expressions of the existing social reality, acting out, consciously or unconsciously, utopian aspirations.

In his 1939 essay "Avant-garde and kitsch," Clement Greenberg had explicitly tied the emergence of what he was later to call "Modernist" art to the rise of a socialist opposition to capitalist society in the nineteenth century. The socialist critique was absorbed, "even if unconsciously for the most part," by artists and writers who drew on revolutionary ideas to define themselves in antagonism to "the bourgeois," their normal public. This antagonism served them well when class conflict threw into question "all the verities involved by religion, authority, tradition, style, . . . and the writer or artist [was] no longer able to estimate the response of his audience to the symbols and references with which he works."[3] Once artistic form—the material of which now destabilized "symbols and references" is made—is detached from its former standardized representational uses, the artist comes to try to make an object which will be meaningful by virtue of having no subject-matter beside itself. This can, in practice, only mean an object whose significance is given by the materials and practices of art-making. "This is the genesis of the 'abstract.' In turning his attention away from subject matter of common experience, the poet or artist turns it upon the medium of his own craft."[4] Modernism in this way turns cultural resistance to the established social order into the formal stuff of art.

In an earlier essay on Greenberg's theory of art, Clark declined to join in with "the patter about art being 'revolutionary'."[5] What then does it mean to speak, more mildly, of art's "resistance" to the dominant culture? Clark's answer in the Pollock essay evokes the familiar "shock of the new": it is to refer to "some form of intransigence or difficulty in the [art] object produced, some action against the codes and procedures by which the world was lent its usual likeness" (p. 364). That Clark means something with more bite to it than such modern art-appreciation bromides suggest emerges in his more detailed discussion of Pollock's abstract painting between 1947 and 1950. In Clark's view, figurative painting by the 1940s was "an agreed order of images . . . overlaid with lies" (p. 364). Pollock's painting, by rejecting figuration in the particular way it did, proposed the existence of "a kind of experience . . . not colonized or banalized by the ruling symbolic regimes," which is "not occupied by the usual discursive forces because it is a wilderness" (p. 335).

But if this was modernism's ambition in the particular conditions of New York City in the late 1940s, the *Vogue* story, Clark writes, actualized "the bad dream of modernism," (p. 308) the thought that "however urgent the impulse had been to

---

3 Clement Greenberg, "Avant-garde and kitsch," in *idem, Art and Culture* (Boston: Beacon Press, 1961), p. 4.

4 Ibid., p. 6.

5 T. J. Clark, "Clement Greenberg's theory of art," *Critical Inquiry* 9:1 (1982), p. 156.

recast aesthetic practice and move out into uncolonized areas of experience," the result could only be the incorporation of new territory into the domain of bourgeois culture. Just as the Bolshevik seizure of power in fact marked not victory over oppression but the inauguration of a new form of it, modernism's aspirations led to a double failure, meeting not only with the inherent weakness of fine art as a form of social action but with its inevitable incorporation into the visual practices of capitalist society. Any success in representing the hitherto unrepresented, the "wilderness"—say, through the use of poured paint as a metaphor for spontaneity—served ultimately to bring it inside the dominant sign system, perhaps providing a vocabulary of images required by the postwar consumer culture. Beaton's photographs literally transformed Pollock's abstractions into grounds for his fashion-plate figures, emblems of class privilege.

> The photographs are nightmarish. They speak to the hold of capitalist culture: that is, to the ease with which it can outflank work done against the figurative, and make it part of a new order of pleasures—a sign of that order's richness, of the room it has made for more of the edges and underneath of everyday life.
>
> (p. 365)

Abstraction, developed in opposition to the banality of figurative art, is absorbed as no more than a new style into bourgeois culture. The wilderness is pacified, developed, cut up into lots for sale. Thus Beaton's pictures "show the sort of place reserved within capitalism for painting like Pollock's." Nonetheless, Clark insists, while doomed to submit, Pollock's painting "fights for room" (p. 365) within and against that place; specifically, the recurring suggestion of the figure (in various forms) in Pollock's work enacts the struggle against bourgeois "codes and conventions" as a central motif. Most generally, in Clark's view, Pollock works "against metaphor: that is to say, against any one of his pictures settling down inside a single metaphorical frame," (pp. 331–9) thus fighting its utilization for new forms of bourgeois expression. The "fact or fear" of its absorption by the society that is its enemy, Clark argues, "is internalized by modernism and built into its operations; it is part, even cause, of modern painting's way with its medium" (p. 308). What this means in Pollock's case is the burden of Clark's essay. The limitations of this way of construing modernism's relationship to modern society is the topic of this chapter.

Pollock's abstraction

The most successful art style in the United States during the 1930s and 1940s was a modernist-inflected form of naturalism that went by the name of Regionalism; its leading practitioners, featured in such national magazines as *Time* and *Life*, were John Stuart Curry and Thomas Hart Benton, Pollock's teacher at the Art Students League in New York. It is not unfair to describe this style, which celebrated an imaginary America of productive farms, muscular workers, and singing, gambling "darkies," as "overlaid with lies." But Pollock was by no means an innovator in painting abstractly in New York in the later 1940s. The 1936 exhibition "Cubism and Abstract Art" that Alfred Barr organized at the Museum of Modern Art presented an organized review of art that artists had been responding to in this city and elsewhere for more than two decades.[6] 1936 also saw the formation of the American Abstract Artists (AAA), an artists' group that mounted regular exhibitions and campaigned in favor of abstraction. By the mid-1930s, the issue of abstraction in relation to representation was hotly debated, in political, general cultural, and purely artistic terms.

I have already cited Greenberg's essay on the avant-garde; to take another example, John Graham, artist and friend of Pollock (whom he was one of the first to promote), wrote in his 1937 book *System and Dialectics of Art* that "academico-impressionist art methods regardless of the subject matter only lull the masses gently to sleep, . . . abstract art with its revolutionary methods stirs their imagination (negatively at first so as to gather speed) to thinking and consequently to action."[7] In *Art Front*, the monthly publication of activist artists grouped in the leftist Artists' Union and Artists' Committee of Action, Clarence Weinstock criticized the work shown in the 1935 Whitney Museum exhibition "Abstract Painting in America" for the "absence of meaning" to which purist abstraction is doomed by its limitation to issues of form. The modern artist should see "that the conflicts of classes of society, insofar as they are embodied in individuals, are as much a part of his . . . aesthetic experience as . . . two planes, grey and yellow, intersecting at a precise angle." Abstract painting cannot deal resolutely with such subject-matter because, confining itself to relations between forms, it is "at the mercy of whatever physical associations the spectator has in mind."[8] In reply, Stuart Davis insisted that while abstraction is not in general the expression of class consciousness, it is "the result of a revolutionary struggle relative to . . . bourgeois academic conditions . . . In the materialism of abstract art in general, is implicit a negation of many ideals dear to the bourgeois heart."[9]

Pollock's innovation, as is often said, lay in using abstraction for the formulation of intense emotional content, as opposed (for example) to the impersonal purity that geometrical abstractionists claimed for their goal. Before 1947 Pollock, influenced by French and Mexican styles, as well as by his teacher Benton, indicated content by way of various kinds of deformed representation, employing a vocabulary of signs drawing on the primitivism and archaism current in his artistic circle. But the tendencies toward abstraction operative in New York had

6 For an overview of this history, see Eric de Chassey, *La Peinture efficace. Une histoire de l'abstraction aux États-Unis (1911–1960)* (Paris: Gallimard, 2001).

7 Marcia E. Allentuck (ed.), *John Graham's System and Dialectics of Art* (Baltimore: Johns Hopkins University Press, 1971), p. 137.

8 Clarence Weinstock, "Contradictions in abstractions," *Art Front* 1:5 (April 1935), p. 7.

9 Stuart Davis, "A medium of 2 dimensions," *Art Front* 1:6 (May 1935), p. 6.

Figure 10.2 Jackson Pollock, *Guardians of the Secret*, 1943, © Pollock–Krasner
Foundation/ARS, New York and DACS, London

a clear effect. Pollock's 1943 painting *Guardians of the Secret* (Figure 10.2) now
seems a prophecy of what was to come: figures at left and right, with "totemic"
elements above and below, stand over a plane on which an imaginary writing
system spells out the secret of the title. In writing, line signifies without representing. It neither indicates the edges of objects nor outlines planes. It shares the
image within an image here with similarly nonrepresentational areas of color
establishing a picture plane on which the linear symbols lie.

The same year saw the production of a gigantic painting—about twenty feet
by eight—designed to fit the hallway of the new apartment of Pollock's dealer
and patron, Peggy Guggenheim. The black linear elements that move across this
work are clearly figural in origin, but color follows these lines or fits into spaces
between them, so that it no longer functions to define a ground. Guggenheim's
friend and adviser Marcel Duchamp suggested the picture be painted on canvas,
making it removable when she moved house. Lee Krasner, soon to be Pollock's
wife, named it *Mural*. Pollock referred to this picture four years later, in his application for a Guggenheim Foundation fellowship, as a precedent for paintings he
hoped to make: "large movable pictures which will function between the easel
and mural."[10]

Pollock did not get the fellowship. But *Mural* pointed in the direction of the
pictures he was to produce in the next few years: often very large, but painted

10 Pepe Karmel (ed.), *Jackson Pollock: Interviews, Articles, and Reviews* (New York: Museum of Modern
Art, 1999), p. 17.

157

on canvas. The works in what became his "signature" style of poured and dripped as well as brushed paint were not made on the easel, however, but on the floor. Neither strictly mural nor easel paintings, Pollock's work of 1941–50 can indeed be said to lie between these in function; I will return shortly to the question of function.

His "drip" technique established the canvas as the ground of the picture: the physical ground is the visual ground. On this lie various sorts of line, which once again define neither planes nor figures. Along with the abandonment of earlier normal functions of line pictorial space tends to vaporize. Differences in value, color, and thickness of line or paint area (as well as other objects that may be embedded in the picture surface) typically generate a hazy, pulsating spatiality in these pictures, like a thinned-out and flowing version of cubist space.

Perhaps it was no accident that it was Piet Mondrian—important influence on the geometric abstractionists in the AAA, a friend of AAA member Lee Krasner—who gave Pollock a big break by urging Peggy Guggenheim to take his work seriously. In Mondrian's "Neo-Plasticist" pictures, too, line neither outlines forms nor defines planes. While planes, rendered as flat areas of solid color, are present, they are not grounds on which figures can appear, and are no more—and no less—than equals of the lines. (In some works the distinction between a thick line and a narrow plane is arbitrary.) One consequence of this pictorial method is that Mondrian's pictures completely fill the picture space, as opposed to the centrality of image typical of Cubism. This edge-to-edge character of Mondrian's paintings combines the exquisite balancing of elements that makes each a totality with the suggestion that what we are seeing stands in for a greater totality that continues beyond the framing edge.

A related idea emerged in the form of a negative judgment on Pollock's pictures when in 1948 *Life* magazine convened a panel of experts to consider the question, "Is modern art, considered as a whole, a good or bad development? That is to say, is it something that responsible people can support, or may they neglect it as a minor and impermanent phase of culture?"[11] This question about modern art had to do particularly with abstraction, which foregrounded the picture as an object of interest in its own right by abandoning the modes of representation and narrative central to the meaning of earlier art. The absence of figurative content seemed to rob Pollock's pictures, in particular, of the formal identity that made serious significance possible. Speaking of the 1947 painting *Cathedral*, panel member Aldous Huxley said, "It raises a question of why it stops when it does . . . It seems to me like a panel for a wallpaper which is repeated indefinitely around the wall."[12]

---

11 Russell W. Davenport and Winthrop Sargeant, "A *Life* Round Table on modern art," *Life* 25 (October 11, 1948), p. 56.

12 Ibid., p. 62. Interestingly, people had already spoken about *Mural* in these terms; according to Clement Greenberg, "People were saying it goes on and on, repeating itself, but I told Jackson,

Such a view is more plausible in relation to *Cathedral* than to most of Pollock's drip paintings. Even in a relatively edge-to-edge work like *Full Fathom Five* (also from 1947) his looping marks draw his images away from the edges; the resulting centeredness is one of the things that links them, in contrast to Mondrian's work, to earlier painting and limits what Greenberg called their "allover" character. But the problem of decorativeness, seen as a fault, had long been raised for abstract painting generally. Clement Greenberg himself—a member of the *Life* panel and by that time Pollock's champion—had written of the very danger evoked by Huxley's criticism in a 1941 review of works by Miró, Kandinsky, and Léger, which showed, he felt, "how easy it is for the abstract painter to degenerate into a decorator." This is "the besetting danger of abstract art" (although, Greenberg also insisted, to be an interior decorator "is still . . . to be more creative than an academic painter").

The rejection of depiction of natural and social phenomena in favor of concentration on the artist's picture-making material and procedures was a major reason, Greenberg thought, why modern painters could not "cover large spaces successfully," as recent mural painting demonstrated:

> We, with our tradition of easel painting, are not satisfied to have our pictorial art in the form of decoration. We demand of a picture what we demand of literature and music: dramatic interest, interior movement . . . It is the task of the abstract artist to satisfy this requirement with the limited means at his disposal. He cannot resort to the means of the past, for they have been made stale by overuse, and to take them up again would be to rob his art of its originality and real excitement.[13]

In 1943 Greenberg described *Guardians of the Secret* as zigzagging "between the intensity of the easel picture and the blandness of the mural."[14] One thing Greenberg found in Pollock's later work, then, was successful large-scale painting, fulfilling the "function" of the easel painting—visual drama—in wall-sized works.

'*That* is great art'" (Jeffrey Potter, *To a Violent Grave: An Oral Biography of Jackson Pollock* (New York: G. P. Putnam's Sons, 1985), p. 76).

13 Clement Greenberg, *The Collected Essays and Criticism*, vol. 1, *Perceptions and Judgments, 1931–1944*, ed. John O'Brian (Chicago: University of Chicago Press, 1986), pp. 61–5. Greenberg's next-written review essay, on Paul Klee, continued this theme:

> The difficulty which besets the abstract painter in so far as he wants to create more than decoration is that of overcoming the inertia into which his picture always risks falling because of its flatness. The easel-painting . . . relies upon the illusion of depth, of composition in depth and upon dramatic interest for the intensity of the effect it must have to overcome its smallness and its isolation.
>
> Ibid., p. 69

14 Ibid., p. 165.

But what function, or functions, belong to the mural? One is what Greenberg identified as the danger run by abstraction: decoration of a surface, that is, a function subordinate to the structural and visual work performed by a wall (or ceiling).[15] This was certainly not a function Pollock wished to fulfill: although he was interested in working with architects, he said to his friend, the architect Peter Blake, "You architects think of my work as being a kind of wallpaper, potentially decorative."[16] What Pollock had in mind was more along the lines of Mies van der Rohe's idea of "an ideal museum in which the paintings would be large walls, free-standing, and with sculpture"[17]—a vision anticipated in part, perhaps, by *Mural*. With painting-walls made to measure, such a museum would be not a repository of the art of the past—even of the modernist past, as in the Museum of Modern Art—but a demonstration of the significance of the contemporary avant-garde.

Decoration

Modernist painters and architects had long shared the condemnation of decoration. In the 1912 text *Du "Cubisme,"* in which Albert Gleizes and Jean Metzinger explained Cubism as a style, they insist that decoration is "the antithesis of the picture," as it is "essentially dependent, necessarily incomplete" while the easel painting "bears its pretext, the reason for its existence, within it." Portable from context to context, it is, as a meaningful object, autonomous in relation to all of them. "It does not harmonize with this or that environment; it harmonizes with things in general, with the universe."[18] The supposedly neutral white cube of the gallery space or the modern house is therefore its ideal home: the undecorated building is the counterpart of the autonomous art object on display within it.

Twelve years after Adolf Loos's 1908 denunciation of architectural ornament as "crime," Le Corbusier and Ozenfant criticized Mondrian's abstractions,

---

15 Curiously enough, it was as decorations that Burgoyne Diller, director of the mural division of the Works Progress Administration's Federal Artists Project in New York between 1935 and 1941, was able to procure abstract mural commissions in a number of public buildings. As he later explained, "they didn't have to be called art—abstract or anything. So the name was a dangerous thing. I found in other places that we introduced abstract work just simply by calling it . . . 'the decoration'" (quoted in Barbara Haskell, *Burgoyne Diller* (New York: Whitney Museum of American Art, 1990), p. 64).

16 Potter, *To a Violent Grave*, p. 94.

17 Ibid., p. 104.

18 Herschel B. Chipp (ed.), *Theories of Modern Art: A Source Book by Artists and Critics* (Berkeley: University of California Press, 1968), pp. 201–10. David Cottington notes the "apparent contradiction between what those artists said in their manifesto and their loan of paintings to the Maison Cubiste's *salon bourgeois*," exhibited in Paris in 1912—an indicator of the complexity of the story of decoration and modernism ("The Maison Cubiste and the meaning of modernism in pre-1914 France," in Eve Blau and Nancy Troy (eds), *Architecture and Cubism* (Cambridge: MIT Press, 1997), p. 28).

"stripped of human resonance," as "ornamental art."[19] What this responded to correctly was Mondrian's at least partial rejection of the ideal of the autonomous art object. Art, in his view, is not autonomous in relation to "everyday life" but manifests, and can itself be among, the forces shaping life. For Mondrian, painting was the area in which aesthetic progress was being made most rapidly. "In our time," he wrote in 1922, "each work of art can only remain isolated." But this is only because architecture and, beyond it, city planning, is limited by financial and political forces that inhibit the modern tendency to an organization of life satisfying the needs of everyone. Painting shows the way, but when it is followed, art as such—easel painting—will disappear. By the same token, in the architecture of the future, ornament—a decorative element distinct from the articulation of the built environment—will also disappear. Beauty will be "no longer an 'accessory' but . . . in the architecture itself."[20]

Mondrian's paintings, as he thought of them, demanded the reconfiguration of the room in which they hung, the house that contained that room, the street in which the house was situated, and the city that contained the street.[21] In reality they ended up in individual homes or—mostly—in the white cubes of museum galleries, where they are set beside non-neo-plastic works as milestones in the history of art. Pollock's *Mural* accepted this fate from the start, its canvas support implying portability, its dimensions fixed by those of Peggy Guggenheim's hallway, not by some necessity of design at the heart of its own existence.

What is the function of the modern large painting such as Pollock made, then? It can only be to make a claim for the importance of art on a scale equal to that of any private or public space. The mural painting of Benton, like those of Clemente Orozco and of the other Mexican muralists who influenced Pollock, presented itself as public art, the present-day equivalent of Renaissance fresco decoration of palaces and city halls. Its association with institutions of state, economy, or education justified its size and suggested its content. Pollock's paintings of the late 1940s suggest this scale without the social support.[22] They address not

19 Quoted from *L'Esprit nouveau* 1 (October 1920) in Christopher Green, *Cubism and its Enemies: Modern Movements and Reaction in French Art, 1911–1928* (New Haven: Yale University Press, 1987), p. 222. This critique was echoed in New York in the 1940s, notably in Barnett Newman's declaration that geometrical abstraction "has reduced painting to an ornamental art" ("The plasmic image," in *idem, Selected Writings and Interviews*, ed. John P. O'Neill (New York: Alfred A. Knopf, 1990), p. 139).

20 Piet Mondrian, "The realization of neo-plasticism in the distant future and in architecture today" (1922), in Harry Holtzman and Martin S. James, (eds and trs), *The New Art—The New Life: The Collected Writings of Piet Mondrian* (New York: Da Capo, 1993), pp. 170, 172.

21 See Piet Mondrian, "Home—Street—City" (1926), in Holtzman and James, *The New Art*, pp. 201–12.

22 As Sidney Tillim expressed it, "if modernism's monumentality has been conceptually circumscribed, it is partly because the distinction between mural and easel concepts [has] been blurred due to a lack of real walls to paint on" ("Scale and the future of Modernism," *Artforum* 6:2 (October 1967), pp. 11–18), p. 16.

the masses (of workers or citizens) but individuals; their goal, as Meyer Schapiro pointed out in a penetrating essay of 1957, is not communication (like the majority of contemporary media), but to offer an experience of "contemplativeness and communion with the work of another human being."[23] Combining mural scale with the individual address of the easel painting, their meaningfulness rests on the assumed significance of the artist's preoccupations and artistic procedures. The drama of the painter's creative struggle to make his work (I will come back, once again, to the artist's sex) and the painting's location in the ongoing history of art must by themselves provide the "interior movement" Greenberg looked for on a scale sufficient to animate a wall-sized picture. Such a painting, Schapiro observed, can compete with its environment, and "command our attention fully like monumental painting in the past."[24] If it is seen as wallpaper, as subject to repetition or as decorative, this means either the failure of the work or the failure of the viewer to grasp its autonomous significance.

Pollock's fellow-artists Mark Rothko and Adolph Gottlieb had attempted a preemptive strike at such readings or misreadings in a public statement of 1943. "We are for the large shape because it has the impact of the unequivocal," they wrote. Professing "spiritual kinship with primitive and archaic art" they asserted that their work "must insult anyone who is spiritually attuned to interior decoration."[25] In 1950, nevertheless, *Vogue* published a photograph of a Rothko painting (again at the Betty Parsons Gallery) in an article entitled "Make up your mind: one-picture wall or many-picture wall" (April 14, 1950). The story contrasted the large-format Rothko with a "wall space used for a composite still-life of small prints, paintings, and objects" arranged in "an abstract pattern." The Rothko was similarly described as "a single still-life composed of abstract gradations of line and color." Despite the apparent differences, the article insisted, "the wall spaces in these two photographs come from the same impulse—the use of a variety of shapes and colors to make a simple design." Abstraction and representation alike serve as "still lifes" of design elements, as decoration for a wall. Gone is the impact of the unequivocal, the primitive and mythic content. In its stead we have interior decoration, a setting—in the case of the Beaton pictures—for the New Soft Look of the new decade. In Pollock's ideal museum, the living figure is a spectator of the space-dominating work of art; in *Vogue*'s version, the work of art is a backdrop for the figure who is herself (again, sex will have to be discussed) the focus of attention.

It is not size per se, therefore, that renders Pollock's drip pictures perfect backdrops for the ball gowns in Beaton's illustrations. The use of art as prop is common enough in *Vogue* and similar magazines. Fernand Fonssagrives shot

23 Meyer Schapiro, "Recent abstract painting," in *idem, Modern Art: 19th and 20th Centuries. Selected Papers* (New York George Braziller, 1978), p. 224. See the interesting discussion in de Chassey, *La Peinture efficace*, pp. 240 ff.

24 Ibid., p. 219.

25 Chipp, *Theories*, p. 545.

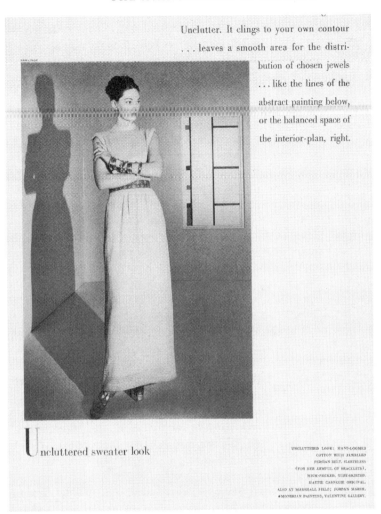

Unclutter. It clings to your own contour ... leaves a smooth area for the distribution of chosen jewels ... like the lines of the abstract painting below, or the balanced space of the interior-plan, right.

Uncluttered sweater look

UNCLUTTERED LOOK: HAND-LOOMED COTTON WITH JEWELLED PERSIAN BELT, SLEEVELESS (FOR HER ARMFUL OF BRACELETS), HIGH-NECKED, TUBE-SKIRTED. HATTIE CARNEGIE ORIGINAL. ALSO AT MARSHALL FIELD; JORDAN MARSH. *MONDRIAN PAINTING, VALENTINE GALLERY.

Figure 10.3 John Rowlings, "Uncluttered Sweater Look," *Vogue*, January 1, 1945, p. 46, © *Vogue*, The Condé Nast Publications Inc.

some fashion plates for *Town and Country* in Mondrian's studio shortly after the artist's death in 1944; a year later Mondrian's *Composition with Red, Yellow, and Blue* (1931–42) appeared in a *Vogue* story. *Vogue*'s copy compares the smooth contour fit of the "sweater look" dress to the lines of the painting, which seems to float beside it as an apparitional equivalent (Figure 10.3). They share a modern, spare version of elegance, setting off jewels on the woman, bars of color in the picture. The Pollocks, in contrast, frame gowns in taffeta and satin; hence the appropriateness of the notes they strike: "intensity of feelings" and connoisseur approval. Beaton's photographs put a positive spin on the dismissal of *Cathedral* by Sir Leigh Ashton of the Victoria and Albert Museum, a member of the 1948

Life panel on modern art, who opined that the painting "would make a most enchanting printed silk." (Professor Greene of Yale remarked that *Cathedral* seemed a pleasant design for a necktie.)[26] In Beaton's images of Pollock's paintings they both serve a decorative function and represent daring, brilliance, and novelty, something not for everyone.

Whatever the suggestion of *Vogue*'s text, they did not yet represent market success: despite some critical approval and growing exposure Pollock's works barely sold in 1951. (From that show only *Autumn Rhythm* found a buyer, Pollock's friend, artist Alfonso Ossorio.) From the artist's point of view, and that of his dealer, Beaton's photographs must have been a welcome boost. But Pollock, who objected to architects' assignment of painting to the task of decoration, certainly did not accept Beaton's relegation of his work to providing background and atmosphere. And it must be said that the dresses, undistinguished and retrograde, despite the "New Look" label, are in no way on the same level as the paintings. Beaton's ingenuity shows in his use of Pollock to give the fashions an excitement and vitality they lack.

Fashion

By the same gesture that exposed the aesthetic disparity between the paintings and the dresses, however, Beaton accentuated their social kinship. Both art and high fashion are, in the first place, primarily possessions of the upper classes, though both provide areas in which those classes can be challenged by others. Fashion, as Georg Simmel explained in an essay of 1904, "is a product of class distinction." It both "signifies union with those in the same class, the uniformity of the circle characterized by it, and *uno actu*, the exclusion of all other groups." In this, fashion resembles the easel painting, operating like the frame of a picture that "characterizes the work of art inwardly as a coherent, homogeneous, independent entity and at the same time outwardly severs all direct relations with the surrounding space."[27] In a society like ours, where some class mobility is possible, a system of distinguishing marks like fashion is subject to emulation—a process in which a magazine like *Vogue* plays an important role, making fashion available to a wider circle than the clients of the couture. But, as Simmel wrote,

> Just as soon as the lower classes begin to copy their style, thereby crossing the line of demarcation the upper classes have drawn and destroying

---

26 Davenport and Sargeant, *"Life* Round Table," p. 62. Ashton's opinion was apparently vindicated by the drip-patterned scarf sold by the Museum of Modern Art in conjunction with its 1998–9 Pollock retrospective; similar patterns appeared on dresses illustrated in *Vogue* already in 1952 and 1953.

27 Georg Simmel, "Fashion," in *idem, On Individuality and Social Forms: Selected Writings,* ed. Donald N. Levine (Chicago: University of Chicago Press, 1971), p. 297.

the uniformity of their coherence, the upper classes turn away from this style and adopt a new one, which in its turn differentiates them from the masses.[28]

The analogy between fashion and avant-garde art in the modern period could be seen at work in Paris in the early twentieth century, where, to quote a recent study, "certain members of the social and aristocratic elite used their sponsorship of the avant-garde to distinguish themselves from the more mainstream taste of new entrants into the art market such as businessmen and professionals."[29] But the analogy need not hold so neatly. In particular, in New York during the 1940s and 1950s, as in Paris, collectors were divided between those interested in the latest art and the accumulators of established artistic (and economic) values. Blue-chip collecting was characteristic of the very rich, executives or owners of significant business enterprises, exercising a taste established, as Deirdre Robson explains, "by historians and critics and confirmed by the most prestigious dealers."[30] Avant-garde collecting was associated with relatively restricted means (which in part dictated the buying of cheaper work). According to Robson, such collectors came in large numbers from two groups: women, spending inherited or marital fortunes, and art professionals, predominantly male, like Alfonso Ossorio.[31] In developing a taste for avant-garde art, collectors with lower degrees of social and economic power substituted for these what Pierre Bourdieu calls cultural capital, investments in knowledge and taste making possible a claim to cultural power and even, as the avant-garde became artistic fashion, huge monetary returns on small investments.

Beaton's pictures associated expensive dresses with as yet relatively inexpensive art that by 1951 had begun to receive recognition within the art world. If they thus suggested a potentially elevated social status for Pollock's work, they also linked the gowns to the newness and originality that—in the context of the postwar political and economic order—American fashion, like American art, was claiming in relation to Paris, since the nineteenth century the international capital of fashion and art alike.[32] This linkage of avant-garde and fashion, as exemplars of the American and the new, posed, as Clark recognizes, a direct challenge to the claim of art to transcend its social context, whether that transcendence be described as spiritual ascendance, as in nineteenth-century aestheticism, or as crypto-political negation, as left modernists like Adorno and Clark would have it.

---

28 Ibid., p. 299.
29 A. Deirdre Robson, *Prestige, Profit, and Pleasure: The Market for Modern Art in New York in the 1940s and 1950s* (New York: Garland, 1995), p. 257.
30 Ibid., p. 153.
31 Ibid., pp. 197 ff.
32 It is interesting to contrast these images with another set that Beaton shot to illustrate "Atmosphere story: airy nightdresses" in the same issue of *Vogue*, which set sleepwear in a traditionalizing (though equally American) context of quilts and framed old-fashioned paintings.

The analogy between art and fashion established by Beaton's Pollock pictures contained a double danger for those who wanted to insist that modern art was, in the words of the question put to *Life*'s panelists in 1948, more than "a minor and impermanent phase of culture." Not only did Beaton bring to the fore the ornamental aspect of Pollock's paintings, his pictures, both in their composition and in their work of promotion, also suggest the truth of the idea that—in the words of Renato Poggioli—"the avant-garde is condemned to conquer, through the influence of [artistic] fashion, that very popularity it once disdained—and this is the beginning of its end." Once Abstract Expressionism had triumphed, becoming the "New York School," new modes of art reacting to it or going beyond it could be expected to arise in accordance with the logic whereby (as Poggioli expressed this version of Clark's "bad dream") "the whole history of avant-garde art seems reducible to an uninterrupted series of fads."[33]

The difficulty this poses for the claim that art constitutes a high and timeless spiritual value was seen already at the start of the modern period. Around 1860 Charles Baudelaire began his essay on "The painter of modern life" by drawing attention to an historical factor active in the production and reception of art. The art of the past, he writes,

> is interesting not only because of the beauty which could be distilled from it by those artists for whom it was the present, but also precisely because it is the past, for its historical value. It is the same with the present. The pleasure which we derive from the representation of the present is due not only to the beauty with which it can be invested, but also to its essential quality of being present.[34]

Baudelaire's text, having opened with an image of an art-loving visitor to the Louvre gazing in rapture at a Titian or a Raphael, turns at once to "a series of fashion-plates" dating from the first years of the French republic and redolent of "the moral and aesthetic feeling of their time." For Baudelaire, art, which seems to transcend its time, and fashion, which seems tied to short periods of time, share both historical location and the ambition to create timeless beauty: "And if to the fashion plate representing each age [one] were to add the philosophic thought with which that age was most preoccupied or concerned—the thought being inevitably suggested by the fashion plate—he would see what a profound harmony controls all the components of history" (pp. 1–3). In terms of the present chapter's starting point, the Pollock today in the museum and the ball gown

---

33 Renato Poggioli, *The Theory of the Avant-Garde* (Cambridge: Harvard University Press, 1968), p. 83.

34 Charles Baudelaire, "The painter of modern life," in *idem*, *The Painter of Modern Life and Other Essays*, ed. and tr. Jonathan Mayne (London: Phaidon, 1964), p. 1. Further references to this text will be placed in parentheses.

long consigned to the dustbin once shared an aspiration and a specific historical moment that gave them shape.

Along with fashion, Baudelaire argues, art presents us both with "the eternal and the immutable" character classicism ascribed to beauty and with "the ephemeral, the fugitive, the contingent" that defines modernity at every historical moment. Once we come to value our modernity, and to seek in art responsiveness to that value, then the "transitory, fugitive element, whose metamorphoses are so rapid, must on no account be despised or dispensed with" (p. 13). The modernist artist must make it his business "to extract from fashion whatever element it may contain of poetry within history, to distill the eternal from the transitory" (p. 12).

Baudelaire assumes the masculinity of the artist; woman, on the other hand, is "a divinity, a star, which presides at all the conceptions of the brain of man . . . the object of the keenest admiration and curiosity that the picture of life can offer its contemplator." She is, in fact, eternal beauty in living, transitory form. Baudelaire is careful—and this represents a crucial break with classicism—to specify that woman's beauty is made not by nature but by artifice. Put otherwise, it is her nature to be shaped by fashion: "Everything that adorns Woman, everything that serves to show off her beauty, is part of herself" (p. 30). Hence cosmetics, face painting, is a model for all painting, and by extension "fashion should . . . be considered as a symptom of the taste for the ideal" (p. 32) which men strive for when they transform the naturally given into art.

Baudelaire was an idiosyncratic thinker and a great poet, not a promoter of the couturier's status, but that his words are in tune with some important aspect of modernity rather than simply a private vision can be seen when we set them beside the assertion of Charles Fréderic Worth, founder of the haute couture: "I am a great artist, I have Delacroix's sense of color and I compose. An outfit is the equal of a painting."[35] And about 70 years after Baudelaire's essay we find Mondrian asserting in almost the same words as the poet's that fashion is "not only the faithful mirror of a period" but also "one of the most direct plastic expressions of human culture." Although unlike Baudelaire, who demanded the domination of nature by artifice, he wished for an equalization of forces between nature and culture; he opposed 1930s fashion for its "tendency to return to natural appearances," a regressive tendency in the era of the skyscraper and the machine. Fashion like architecture had, in Mondrian's opinion, to follow the dictates of Neo-Plasticist design, "to oppose the undulating lines and soft forms of the body with tautened lines and unified planes,"[36] a demand met only in 1965—by this time flavored by nostalgia and irony—in the form of Yves Saint-Laurent's "Mondrian" dress.

35 Quoted from an 1895 newspaper interview in Marie Simon, *Mode et peinture. Le Second Empire et l'impressionisme* (Paris: Hazan, 1995), p. 128.
36 Holtzman and James, *The New Life*, p. 226.

In an essay on Mondrian, Meyer Schapiro pointed out that in a picture like Degas's *At the Milliner's* (1882, Metropolitan Museum of Art), the woman trying on a hat before a mirror "is the artist-critic of her own appearance, her object of contemplation . . . In Degas's pastel the woman is testing the fitness of a work of art that is not at all a representation, yet as a part of her costume will symbolize her individuality and taste in shape and color," in the same way that the artist's handling of his visual materials may signify his.[37] Degas himself brought the two ideas together—visual art and the fashionably dressed woman as a living work of art—in a drawing of his friend Mary Cassatt as a well-turned-out museum visitor (*ca.* 1871–80, Boston Museum of Fine Arts). The similar operation accomplished by Beaton's photographs has a different effect, not only because of the scale of the paintings and the danger of decorativeness inherent in Pollock's abstraction but also because of their function as fashion plates rather than artworks. The fashionable woman, whatever her Baudelairean significance as incarnation of beauty, remains here as in the nineteenth century a male construction and object of enjoyment. But Beaton draws Pollock's work from the gallery or museum into the shop window: Pollock's male creative ambition is made to serve the female consumer (whomever she in turn may serve). The pictures thus link the relations of social power between the sexes to the issue of the relation between creativity and commerce that lies at the heart of the modern practice of art.

Despite the verbal self-assurance with which Baudelaire articulated his wish for an art at once modern and eternal, this proved difficult to achieve. His own lack of monetary success as a writer (not to mention the censor's banning of his greatest work, *Les Fleurs du Mal*) testifies to the gap typically experienced at first between avant-garde art and its potential public. It is noteworthy that Baudelaire found "the painter of modern life" in neither of the plausible candidates among his artist friends, Courbet and Manet, but in the fashion illustrator Constantin Guys, who has lived on in art history largely because of Baudelaire's essay. Although as a late Romantic Baudelaire rejected the possibility that photography could produce works of art, it was surely a brilliant idea to locate the specifically modern home of beauty in pictures made for mechanical reproduction in the illustrated press.

Art and ideology

Considering the same issues nearly a century later, Clement Greenberg was less sanguine about the relation of mass produced culture to the handmade goods of the art trade. He recognized, as Baudelaire had, that both are produced for sale. On the one hand (to cite a passage quoted earlier in this book), the avant-garde

---

37 Meyer Schapiro, "Mondrian: order and randomness in abstract painting," in *idem, Modern Art,* p. 240.

had its "social basis" in "an elite among the ruling class . . . from which it assumed itself to be cut off but to which it has always remained attached by an umbilical cord of gold." On the other hand, industrial capitalism produced the phenomenon called in German *Kitsch*, "popular, commercial art and literature." Both "a painting by Braque and a *Saturday Evening Post* cover" are products of "one and the same civilization."[38] But today as in the past, in Greenberg's view, art attempts to create occasions for experiences apart from the assumptions and values of everyday life, while kitsch borrows art's techniques and imagery to provide comfortable versions of the experiences people already have. If Pollock's *Autumn Rhythm* is a perfect representative of art as Greenberg understood it, Beaton's photograph including it is a perfect representative of his concept of kitsch. The intimate relation between avant-garde and kitsch only shows, in Greenberg's view, that "advances in culture, no less than advances in science and industry, corrode the very society under whose aegis they are made possible."[39] In the same way that modern science makes possible ever more destructive weaponry, artistic advances provide new stylistic means for the culture industry's destruction of sensibility. Where Baudelaire hoped to discover the beautiful in the spirit animating commercial culture, Greenberg believed the history of capitalism led instead in the direction of the swallowing up of art by the cultural complacency of the market.

In this, an obvious ancestor of T. J. Clark's analysis, Greenberg drew on the opposition of culture and capitalist economy fundamental to the modern idea of art. As we saw in Chapter 3, art has been conceptualized since the eighteenth century in terms of distance from the mundane world of getting and spending— from what art talk typically refers to as "everyday life." In his classic text of 1913, Clive Bell put it this way: "Art transports us from the world of man's activity to a world of aesthetic exaltation."[40] Greenberg's thinking similarly rests on a distinction "between those values only to be found in art and the values which can be found elsewhere."[41] While in Clark's use the phrase "everyday life" carries a whiff of the Situationist critique of bourgeois "banality" present also in the language of "colonization," it indicates that his thinking, however original, remains within the terms of the modern ideology of art.

Like all ideology, this view is based on a reality: the distinctive social character of art objects, as handmade luxury goods in a world dominated by mechanized mass production. This difference provides art producers with a domain for the exercise of individual creativity ("genius"), as opposed to the alienated labor under the direction of others that is the lot of most people, and allows the products of genius to provide their consumers with an experience outside the

38 Greenberg, "Avant-garde and kitsch," pp. 8, 9, 3.
39 Ibid., p. 21.
40 Clive Bell, *Art* (London: Chatto and Windus, 1948), p. 27.
41 Greenberg, *Art and Culture*, p. 13.

constraints of the market. Expressive, in its very freedom from monetary consid-erations, of the power of money and of the access to free time made possible by money, art is a token and a perk of social distinction for those who own and even for those who merely appreciate it. The artist, as producer of this token, shares in the distinction, though (for the most part) not in the wealth that sup-ports the social practice of art as a whole. As Bourdieu has explained the meeting-place of economic and cultural value in modern society, "The structural ambiguity of their position in the field of power leads writers and painters, those 'penniless bourgeois' in Pisarro's words, to maintain an ambivalent relationship with the dominant class within the field of power, those whom they call the 'bourgeois,' as well as with the dominated, the 'people.'"[42]

The artist's ambivalent social identity, whose first important form was Roman-ticism and which reappeared in both Realism and Aestheticism, since the late nineteenth century has powered avant-garde activities within such varied orientations as geometric abstraction, Dada, the surrealist plumbing of the unconscious, and the Abstract Expressionism of the late 1940s. The element of misrepresentation involved in all these artistic self-representations appears in Clark's writing in the use of concepts like "colonization," implying the existence of a psychic hinterland to be invaded and conquered by bourgeois culture. Despite the conflicts of ideas and modes of life that distinguished vanguard artists from the bourgeois public, the oppositions—of self to society, spontaneity to con-vention, freedom to conformity, "wilderness" to social order—that articulate the meaning of avant-garde activity lie well within the "normal understandings" of bourgeois society. Both sides of these oppositions represent bourgeois virtues as well as vices.[43]

This is not to say that they cannot also be taken to express a conflict between two social principles. Like anyone else, an artist—in his or her artistic work as well as in more directly political action—can call into question central features of present-day society and imagine future alternatives. But the elements of any such critique can only be discovered inside social reality, not in a mythical exter-nal area of wildness. And this—not just the inherent polysemy of abstract art that Clarence Weinstock complained of—is ultimately what makes it possible for the dominant culture to absorb the most resistant art, figurative and nonrepre-sentational alike.

Though it seemed to Greenberg when he wrote "Avant-garde and kitsch" that vanguard culture was "being abandoned by those to whom it actually belongs—our ruling class,"[44] as we now know, he could not have been more

---

42 Pierre Bourdieu, *The Field of Cultural Production: Essays on Art and Literature*, ed. Randal Johnson (New York: Columbia University Press, 1993), p. 165.

43 For an argument to a similar conclusion, but carried out at convincing length, see Jerrold Seigel, *Bohemian Paris: Culture, Politics, and the Boundaries of Bourgeois Life, 1831–1930* (New York: Viking, 1986).

44 Greenberg, "Avant-garde and kitsch," p. 10.

wrong. Avant-garde art, whatever the wishes of its makers and propagandists, became the official art of the dominant class, to such an extent that the concept of the avant-garde has not been able to maintain its original connotation of cultural negation.[45] I do not mean to express by pointing this out what Clark describes as the view "that any culture will use art as it sees fit, and that the very idea of art resisting such incorporation is pie in the sky."[46] This view involves a misconception fundamental to the ideology of art, a misconception fatal also to Clark's more sophisticated view. Art does not need to be "incorporated," because it is not outside society to begin with; avant-garde production cannot be "used" in this sense by bourgeois society (as, say, African art could be) because it is a part of that society's operations.

In identifying the idea that it is both subject to such utilization and strives to resist it in the formal nature of Pollock's abstraction, Clark attributes to Pollock something like his own version of the ideology of art and of modernism in particular. Given the centrality of the avant-garde idea for Pollock's circle and for him personally, this is a more believable reading than, for instance, Thomas Crow's claim that Beaton's pictures reveal that the large-scale painting of Abstract Expressionism "would always carry the meaning of stage and backdrop" for the "courtly culture" of the art-loving American rich.[47] However Peggy Guggenheim saw the painting Pollock made for her hallway, the image itself embodies the artist's response to the opportunity to work on a large scale, transmuting the claim to public significance made by Mexican and North American muralists into the assertion that his own artistic powers could stand measurement against those of Picasso and Matisse.

Beaton's photographs, Clark writes, are important because by subduing the challenge of the paintings "they raise the question of what possible uses Pollock's work anticipated, what viewers and readers it expected, what spaces it was meant to inhabit, and, above all, the question of how such a structure of expectation entered into and informed the work itself, determining its idiom."[48] Though

---

45 Greenberg himself, considering the problem in 1967—in an article written for *Vogue*, no less—defined the avant-garde without reference to politics as "constituted by the highness of its [aesthetic] standards, which depend on distance from those of society at large" ("Where is the avant-garde?," in *idem*, *The Collected Essays and Criticism*, vol. 4, *Modernism With a Vengeance, 1951–1969*, ed. John O'Brian (Chicago: University of Chicago Press, 1993), p. 264. While he thought it was possible that "the avant-garde as an historical entity may be approaching its definite end," Greenberg considered it likely that "the production of high art would . . . be taken over by some other agency" (ibid., p. 265).

46 Clark, *Farewell to an Idea*, p. 363.

47 Thomas Crow, *Modern Art in the Common Culture* (New Haven: Yale University Press, 1996), p. 48. I cite this view—despite the unconvincing character of an argument about "the origin of this kind of object" (p. 47) that mentions neither 1930s muralism nor earlier modernist large-format painting, and that makes much of a myth about the cutting down of *Mural* to fit Peggy Guggenheim's wall—because of its author's distinction as a social historian of art.

48 Ibid., p. 176. Unfortunately, he pursues these questions only negatively, in terms of what he takes to be the pictures' attempt at formal resistance to conventional reading.

Clark himself does not try to answer these questions, they are good ones. To do no more than sketch some answers: the large size of pictures like *Autumn Rhythm* suggests large intended spaces; given the visible effort to be more than wall decoration, the most likely ones, after the studio, are those of the art world: galleries and museums. The "work against metaphor" Clark, like others, identifies as determining the paintings' formal method indicates as expected viewers the normal inhabitants of those art-world spaces, no doubt in the first place other artists, who could be expected to come equipped with the habit of reading modern artworks metaphorically. In addition, *as works of art*, and in particular as paintings on canvas, they anticipated or at any rate hoped for buyers.

In Beaton's pictures, the Pollocks function neither as mural nor as easel paintings; visible only in part, they are subordinated as décor to the model and the dress. Fifty years later, the paintings have long since triumphed culturally and economically over the fashions and the photographs. The fame of these photos today is largely due to their connection with Pollock. Even if fashion has now made it into museums, it lives, when not segregated in institutions of its own, in the basement or in period rooms, along with the other *arts décoratifs*. The catalogue of a 1999 exhibition of the Metropolitan Museum's Costume Institute devoted to "The Four Seasons" in dress featured a detail of *Autumn Rhythm* on its cover. A Pollock retrospective would never have a Beaton up front.

Yet the illustrations for *Vogue* still irritate art historians and theorists. For all the conventionality of their daring, these photographs can be as subversive of received ideas about art as Pollock's work once was. By bringing highpoints of both personal expression and formal exploration into collision with *mondaine* elegance they raise questions not only within but also about the discourse of art, and in particular about the intimate relations of art to the social environment from which, as "everyday life," that discourse wishes to distance it. For instance, they expose the interrelation between a conception of art linking masculinity with creative intensity and an idea of the feminine as the decorative embodiment of powers of consumption and display. Most generally, they suggest the idea that the meanings of artworks are not given simply by the physical and visual nature of the works themselves but—to emphasize a commonplace—by the uses to which they can be put.

The paintings in which Pollock worked out his ideas about art in New York in the late 1940s, about his personal life experiences, and about the relation between the two in the practice of painting, provided others at the time with signifiers of fashionable excitement, sophistication, and privilege. Today they provide Professor Clark with exemplars of the idea that political opposition to capitalist society can be located in cultural activity, if only imbued with the grandeur of inevitable failure. Beaton's use of them reminds us that the sense of failure depends on the claim to political grandeur. After all, the idea that art—whatever the artist's wishes—can "resist" the culture that produces it is as dubious as the hope that an economically underdeveloped country could have been the scene of a communist revolution in 1917.

One can easily object to social reality, and even imagine a different one. But an individual person cannot resist society and live; the most militant revolutionary must obey the law of value regulating capitalist economic processes, must find money to pay the rent. A painting, even if made in an effort to live and produce in a way at radical odds with modern society, lives on in the world in independence of its maker's—or any particular viewer's—intentions. It was a dream of some early twentieth-century modernists that artists could change the world, a version of the fantasy, shared by producers and lovers of culture since the nineteenth century, that art could exist in independence of the dominant structures of social power. Today artists by and large have given up such ambitions, though they may still wish to enact a kind of personal autonomy in their work hard to find in other social locations. It is more likely to be critics, theorists, and historians of art who hold onto the idea of art's transcendence and subversive power, for its reflection can give them a sense of their own wished-for independence and importance. Discovering the limits of culture's social force, however, need not be experienced as a nightmare; it can also be an awakening.

11

CLASSLESS TASTE

In memoriam Pierre Bourdieu, 1930–2002

The concept of taste developed in the course of the eighteenth century, together with the idea of aesthetic experience and, indeed, with what in the next century would become the modern idea of art. Kant located taste in a mental faculty of aesthetic judgment, establishing the beauty (or sublimity) of some object of sense experience as a property of the human subject's response to it. Similarly, Hume took taste to be a matter of "the common sentiments of human nature" excited by objects of beauty. Beside these philosophically canonical authors stand the writers of essays, pamphlets, poems, and treatises exploring taste as a human response to the worlds of nature and art. What they all share is the idea that taste represents a natural response of human beings to sensory experience, providing a basis for judging degrees of beauty (or, as a more recent terminology has it, of quality).

Although it has lost its preeminent place as a philosophical concept, taste remains an important category of everyday life, both to describe the range of human preferences and to serve as a standard for judging those preferences. However universal the faculty of judgment may be, tastes notoriously differ. Furthermore, difference—so class society operates—implies inequality, and to the ranking of objects corresponds a hierarchy of subjects, from the sensitive and knowledgeable connoisseur to the ill-informed vulgarian. As Pierre Bourdieu puts it, "taste classifies, and it classifies the classifier."[1] Those with taste recognize others like themselves by their agreement on judgments of quality, or at least by disagreements within an accepted range of preferences. In this way judgments of taste produce social classifications. This is particularly true, Bourdieu argues, with respect to taste in art.

Since the capacity for a judgment of taste about a work of art requires knowledge of its place within the array of objects and performances making up the domain of art, and thus a familiarity with that domain, the capacity for aesthetic experience depends on certain formative experiences—having art in the

---

1 Pierre Bourdieu, *Distinction: A Social Critique of the Judgement of Taste*, tr. Richard Nice (Cambridge: Harvard University Press, 1984). Henceforth cited in the text.

home or being around artists; being encouraged in artistic activity at school; visiting museums and attending concerts, etc. A simple example of familiarity with art is the presence of small art museums at elite universities in the United States, and their absence from lower-class schools. Even if many students at Harvard, Mount Holyoke, or Berkeley never visit their campus collection, the fact that the collections are there to be visited corresponds to the high likelihood that students at those institutions will have grown up in households taking an acquaintance with art and its history for granted, just as that fact helps to maintain that likelihood. Similarily, students attending museum-less Adelphi University, where I teach, are highly unlikely to have gone to an art museum (or classical-music concert) outside of school trips, which teach at once the social legitimacy of such institutions and their distance from the young person's out-of-school experience.

The social distinction manifested in taste is effected not so much on the plane of formal knowledge as on that of unconsciously formed and maintained habits of social and therefore physical interaction with art. Passing the Fogg Museum on a walk across the Harvard campus reinforces the feeling that art is a natural part of the environment, which one may choose to attend to or not on a given occasion, that a student is likely to have derived from growing up with art in the home, on the walls and in adult conversation. Such a student has acquired what Bourdieu calls the habitus of his or her class, the set of dispositions to act, in a range of social situations, in ways "appropriate" to a person of his or her sort. It is habitus which generates a unified "lifestyle" involving such diverse practices as eating cheese after dinner, the adoption of certain styles of dress, ownership of books, the reading of particular magazines and not others, ownership of a country house or summer place, and having tastes in art. In generating this style, habitus is embodied in what one might call micropractices of life—ease in wearing a suit or ordering food in a restaurant, for instance, along with ill-ease in other social circumstances, such as wandering into a working-class neighborhood.

In the concept of habitus Bourdieu has revived a concept from the seventeenth-century origin of aesthetics, the idea of taste as an unconscious propensity (Pascal's "second nature," for instance) to make the right judgment and do the right thing in response to the *je ne sais quoi* characterizing different situations. Habitus creates a class identity in the form of a unified practice of classification, as choices are made. Because these choices exist within a social space of different possible choices they necessarily have meaning as the rejection of different choices. This is how taste classifies the classifier; because in a class society all distinction has status implications,

> Distinction does not necessarily imply [as in Veblen's theory of conspicuous consumption], a quest for distinction. All consumption and, more generally, all practice, is *conspicuous*, visible, whether or not it was performed *in order to be seen* . . . hence, every practice is bound to function

as a *distinctive sign* and when the difference is recognized, legitimate and approved, as a *sign of distinction* (in all senses of the term).[2]

Distinction is, as noted, more than difference, in the realm of tastes and in that of the possessors of taste: "to the socially recognized hierarchy of the arts, and within each of them, of genres, schools or periods, corresponds a social hierarchy of the consumers" (p. 4).[3] This hierarchy is complex and more accurately rendered as a space of positions defined by the different forms of power that structure social life. If we look, for instance, at the subset of American art collectors buying modernist art in the 1950s we find, within a generally wealthy and educated group, wealthier and more socially established men collecting "blue-chip" pictures by artists like Picasso and Matisse, and possessors of lesser and more recently acquired wealth, often women and people professionally close to the art world themselves, initiating the patronage of Abstract Expressionist artists, while sharing the estimation of the blue-chips as the artistic masters of the time.[4] Meanwhile, for the majority of Americans, "Picasso" was a synonym for "far-out" rather than a maker of images actually enjoyed, and a mass-market publication like *Life*, operating in the space between upper- and lower-class taste, insisted on the inclusion of the French master in the artistic canon and hedged its bets on Pollock, both citing experts on his greatness and mocking him for his drips.

It would be wrong to say that in Bourdieu's understanding taste reflects class; rather, taste is for him a constituent of class, a possession that helps to gives a person his or her social position. My ability to wear the clothes appropriate for professional occasions (despite the slight trace of discomfort I experience when engaging in what the voguing masters of disguise featured in the film *Paris is*

---

2 P. Bourdieu, "Social space and the genesis of 'classes'," in *idem, Language and Symbolic Power* (Cambridge: Harvard University Press, 1991), p. 237.

3 As sociologist Alvin Toffler made this point in his celebratory book on arts consumption in the United States, written at around the same time as Bourdieu's first systematic studies in the anthropology of culture,

> There are a finite number of automobiles for a consumer to choose from, a finite number of exotic meals that he can eat, and even a finite number of places to which he can, at the moment, travel. Art, by contrast, is infinite in its variations and possibilities. It is for this reason the broadest of all possible fields within which the individual can express his one-and-onlyness.
>
> *The Culture Consumers: Art and Affluence in America* (Baltimore: Penguin, 1965), p. 63

The typically American substitution of individualism for the French theorist's class analysis is contradicted by Toffler's own description of his "culture consumers" as members of a particular income and lifestyle class, characterized by features quite similar to those identified by Bourdieu; see pp. 39 ff.

4 See A. Deirdre Robson, *Prestige, Profit, and Pleasure: The Market for Modern Art in New York in the 1940s and 1950s* (New York: Garland, 1995), esp. pp. 135 ff.

Burning call "academic realness") is not of course sufficient to give me the powers that accompany my (sub)class position as a professor. But, more than a mere sign of that position, these things demonstrate my acquisition of the habitus that that position requires because they are that habitus in action. The practice of class taste is part of the process by which my classification as an academic is realized, that is, it is part of my occupying that class position. This is evident as soon as we remember with Bourdieu that taste is "the propensity and capacity to appropriate (materially or symbolically) a given class of classified, classifying objects or practices" (p. 173): my ability to enjoy fine art, classical music, and rare wines, as well as my relation to the processes of social production, which makes the exercise of that ability possible, help define my membership in a particular fraction of what Bourdieu calls "the dominated fraction of the dominating class."

Art objects have specific properties, requiring particular elements of habitus for their adequate consumption. As already mentioned, they function particularly well as social classifiers because, Bourdieu notes, they "enable the production of distinctions ad infinitum by playing on divisions and sub-divisions into genres, periods, styles, authors, etc." (p. 16). In addition, peculiar to the modern concept of art, in contradistinction to its historical relatives in other social orders, is the use to which the name "autonomy" has been given: as embodiment of the "higher" (noncommercial) interests of the dominant classes in society, providing opportunities for the cultivation of a capacity for perceptual experience independent of normal practical function. This is what is signaled by the idea of the "aesthetic attitude" as one of detachment from the claims of "practical life." According to Bourdieu,

> the aesthetic disposition, a generalized capacity to neutralize ordinary urgencies and to bracket off political ends, a durable inclination and aptitude for practice without a practical function, can only be constituted within an experience of the world freed from urgency and through the practice of activities which are an end in themselves, such as scholastic exercises or the contemplation of works of art.
>
> (p. 54)

Thus, as Bourdieu describes it, it is not only that art is accessible primarily to those who have the wealth, leisure, and education to encounter and appreciate it. Art itself, in its modern form, represents "the primacy of form over function," of a "stylization of life," of the detachment from the practical and the exercise of taste peculiar to the aesthetic attitude (p. 176). In this it emblematizes the social position of the executive, as opposed to the operative: the decision-maker who looks for "results" without getting his or her hands dirty. The love of art is an expression of the upper-class habitus in the cultural sphere; "the aesthetic disposition is one dimension of a distant, self-assured relation to the world and to others which presupposes objective assurance and distance" (p. 56).

For this reason, Bourdieu objects to the idea of "popular art": "The populist aestheticism which leads some to credit working-class people with a 'popular aesthetic' or a 'popular culture' . . . performs a tacit universalization of the scholastic viewpoint which is not accompanied by the slightest intention of universalizing its conditions of possibility."[5] "Culture" in the modern sense is not just a historically specific concept, it is a class-specific one; to speak of "popular culture" is to treat those excluded from full access to that which "culture" primarily designates as if they were simply people with a different taste, one equally valid though unrepresented by any of the institutions charged with the collecting and display of art.

The working-class relationship to fine art, Bourdieu insists, does not just represent an alternative taste. While the aesthetic attitude expresses a sense of freedom, adaptation to a dominated position "implies a form of acceptance of domination" (p. 386). This has certainly been borne out by my experience of students from a regional working-class and lower-middle-class milieu. When I send them, in connection with class work, to New York's Museum of Modern Art—visited by most of them for the first time at my direction—they typically experience it as a foreign environment, whose contents they are mostly at a loss to understand. They commonly describe both the artists and museum visitors who seem to understand and enjoy the works on display as either fools or fakers.[6] The hostility expressed in this judgment suggests a defense, not just the registration of a difference—a defense against the alternate possibility that they are inadequate to the demands of what are evidently socially legitimated objects. While they cannot understand how many of the things on view came to enter an art museum, it remains incontestable that it is an art museum and that those things are valuable and, however mysteriously, important.

Since taste is a relational system, the near abandonment of fine art to those with the appropriate habitus goes along with the confinement of the dominated to mass-marketed cultural goods that, whatever their quality, lack the character of rarity and luxury typifying the fine-art commodity. And in the realm of non-art consumer goods, it is not only the desire for cheap versions of upper-class objects—imitation leather, designer underwear, posters of artworks—that signifies acceptance of the high social valuation of the real thing. In addition, there is the construction of class-marked objects of conspicuous consumption—expensive sneakers, elaborate fingernails, dubious gold jewelry—that take the place occupied among the dominant classes by expensive and well-made clothing and accessories.

---

5 P. Bourdieu, *Pascalian Meditations*, tr. R. Nice (Stanford: Stanford University Press, 2000), p. 75.

6 Similarly, David Halle's research into class taste in the New York City area showed that "the two main criticisms made by working-class people" are "that the artists are charlatans who cannot draw and cannot paint" and the related objection that abstract art "has no meaning" (D. Halle, *Inside Culture: Art and Class in the American Home* (Chicago: University of Chicago Press, 1993), pp. 121–5, 127).

It would be perverse not to read Bourdieu's analysis of social being as an indictment of a system in which the freedom of some depends conceptually and practically on the unfreedom of others. The indictment is a radical one—more radical, indeed, than the responses Bourdieu himself seemed able to imagine, forms of pressure on the political institutions of the very system whose working he criticized. For example, he remarked in a dialogue with artist Hans Haacke that

> there are a certain number of conditions for the existence of a culture with a critical perspective that can only be assured by the state. In short, we should expect (and even demand) from the state the instruments of freedom from economic and political powers—that is, from the state itself.[7]

The absurdity of this suggestion is evident. Apart from the continual failure of schemes for "democratization of the arts" such as those advanced in the United States by well-meaning foundations and government agencies like the National Endowment for the Arts, schemes which never succeed in expanding the arts audience much beyond a well-educated and relatively well-off minority, it is odd to find such a self-contradictory suggestion by a writer who has analyzed the functions of the "state nobility" within the apparatus of domination.

But Bourdieu's own theory explains the limitations their social position places on the capacity of intellectuals to draw the furthest consequences of their own ideas. Exercise of their power as the possessors of "cultural capital"—socially legitimated knowledge, degrees, institutional connections, mastery of certain jargons, etc. yielding "a profit in distinction" (p. 228)—requires their maintenance of belief both in the autonomy of their field of activity and in their unique fitness to exercise it. Despite what one can fairly call Bourdieu's heroic attempts to overcome the social blindspots inherent in his own social position, even he was unable to imagine a politics born outside of the existing political languages and institutions, in which a professional thinker like himself might play a relatively minor role—a politics ultimately centered not on the transformation of the state but on its abolition.[8]

It is hard today for anyone to imagine a politics capable of reorganizing present-day society on a sufficiently radical level to do justice to Bourdieu's indictment. But it is not impossible, and the alternative, the unbounded continuation of the present order of exploitation, war, and ecological destruction, is both unlikely and frightful to contemplate. If we make the effort to imagine a

---

7 P. Bourdieu and H. Haacke, *Free Exchange* (Stanford: Stanford University Press, 1995), pp. 71–2.

8 For a brief discussion of the limits of Bourdieu's theory of class, see P. Mattick, "Class, capital and crisis," in Martha Campbell and Geert Reuten (eds), *The Culmination of Capital: Essays on Volume III of Marx's* Capital (London: Palgrave, 2002), pp. 31 ff.

future renewal of revolutionary social movements, what effects might a radical social upheaval have on the nature of art and aesthetic experience?

If we imagine a world in which the working class, the actual producers of social wealth, would take for themselves the power to regulate their activities of production and distribution, we imagine a society in which the assertion of control over economic goods would include the appropriation of cultural goods. But such a social revolution would mean more than a redistribution of goods and privileges. First of all, it would both make possible and necessitate a reorientation of production, to meet not only old needs but newly defined ones. And it would involve a transformation of working-class habitus, utilizing for wider social purposes the principles activated in those areas of life, both at work and during leisure time, in which even today the dominated find resources for creativity and autonomous action.

It was in the framework of some such vision that Marx imagined the ultimate goal of socialism as the limitation of working hours to expand the time available for creative activity. Without the need to support a parasitic ruling class and its apparatus of repression and mutual competition, and with a more rational allocation of productive resources and activities, the social working day would be shorter

> and, as a consequence, the time at society's disposal for the free intellectual and social activity of the individual is greater, in proportion as work is more and more evenly divided among all the able-bodied members of society, and a particular social stratum is more and more deprived of the ability to shift the burden of labor . . . from its own shoulders to those of another social stratum.[9]

With the abolition of commodity production, capital *strictu sensu* would lose its social significance: means of production would no longer also be the means of the exploitation of labor, and would therefore require reconceptualization under new schemas of property and social function. Analogously, cultural capital would no longer function as a means for generating class distinction. The meaning of taste would change fundamentally once the experience of actually altering society removed the appearance of naturalness from today's cultural categories. The role of education in reproducing and altering habitus could become an object of conscious attention, and with it public discussion and decision-making about what modes of perception and activity to foster and inhibit.

It is imaginable, perhaps even likely, that art would lose the special social value which today stems from its contrast with industrial production and consumption, and which enables it to function as an emblem of class superiority. Interestingly, something like this change in social character is already happen-

---

9 Karl Marx, *Capital*, vol. 1, tr. Ben Fowkes (Harmondsworth: Penguin, 1976), p. 667.

ing, as the boundaries between art and such lifestyle fields as cuisine and design, on the one hand, and commercial entertainment, on the other, are becoming increasingly permeable (a permeability exemplified by Damien Hirst's expression, in a 2001 *New Yorker* interview, of indecision as to whether to put more energy into making art or into running restaurants). Under contemporary conditions, this decay of the distance between the aesthetic attitude and commercial practicality has taken the form of an apparent devaluation of culture, in the nineteenth-century sense, as such.

How would people look at the arts in a society in which the opportunities to make art and to enjoy it would be generalized and in which commerce would no longer exist? Would art, as a nineteenth-century thinker like Marx would no doubt have imagined, reassert its dignity as the exercise of "free activity"? Or should we expect something like a realization of the high-modernist utopia dreamed of by artists like Piet Mondrian and the Russian Constructivists, the dissolution of art into "everyday life"? As Czech architectural theorist Karel Teige expressed this idea in 1925,

> If today we still use and will continue to use the word *art* as an auxiliary term, it does not signify the sacred and exalted art with a capital A, the beautiful academic art, *ars academica, les beaux arts* that the modern era has unseated from its throne . . . [I]t is a word that simply designates every artificial skill and proficiency. In this sense we can talk about building art, industrial art, theater and film art, much in the same way that we can talk about the art of cooking, poetry, photography, the art of travel, or the art of the dance . . . Art is simply a way of using certain means in a certain function.[10]

Interestingly, a page later Teige contradicted his rejection of a special status for art and artists by asserting that "Constructivists make no proposals for a new art, but rather they propose a plan for the new world, a program for new life."[11] Like Mondrian, even in forecasting the end of art Teige made the artist the hero of the story.

But while art was not, after all, "liquidated" by the realization of cultural imperatives embodied in modernist works, it seems also unlikely that it will lose the identity it has acquired through its history as an autonomous field, institutionalized in art schools, museums, and art history as an academic discipline and popular subject, represented by the multitude of books, musical compositions, paintings, and sculptures occupying cultural and physical space throughout the

10 K. Teige, "Constructivism and the liquidation of 'Art'," in *idem, Modern Architecture in Czechoslovakia and Other Writings*, tr. Irena Zantovská Murray and David Britt (Los Angeles: Getty Research Institute, 2000), pp. 331–2.

11 Ibid., p. 333.

world. Alexander Dorner's meditations on the fact that "our conception *art* is but a temporary fact in human history" offer a more plausible direction for speculation: "The present thus becomes a re-formation of the past; the elements of the past live on in it in a new and much more dynamic fashion." This is a radical reformulation of Baudelaire's definition of *modernité* as the appearance of the eternal in the ephemeral. The "growth of the present," in Dorner's view, "contains no longer any eternal elements which may be conserved and, at best, rearranged."[12] The elements with which the future will have to work are those created in the past and re-created in the present. Art has been and so far remains such an element of social reality.

Musing on the future of the arts "in a more rational, more sociable society" in 1957, Meyer Schapiro thought it likely that "in a socialist society the painter would cease to be a professional and would become an amateur like the lyric poets and the photographers." At present, the artist lives, when successful, thanks to "an excessive valuation of his works that only a capitalist society can sustain." Society in general cannot sustain artists "for the simple reason that only a few are good artists and every man today can be an artist." This situation is related to another important trend Schapiro discerned: "the reduction of painting to a nonprofessional activity" ongoing since the nineteenth century, carried in the twentieth to a point where painting "requires no elaborate skill in drawing, no stock of conventional knowledge, but sensibility, feeling, and a strong impulse to creation."[13] Perhaps the philistine complaint about modern art—"But anyone can do it!"—will appear as a virtue. Perhaps only a few fanatics will give the time and effort necessary to create objects and performances responding to what they, under novel circumstances, will judge the great works of the past. That in itself would be not so different from the situation at present.

Such thoughts admittedly take us beyond the point at which speculation can yield much of interest. But it is still worthwhile thinking about the possibility of classless taste. Imagining a different social world helps reveal aspects of our world we take for granted but need not. It is important to remember that just as taste, aesthetic experience, and art as we know them came into existence at some time—and not so long ago—we can expect them to be transformed in fundamental ways if the political, economic, and ecological dangers we have created leave us enough time to grapple with the need to change our world.

---

12 A. Dorner, *The Way beyond 'Art': The Work of Herbert Bayer* (New York: Wittenborn, Schultz, 1947), pp. 15, 16. Teige is equally explicit: "There is no truth other than the occasional, ephemeral truth. The basic feature of the modern spirit is skepticism against every dogma, every absolute validity, every eternal value" ("Constructivism," p. 333).

13 M. Schapiro, "The future possibilities of the arts," in *Worldview in Painting: Art and Society: Selected Papers* (New York: Braziller, 1999), pp. 192, 196.

INDEX